Barrier Canyon Style

BARRIER CANYON STYLE

STYLE

Thousands of Years of Painting on Rock

Text by Phil R. Geib
Photographs by Goodloe Suttler

The University of Utah Press
Salt Lake City

The Defiance House Man colophon is a registered trademark of the University of Utah Press. It is based on a four-foot-tall Ancient Puebloan pictograph (late PIII) near Glen Canyon, Utah.

LIBRARY OF CONGRESS CATALOGING-IN-PUBLICATION DATA
Names: Geib, Phil R., 1956- author. | Suttler, Goodloe, 1951-2024 photographer.

Title: Barrier canyon style : thousands of years of painting on rock / text
  by Phil R. Geib ; photographs by Goodloe Suttler.
Description: Salt Lake City : The University of Utah Press, [2025] |
  Includes bibliographical references and index.
Identifiers: LCCN 2024016340 | ISBN 9781647691998 (cloth) | ISBN
  9781647692001 (paperback) | ISBN 9781647692018 (ebook)
Subjects: LCSH: Rock paintings—Utah. | Rock paintings—Colorado. |
  Picture-writing—Utah. | Picture-writing—Colorado. |
  Paleo-Indians—Utah—Antiquities. |
  Paleo-Indians—Colorado—Antiquities.
Classification: LCC GN799.P4 G45 2024 | DDC 978.8/201--dc23/eng/20240815
LC record available at https://lccn.loc.gov/2024016340

Errata and further information on this and other titles available at UofUpress.com

In Memoriam

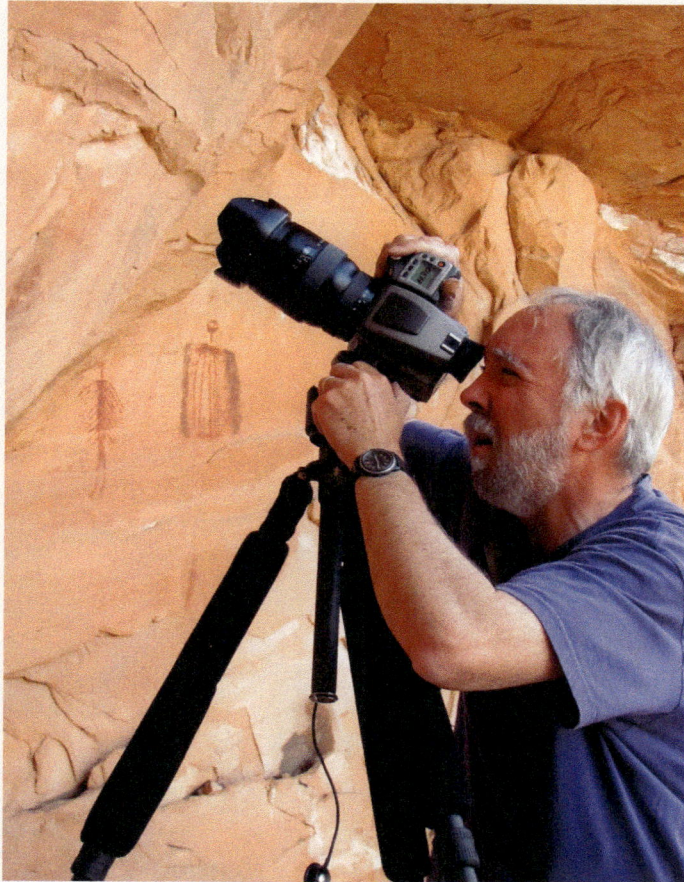

HENRY GOODLOE SUTTLER 1951–2024

"Life is your art. An open, aware heart is your camera. A oneness with your world is your film. Your bright eyes and easy smile is your museum."—Ansel Adams

Contents

Preface

My interest in Barrier Canyon Style rock art developed slowly and organically. It traces back to the fall of 1979 when I studied ancient yucca leaf sandals from Dust Devil Cave in southeastern Utah. I was in my first semester as a graduate student at Northern Arizona University (NAU) so I knew little about archaeology and less about perishables. Fortunately, J. Richard (Dick) Ambler entrusted me to examine the fragile footwear from his 1970 excavation of the cave. So began a lifelong interest in the hunter-gatherers who made these sandals and used them when trekking Utah's canyon country more than five thousand years ago.

The Dust Devil Cave sandals represent the earliest type of footwear on the Colorado Plateau, but published descriptions of comparable artifacts were few in 1979. Dick was aware that similar sandals were recovered from Cowboy Cave by Jesse Jennings's University of Utah field school in 1975. His 1980 report showed and described sandals just like those from Dust Devil Cave, though much better preserved. Cowboy Cave also contained a far richer set of material remains, perhaps in part because of its considerably larger size. My copy of the Cowboy Cave report soon became heavily thumbed through. The perishables were just one interest. By 1981 I had begun an analysis of Dust Devil Cave stone artifacts, so I commonly referred to the Cowboy Cave report, along with one on Sudden Shelter.

Cowboy Cave had many intriguing artifacts including items of a symbolic nature such as painted and inscribed stones and anthropomorphic clay figurines. The figurines closely resemble the BCS rock art downstream from Cowboy Cave within Horseshoe Canyon, but this was not obvious until my first visit to the Great Gallery in the spring of 1985. I brought along Polly Schaafsma's monograph *The Rock Art of Utah* and added various notations in the margins. Some of my notes and observations, along with ones made a few years later, proved useful for this book, although I never would have imagined then what would transpire more than thirty-five years later.

My initial Great Gallery visit occurred while in the area conducting an archaeological survey of North Point, a plateau that overlooks the Green and Colorado River confluence. That survey was part of a project I directed for the NAU Archaeology Laboratory under contract to the National Park Service. The work involved survey and limited excavation on lands in and around Lake Powell within the Glen Canyon National Recreation Area. One research focus was cultural continuity and how the people that archaeologists call Fremont related to people who came before as well as to Basketmakers and later Puebloans. Rock art seemed a useful way to examine this issue and the NAU project happened to record several outstanding Fremont pictograph panels. Additional visits to Horseshoe Canyon and the Great Gallery, along with several other BCS sites in the region, occurred in the late 1980s. Despite conducting considerable survey in the Orange Cliffs area, where such notable sites as the Perfect Panel occur, the NAU crew did not locate any previously undocumented BCS rock art. We did, however, locate additional shelters with early style yucca leaf sandals and confirmed that they were indeed ancient by radiocarbon dating: made and used more than eight thousand years ago.

Through the decades since 1979 my interest in the Archaic Period hunter-gatherers of canyon country continued and involved survey, excavation, and research with old collections, including those from Cowboy Cave. One study involved radiocarbon dating of sandals found next to the largest clay figurine recovered, one that seems so analogous to BCS spirit figures and shown herein. I also kept coming across traces of the hematite that is central to BCS imagery at Archaic sites in various ways. Some of the flaked stone tools from Dust Devil Cave were stained by red ocher, and I found the same when analyzing the flaked tools from Old Man Cave, which also yielded ocher pieces. Some grinding tools at this site and Atlatl Rock Cave were red stained from pigment preparation. Most notable of all is the pigment stick, basically a fat crayon, from Cottonwood Cave, Utah, that is also reported here.

All of this was groundwork of sorts for my role in this monograph, but none of it would have mattered had I not received an email out of the cold from Goodloe Suttler back in 2016 inquiring if I had any interest in working on a book about BCS rock art. So began my official journey on this project. There were plenty of twists and turns along the way including my own personal medical challenges. Suffice it to say that this final version is far different from the initial rough draft sent to Goodloe in 2021 or the version sent out for peer review. BCS rock art is endlessly fascinating and provides a glimpse into the lives of people that cannot be acquired by other means, even if the messages are undecipherable.

—PHIL GEIB

For decades now, I have enjoyed experimenting with cameras, enlargers, and printers. This book is the result of my most recent experiment: could faded rock-paintings, created thousands of years ago, be "virtually restored" using the advanced math employed by NASA to photographically explore Mars in 2004? I was intrigued by the prospect of something very new helping the human eye to see something very old.

After conducting thousands of image-processing experiments, I discovered a way to choose the degree of restoration that best suits a selected audience. The Barrier Canyon Style (BCS) rock art photographs in this book contain varying degrees of digital paint restoration to help viewers appreciate both the rock art and the extraordinary painting skills required to create it. The photos of BCS panels and motifs play a central role in the larger purpose Phil Geib and I had in mind for this book.

We wanted to provide readers an easy way to vicariously visit the most visually interesting BCS sites, many of which are difficult to access. We also wanted to offer readers help in interpreting BCS motifs, and to make it easy for readers to understand BCS artwork through the lenses of several different contexts. Here in 2024, this is the only rock art book 100 percent dedicated to BCS. If you are curious about BCS rock art but don't know where to start, look no further.

In 2009, while planning a trip to Moab, Utah, to photograph regional landscapes with friends, I became curious about BCS rock art without knowing that it had a name. Several online photographs of BCS panels caught my eye and I simply couldn't look away! The more BCS images I saw, the more I felt that I had to see these panels for myself and photograph them if possible. After a couple of months of online BCS research, an exciting trip-plan emerged: I would spend two weeks in Utah, one week shooting in the Moab area with friends, and one week shooting solo at ten carefully researched BCS sites.

Once back home from the Moab trip, as I began printing the images from the BCS sites, I knew I had found my next exhibition series. The motifs on the rock panels were mesmerizing in print form: the camera had captured textures and details that were invisible while visiting the panel.

My camera of choice for the Moab trip was the state-of-the-art 39-megapixel Hasselblad. My backpack also contained four new Hasselblad lenses capable of resolving details far beyond the limits of my camera's sensor. Designed with the needs of professional photographers in mind, this camera system could produce a 16x20-inch print sharper than images rendered in the human eye. Subtle textures and color changes in the motifs were captivating in the final prints. Many prints appeared to be three-dimensional because of the extraordinary sharpness of tiny edges combined with visible details in shadow areas.

From the week I spent visiting BCS sites in 2009, I generated a variety of exhibition-quality prints. I was very fortunate to be a given an opportunity to create an exhibit of BCS prints at the University of North Carolina's (UNC) Ackland Museum in 2011. The Ackland's head curator, Peter Nisbet, PhD, invited BCS expert Michael Firnhaber, PhD, to give a talk at UNC while my BCS prints were on display. Following his UNC presentation, Michael and I began talking about photographing twenty-five of the sixty BCS sites he had visited when writing his doctoral thesis a few years earlier. We developed a BCS site-visitation plan and executed the plan a few months later.

Adobe's Photoshop was used for image processing and print file preparation. DStretch was the most useful auxiliary postprocessing tool, becoming a standard layer within my BCS images after I learned how to weave its color outputs into final prints. Jon Harman's DStretch application was based upon math originally developed at NASA's Jet Propulsion Lab for stretching narrow color spaces. Jon adapted the math to help rock art researchers find faded or overpainted motifs. Today, the DStretch app has become a popular tool both for postprocessing images from rock art sites and for real-time use in the field using cell-phone cameras.

After a few thousand postprocessing experiments, I realized that a single field capture could enable five distinct end-purposes:

(1) Basic documentation of what the panel looks like today; no alterations are made to the image except for essential adjustments to color temperature & tint, and to exposure.

(2) An exploratory site survey using a variety of DStretch color spaces to bring out motifs.

(3) An interpreted image, derived from **(1) and (2)** above, of how the panel could look today with optimal lighting conditions present, and with touch-up removals of distracting faults & defacements.

(4) A restoration of original paint colors from **(2) and (3)** above.

(5) The creation of new art from using combinations of **(1), (2), (3), and (4)** above.

DStretch software plays an essential role in all end-purposes except (1). Each of the five end-purposes has a unique workflow, but all start with a color-accurate and detailed field capture. The workflows for (3), (4), and (5) images use multiple outputs from DStretch and Photoshop as inputs to the final assembly of an image in Photoshop. Several BCS images that I prepared for an exhibition needed three different DStretch color spaces in the final Photoshop file.

These five end-purposes serve the interests of very different audiences. Science is usually best served by being able to verify or replicate results, so (1) and (2) are used for academic and scientific inquiries. Aesthetics and interpretation are best served by combining the outputs from (3), (4), or (5) in ways that help the eye and the brain absorb a given field capture.

The accuracy of the field captures, coupled with individualized postprocessing workflows, enable the readers of this book to view archaic artistic skills that are still spellbinding thousands of years later. I can attest to the difficulty of seeing everything that a BCS panel has to offer while standing right in front of the panel. Advancements in electronics, software, and optics can help inform us about early art which millennia of weather has rendered almost invisible in some panel sections. Being able to more clearly see brush strokes, textures, and colors on a panel allows the original artwork to become informative and magical once again.

—GOODLOE SUTTLER

Acknowledgments

Many people deserve mention of gratitude for help on the specific topic of BCS rock art or more generally. Dick Ambler is certainly one of these in the general sense: he was the reason I embarked on an archaeological career and have an interest in Archaic period hunter-gatherers. I am sure he had thoughts about BCS rock art, but I cannot recall what these might have been and I unfortunately missed the trip he led with students to Cowboy Cave and the Great Gallery in 1981. The night in 1979 when we took refuge in Dust Devil Cave in the face of a wicked late October storm provided vivid insight as to how comforting such a shelter can be and why Archaic foragers called the place home on many occasions. Helen Fairley can testify to that and was key to the success of the NAU Glen Canyon project.

Nancy Coulam and Alan Schroedl deserve thanks for advice and assistance on this project and for their many contributions to our understanding of the Archaic Period in Utah. Both participated in the original excavation of Cowboy Cave and have gone back to the records and collections from that rich site to make new insights. Nancy was also instrumental when she served as archaeologist for Canyonlands National Park in the early attempts at direct radiocarbon dating of BCS rock art.

Joel Janetski and Jody J. Patterson are thanked for their thoughtful review comments on an early draft of this book. People who have helped in various ways for my understanding of BCS rock art or with images and dating include Richard Ansley, George Cathey, Laura Costello, Gary Cox, Alan Cressler, David Crompton, Karen DuBroff, Stephen Hall, Ed Jolie, Randy Langstraat, Anne Lawlor, Brian Lee, Cynthia Mackey, Steven Manning, Carol Paterson, Richard Reed, Lee Rentz, Kara Schneiderman, David Susec, Eric Trenbeath, Alan Watchman, and Alyson Wilkins.

Finally, a heartfelt thanks to Carrie Heitman who lights up my life and helped me through the rough patch in 2020.

—Phil Geib

This book would not have happened without a unique and essential contribution from each of the following people: Charles Cramer, Michael Firnhaber, Phil Geib, Jon Harman, Diane Heerema, Peter Linden, Peter Nisbet, Margo Taussig Pinkerton, Reba Rauch, John Sexton, and Arnold Zann. I thank each of you for generously helping me at the exact right moment along an unknowable fifteen-year path.

—Goodloe Suttler

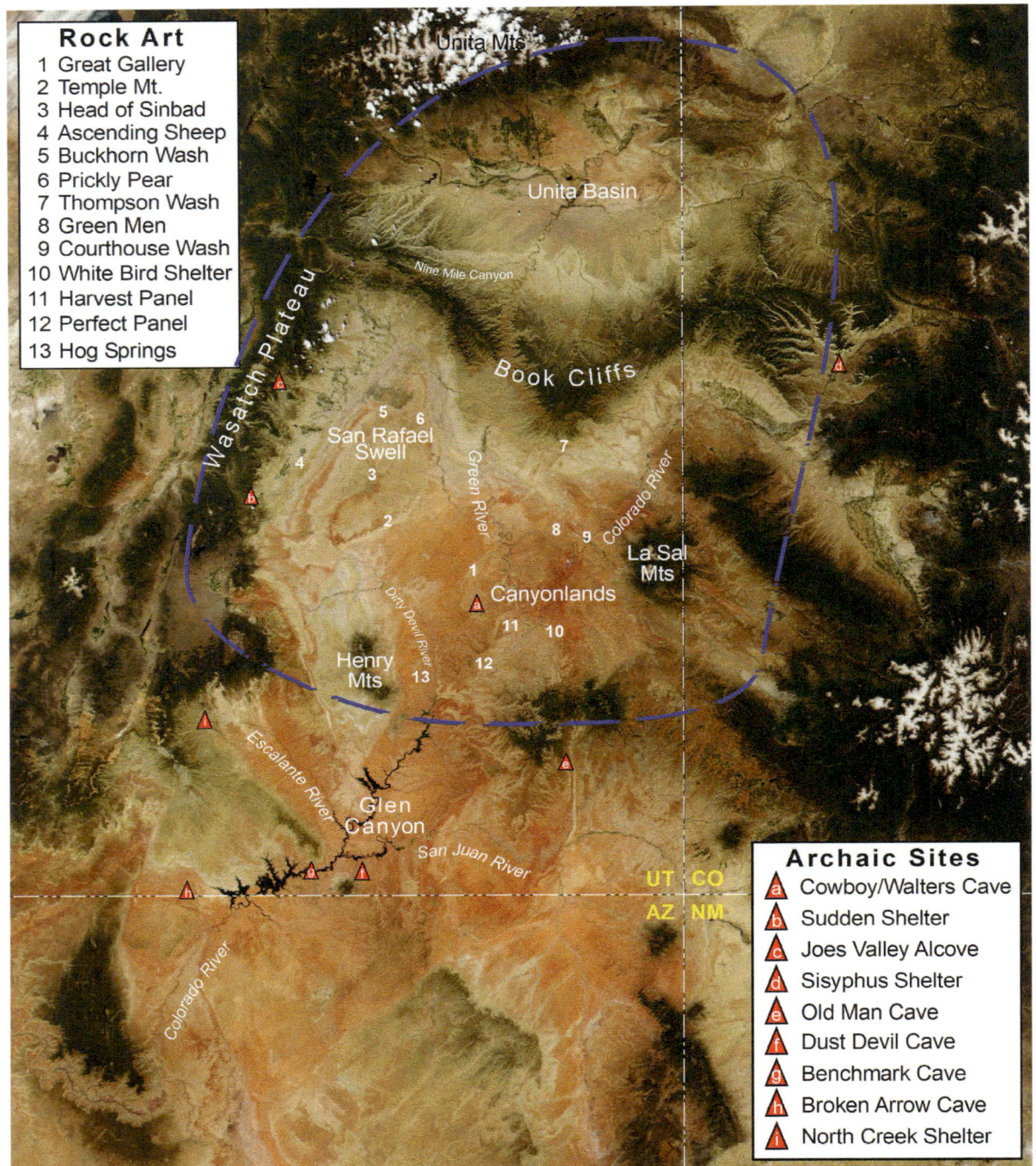

Rock Art
1 Great Gallery
2 Temple Mt.
3 Head of Sinbad
4 Ascending Sheep
5 Buckhorn Wash
6 Prickly Pear
7 Thompson Wash
8 Green Men
9 Courthouse Wash
10 White Bird Shelter
11 Harvest Panel
12 Perfect Panel
13 Hog Springs

Archaic Sites
a Cowboy/Walters Cave
b Sudden Shelter
c Joes Valley Alcove
d Sisyphus Shelter
e Old Man Cave
f Dust Devil Cave
g Benchmark Cave
h Broken Arrow Cave
i North Creek Shelter

Unita Mts
Unita Basin
Nine Mile Canyon
Wasatch Plateau
Book Cliffs
San Rafael Swell
Green River
Colorado River
La Sal Mts
Canyonlands
Dirty Devil River
Henry Mts
Escalante River
Glen Canyon
San Juan River
Colorado River

UT CO
AZ NM

Figure 1.1 Canyon Lands Section of the Colorado Plateau showing the core area of Barrier Canyon Style rock art, some of the key panels mentioned in the text, and some of the archaeological sites that have greatly added to our understanding of Archaic Period hunter-gatherers. Numbering of rock art starts centrally at the Great Gallery then proceeds northwest and clockwise ending in the southwest. Same applies for sites starting at Cowboy Cave, also near the center.

1
INTRODUCTION

This book concerns depictions on rock surfaces made by Native Americans living long ago. For thousands of years, these images, usually painted but also pecked or etched, have survived in a few hundred select locations of rugged canyon country in eastern Utah and far western Colorado. This visually stunning rock art tradition is known as the Barrier Canyon Style (BCS). Its boldly painted motifs and otherworldly subject matter have an uncanny ability to capture the modern imagination, spurring a host of questions. Who created these magnificent murals? How long have these figures been tucked away in remote desert canyons? Why did people make these images and what might they mean? What was life like for the creators of this art?

Barrier Canyon Style rock art is famous among rock art enthusiasts around the world and has nearly universal appeal among those who have experienced the images directly. The style is among the best known of any rock art from the Americas. A life-size mural of the most spectacular example of this style, known as the Great Gallery, hung in the Museum of Modern Art in New York City as part of their *Indian Art of the United States* exhibit during the first half of 1941. This sixty-foot-wide by twelve-foot-high canvas, painted by artists of the Works Progress Administration, now hangs on permanent display at the Natural History Museum of Utah in Salt Lake City. The original pictograph panel of this replica occurs in a secluded canyon tributary of the Green River in east-central Utah.

The Great Gallery's impressive ancient paintings came to the attention of archaeologists in the late 1920s when a Peabody Museum expedition documented them during a wide-ranging reconnaissance throughout eastern Utah.[1] Expedition archaeologists photographed and marveled at the paintings but did not assign a style name. That initial designation occurred in 1971, when Polly Schaafsma applied the canyon name in her publication *The Rock Art of Utah*. Barrier Canyon was the type location for this style and the Great Gallery became the official "type site," since it is the most striking and awe-inspiring panel in that gorge, if not in all of Utah. The commonly dubbed "Holy Ghost" group, artfully framed by a naturally spalled rock arch, is perhaps the best-known portion of the Great Gallery because of numerous photographs published in books and online.

Barrier Canyon is now known as Horseshoe Canyon and its drainage is Barrier Creek. The cluster of pictograph panels found in this canyon is but a small sample of a few hundred BCS rock art panels. The map included here shows the general distribution of rock surfaces that have images classified as part of this distinct style. The photos in this book include most of the main geographic range for this style and many of its great exemplars. New BCS rock art panels are still being discovered, even large ones.

Our intent in publishing a book on BCS rock art is to make many prominent panels of this style vicariously accessible to interested readers through imagery and explanation. Most rock art aficionados of the American Southwest know something of the Barrier Canyon Style, and many visitors who pass through Utah's canyon country catch a glimpse of the BCS figures, whether firsthand on desert rocks or through endless reproductions used in advertising, decoration, and souvenirs. Several regional rock art volumes touch on BCS images, but none focus completely on the art, its context, the people who made it, and its possible meanings. We do not pretend to know what Barrier Canyon Style images meant to their creators; those quite-specific reasons were soon lost to the inexorable passage of time, death of individuals, and culture change. Rather, we posit plausible accounts as to general reasons for image creation.

Archaeologists do not know with any certainty who the people were that created Barrier Canyon Style rock art. This uncertainty occurs for several reasons. Central is an unsettled debate about the antiquity of the rock art style. Providing a plausible age range for specific rock art styles is important for placing them into proper historical context. How do we know what life was like for a painter without any idea of when in time they lived? The temporal span of this tradition, when it started and ended, is a topic likely to remain controversial for years to come.[2]

In a related way, the depictions lumped together today as part of the Barrier Canyon Style have variability that reflects both temporal and spatial changes in who the people were. BCS rock art is the product of multiple different authors. Variability in BCS rock art both within and between areas likely stems from two aspects. First is having somewhat distinct learning traditions within a widespread group of people who shared much in common, including belief systems. Second is change through time in a long-lived practice of adding culturally significant symbols to rock surfaces. BCS was not an artistic event, the expression of some small group, or even a short-lived art florescence of a larger group. BCS rock art formed part of a living and dynamic cultural tradition spanning thousands of years that was never frozen in time or unchanging.

The first section of this book provides a sweeping visual overview of BCS rock art. We highlight about two dozen well-preserved panels to get readers immersed in the subject matter. Every BCS panel is in many respects unique, such that a compendium of all would be useful, but more so for an avid researcher. Scores of BCS panels are faded and damaged by age, which can limit appreciation by the average viewer, at least when experiencing the rock art for the first time.

After exposing readers to BCS rock art by showing entire panels or portions of panels, the second section of this book answers the question "What Did We Just See?" Here the focus is on many of the common elements or motifs that comprise BCS rock art, those repeated at many different sites. Accompanying the visuals of motif examples are descriptions that explain what they are about, at least to the extent that this can be known by modern viewers. It must always be kept in mind that identifiable images can symbolically stand for something other than what is literally represented.

The third section takes a deeper dive into the archaeology of BCS rock art. A variety of topics are explored, including how the images were created, at what periods in the past they were likely created, what life was like for the people who made them, and what might have motivated such activity. This section is geared toward examining what role the images might have served in the past societies that created them.

We now embark on a sweeping visual overview of BCS rock art, starting with the panel that remains as impressive today as when it was created in the distant past: The Great Gallery.

2
BARRIER CANYON STYLE SITES

Figure 2.1 A life-sized, highly decorated anthropomorph located in Canyonlands National Park. The vivid colors shown here are digitally restored approximations of how the image may have looked when first created thousands of years ago. Many centuries of sunlight and weather have reduced the intensity and vibrancy of the paints. This panel is in relatively good shape compared to some BCS panels that are nearly invisible now.

The Great Gallery

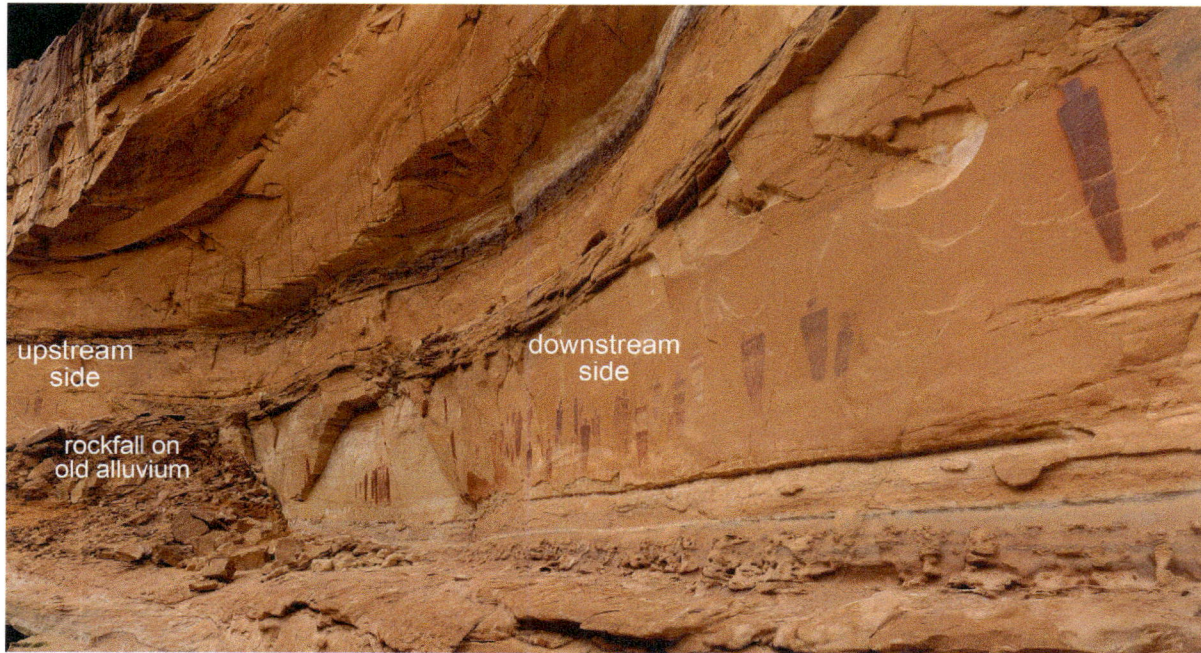

Figure 2.2 Great Gallery in Horseshoe Canyon as captured from a 3D model of the panel created by the Ancient Art Archive. The main panel lies on the downstream side to the right of a large talus pile that overlies and preserves an ancient alluvial terrace. BCS paintings also occur on the upstream side above the top of this alluvial terrace.

We begin with the Great Gallery, the largest and most impressive BCS panel, which extends for 300 feet along the west wall of Horseshoe Canyon. Had the panel occurred elsewhere, this rock art style would doubtless have a different name and visitation to the Horseshoe Canyon would be scant. The Great Gallery is what visitors want to see, and some quickly skip past the three other panels along the commonly used trail that accesses this site.

The Great Gallery is impressive for its size and degree of preservation, and for the intricacy of the renderings. The size aspect refers both to the extent of the painted sandstone wall and the scale of the images, with many human-like forms that are life-sized or larger. These numinous anthropomorphs are characteristic of BCS rock art. They are often described as ghost-like or as resembling an Egyptian mummy, characterized by rather elongated torsos with heads but no arms or legs. The "Holy Ghost" group at the Great Gallery epitomizes this basic element, as do most of the figures at this panel. David Sucec of the BCS PROJECT team refers to the hovering anthropomorphs as "spirit figures," a term that seems more appropriate than referencing ghosts or mummies. These images seem related to and supportive of life rather than connected with death.

The Great Gallery has two main groups of paintings. Most images occur on the downstream side of a large talus pile that buries and preserves an ancient alluvial terrace. A smaller group of paintings occurs above this talus pile on the upstream side, above the top of the alluvial terrace. Multiple hands seem involved in the basic

Figure 2.3 Great Gallery, downstream side left half.

Figure 2.4 Great Gallery right half.

painting, aside from those implicated in subsequent enhancements or other modifications. The Great Gallery was a temporal accretion across a span of time, likely a lengthy one.

The Great Gallery's left side of the main downstream panel includes the Holy Ghost group. Rock spalled from the arch that frames these figures is scattered at the base. Some of the spalls retain paint from figures once present to the left of the Holy Ghost group and two of these have radiocarbon dates. To the right of the Holy Ghost

group are depictions of small-scale humans and animals actively involved in mundane activities, including a bighorn sheep hunt scene that involves a dog. Large scale and smaller spirit figures occur around this hunt.

Nearly all images on the right side of Great Gallery's main downstream panel are large-scale spirit figures. One has a smaller human assistant holding a staff up toward it in a gesture of help. Another is approached by a line of sheep or other hoofed animals. Still others have animals painted on shoulders or as body decoration. The last figure on the far right is a dog barking down canyon next to a ten-foot-high anthropomorph with paired upright feathers or horns.

The focal figure of the Holy Ghost group exhibits a variety of different paint application techniques as well as incising and abrasion. This figure, like most at the Great Gallery, has extensive surface modification of pockmarks in the sandstone from being stuck with sharp hard objects, mainly after the images were in place.

There are more painted images above an ancient alluvial terrace high on the upstream (left) side of the Great Gallery (figure 2.6). The main set of painted anthropomorphs closely compare to BCS pictographs at the Perfect Panel near the Maze Area

Figure 2.5a Great Gallery Ghost group including Holy Ghost.

Figure 2.5b The figure that looks white had the rock surface first abraded and then mud painted.

Figure 2.6 Great Gallery Anthropomorphs, upstream side above an ancient alluvial terrace.

of Canyonlands and in North Wash near Hog Spring. They are also similar to some images on the right side of the Great Gallery, but many there are qualitatively different.

Many of the anthropomorphs in the entire panel have elaborate body and sometimes head decorations created by using other colors in addition to red ocher, as well as incised lines and other techniques. Great Gallery's images are not crowded together, perhaps because the accessible protected canyon wall was so extensive. The torso area of many anthropomorphs have parallel lines that might symbolize rain. Zig-zag lines may represent lightning or snakes, depending on the context. Torso areas containing other anthropomorphs or animals are telling of a special relationship with those internalized figures, perhaps as predecessors or helpers during trances. Most anthropomorphs shown here are life-sized.

Most anthropomorphs at the Great Gallery are large, with some reaching heights of ten feet. Yet, there are also small, delicately painted figures including the group of anthropomorphs and probable dog (figure 2.8). The three spirit figures measure only about fourteen inches tall. Despite the small size, their elongated bodies were painted in detail. In association are realistic animals such as birds and quadrupeds painted

Figure 2.7 Great Gallery anthropomorphs.

at tiny size relative to the spirit figures. The scale relationship between spirit figures and animals seen in large paintings is maintained, which means that some of the animals are less than one inch in height. The quadrupeds consist of a probable bighorn sheep on the left side of the middle figure and a possible deer over the head of the left figure. The right figure has birds flying at its shoulders and up its body, with a crane on the left side of its upper chest. The bird on the right side of the central figure near the chest is the uppermost of a vertical ascending line of at least fourteen birds, with the rest about one-half the size of the top specimen. In the bottom right is a spirit figure less than six inches high. It appears to hold a wavy leash attached to a miniature quadruped that stands about one-half-inch tall and less than one inch long. Again, a relative size relationship between spirit figure and accompanying animal is retained. The leash-like connection is likely a snake symbol, as is common in BCS art. Another

Figure 2.8 Great Gallery small anthropomorphs, upstream side.

snake-like wavy line extends from the other side of the torso down toward another zoomorph, too indistinct to identify as a result of damage to the painting. The beautifully rendered miniature figures of this scene occur at many other BCS panels, some of which consist entirely of small-scale rock art.

The central scene of the Great Gallery depicts a sheep hunt surrounded by various spirit figures, including three life-size or larger examples (figure 2.9). The central-most of these has an eyeless head and elongated red torso embellished with white decorations. This image is painted over two smaller spirit figures and an even smaller citizen figure. A human-like figure turned sideways holds a staff up toward this central spirit figure. Their staff expands near the spirit figure, and likely once touched this image, but abrasion along its edge after being painted has removed this detail. Similar abrasion mostly erased other small anthropomorphs placed immediately above the attendant. The larger spirit figure to the left with the white eyes exhibits elaborate details in its core form as well as subsequent decoration with white paint.

Figure 2.9 Great Gallery spirits and civilians.

The Harvest Panel

Figure 2.10 Harvest Panel left.

Deep within the Maze of Canyonlands National Park occurs a BCS panel named after several motifs pertaining to the harvesting of plants. A spirit figure at the far-right side has a plant emerging from the middle finger of a greatly enlarged hand. A bird hovers before the plant and two rabbits run down the figure's arm. The plant closely resembles Indian ricegrass, the seeds of which were an important food for Native Americans throughout the Southwest and Great Basin. A similar plant is held by the small figure with large antennae slightly to the left. Trudging below and toward the spirit figure that nurtures plants and attracts animals are two human forms, bent forward under the weight of burden baskets. These baskets are carried on their backs attached to tumpline straps that run over their foreheads. Native American women throughout the West commonly used such burden baskets while harvesting seeds and other plant foods. Both figures hold implements used for seed harvesting, as documented ethnographically: one a probable winnowing basket, and the other a seed beater or tongs for picking cactus fruit. Arrayed to the left of the burden carriers are a dozen additional, roughly life-sized, mystical spirit figures. Many have upright horns or feathers and hair bobs or earrings; many torsos consist of parallel lines, often painted in white. Several hold snakes or these zigzag motifs are positioned alongside bodies. The rain essential

Figure 2.11 Harvest Panel right.

to plant growth and animal life might be represented by vertical finger streaks of red and sprays of red dots around a few of the figures, especially those with serpents.

Accessing the Harvest Panel is rather arduous, requiring a long drive on an unimproved road followed by a several-mile hike that involves climbing down hundreds of feet to the canyon floor where the panel resides. Visiting the panel imparts some sense of what life might have been like for the creators of BCS rock art. But the environment seen today is not what the creators of this panel likely experienced. A small stream probably flowed across a canyon floor covered with alluvium that sustained a riparian plant community. As a result, other plants and animals would have flourished in greater abundance. The alluvium that once covered the canyon floor provided the working surface that the artists stood upon to paint this panel. That alluvium is now gone from the panel and most of the canyon bottom, having eroded away in the distant past.

This delicately painted anthropomorph (figure 2.12), less than two feet tall, occurs upstream of the main Harvest Panel. White circles outline the eyes with white dots extending down the neck to the shoulders and beyond. White also decorates the

Figure 2.12 Harvest Panel far left.

Figure 2.13 Spirit Figures, Bear, and Burden Bearer.

head feathers or antennae. One hand holds a stick or atlatl dart with a white feather attached midway along the length. An attendant bird is attracted to the figure at the stick-holding hand. In the other hand is a probable flowering plant as represented by white dots on stem tips. The figure's feet terminate in long white claws. This depiction is perhaps of a real person rather than a spirit, but one that specializes in the supernatural—a shaman or medicine person. The white goggle eyes might represent a trance state, with the white facial dots representing blood from nasal hemorrhaging, something documented to occur during intense exertions brought about to enter trances.[1] The clawed feet are likely indicative of special abilities held by this individual for supernatural intervention.

Upstream from the main Harvest Panel is this scene with elongated spirit figures (figure 2.13), a probable bear, and a burden bearer. The tallest figure is less than thirty inches high. At far left is a human carrying a burden basket on their back much like the two figures shown previously for the main panel. This individual and the large animal face toward the largest spirit figure, which holds vertical a pole such as an atlatl dart. Each of the animal's four feet have pecked areas that likely stem from ancient visitors sampling the pigment to obtain spiritual power or protection. Similar sampled areas occur on some figures of the main Harvest Panel and at other BCS sites. The small goggle-eyed anthropomorph immediately right of the tallest figure closely resembles the previously shown shaman, though this one holds a snake in each hand. Both this figure and the similar example wear a lower wrap of a probable animal hide as indicated by the dangling, slightly flared strips on either side, which represent leg skin.

Buckhorn Wash

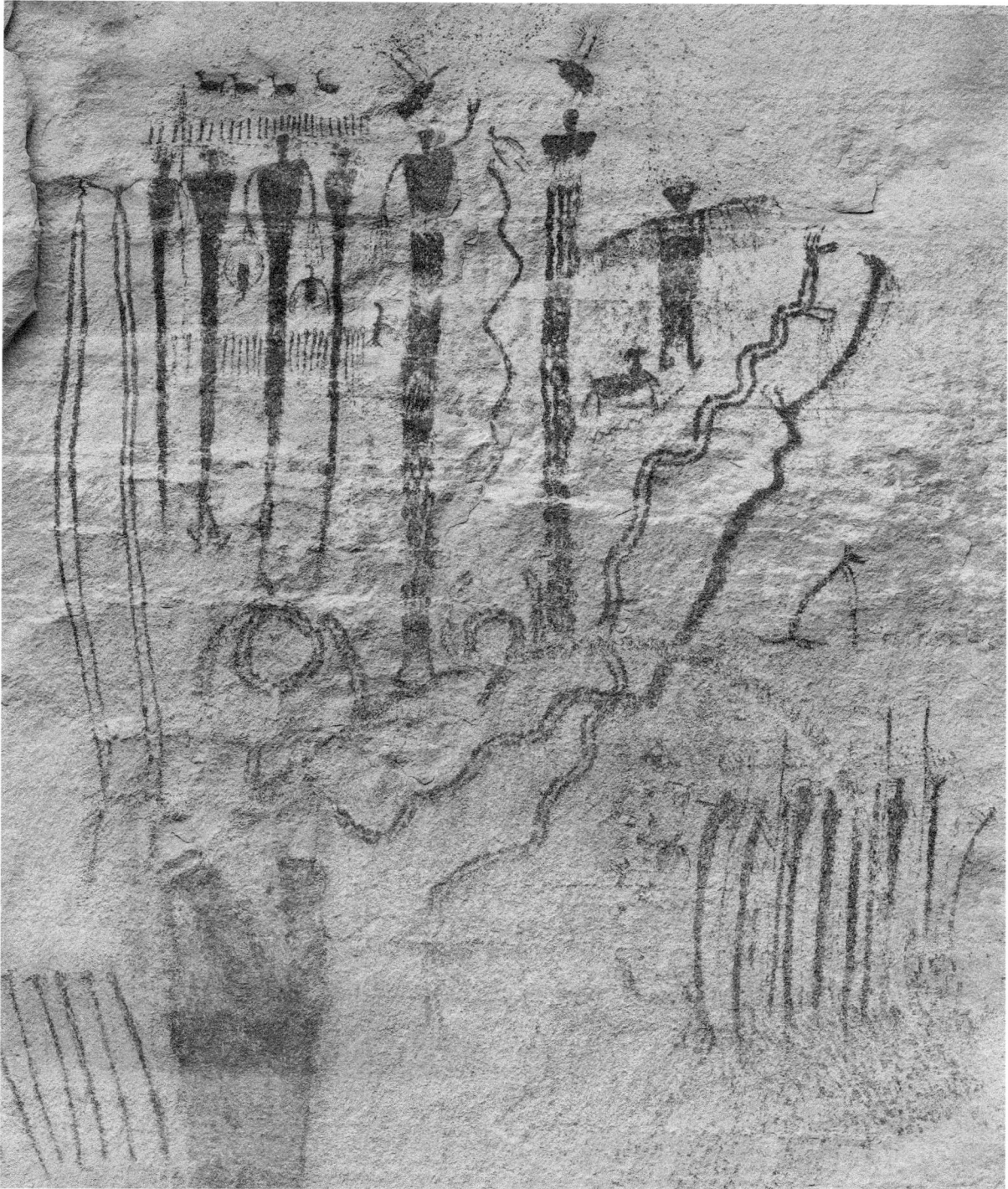

Figure 2.14 Buckhorn Wash overview.

Figure 2.15 Rainbows, snakes, and rain.

Figure 2.16 Buckhorn Wash shaman group.

The Buckhorn Wash site has several interesting panels and is one of a few BCS sites accessible by regular vehicles. The panels received expensive restoration to remedy extensive human damage done during previous decades by thoughtless modern visitors.[2] While some damage is still detectable, the panels are in decent shape for viewing a wide variety of BCS artwork.

Three panels at this site are shown here. The most complex one contains many recurring BCS elements: elongated anthropomorphs; attendant birds, snakes, and quadrupeds; polymorphs of different life forms combined; and other motifs such as flying circles.

This panel displays elements that, taken together, suggest fertility and rebirth were valued and sought. This is a common theme in BCS rock art. Parallel lines coming from the hands and arms of two spirit figures are thought to represent rain. The rainbow that arcs above the right figure is a motif repeated at several BCS panels. Roots descending from the feet represent an obvious beneficial link to precipitation. Snakes, such as the one held aloft by the central figure, are often seen as messengers to the supernatural and metaphorically linked to change and rebirth from their shedding skin.

The Buckhorn Wash Panels depict anthropomorphs with arms and legs in greater numbers than at many BCS sites, and the images are qualitatively different from those at the Great Gallery. This is part of the subregional diversity that occurs within BCS rock art.[3] Stylistic diversity also occurs at this single panel, with the broad-shouldered, stocky figures shown here left undecorated, perhaps to appear more powerful than celebrated. Some diversity in this rock art style is suggestive of change through time. Certainly, the central largest figure is somewhat more recent than the images it superimposes. The partial overpainting seen here occurs on other BCS panels.

Sego Canyon at Thompson Wash

Figure 2.17 Sego Canyon overview.

Sego Canyon at Thompson Wash, along the southern foot of the Book Cliffs, is another BCS site directly accessible by vehicle. The four different panels here include rock art that is not part of the Barrier Canyon Style. Most painted images of this panel are BCS, though petroglyphs of a later style, some of which superimpose the BCS images, appear lower down on the rock face. A few pecked figures occur over BCS paint and over areas where the pigment spalled away naturally. This indicates a substantial time difference between the distinct rock art styles. Even the BCS paintings exhibit stylistic differences and some partial superimposing that stem from temporally distinct periods of BCS art creation. The largest figures are just under life-sized.

Figure 2.18a Sego Canyon snakes.

Figure 2.18b Sego Canyon Antennas.

Vacant eyes, snakes, parallel line motifs, headdresses that resemble antenna or horns, and flying circles are recurring BCS elements on full display. Sandstone spalling has removed portions of some anthropomorphs. An overhanging ledge just above the panel protects it from normal rain, so the figures are in relatively good viewing condition. This is especially true for the higher images; the paint on lower figures has varyingly run and blurred. Sunlight on this panel is plentiful in the morning, which can help visibility of some smaller details while making some larger figures more difficult to see.

Pond Site

Figure 2.19 Pond Site Panel.

Most of this intimate BCS rock art panel is shown here. The artwork is small, with the largest figure in the upper left just thirty-six inches tall. This site is at the back of a small alcove providing ample protection from rain and better-than-normal shielding from direct sunlight. Petroglyphs occur as a band below the painted images and clearly postdate them since there are a few instances of cutting through the pigment. Bird tracks are a common element of these later additions, one of which is seen partially cutting through the bottom of the large central painted spirit figure that holds aloft a snake in one hand and perhaps a pair of snakes or a tassel in the opposite hand. Underlying the BCS paintings are fine lines of purple pigment that seem abstract.

Many figures appear to have been painted with fingers, though images with fine red lines indicate use of brushes. The anthropomorphs depicted here with their blocky bodies or chevron-like designs have a different look than many BCS panels. A few distinct painting episodes or repainting and retouching are indicated. Heavy abrasion of the sandstone surface between anthropomorphs on the right mostly obliterated painted elements.

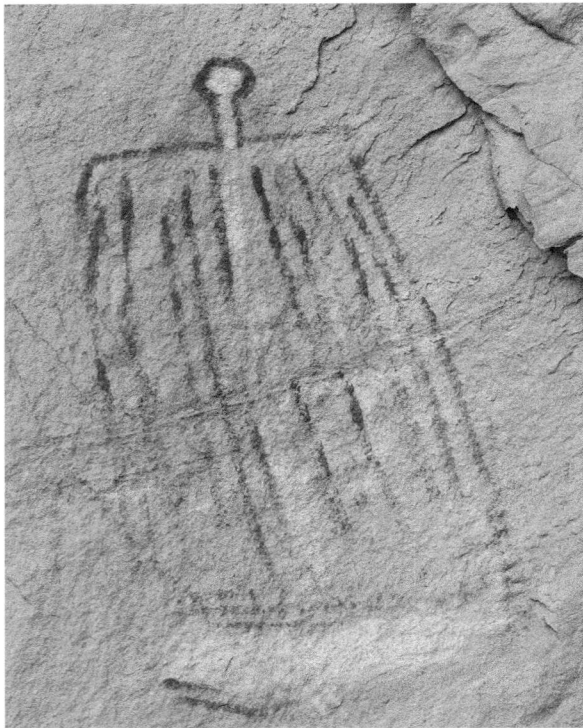

Figure 2.20 Pond Site anthropomorphs.

Head of Sinbad

Two panels occur at this location, separated by a sandstone face that could not preserve painted images. The rock art occurs at the base of a sinuous sandstone formation that rises above an expansive grassland near the center of the San Rafael Swell. The right-hand scene is iconic, a simple yet elegant composition containing a BCS anthropomorphic representation of a likely supernatural entity. This spirit figure, with short arms outstretched, is flanked on both sides by elongated tassels or comet-like forms. A snake and circle hover overhead, with the snake's undulations following the contour of the figure's bug-eyed head. To one side stands a small, human-like form with animal qualities, a polymorph that appears to be a supplicant or attendant to the central figure. The central figure is about two feet in height.

This adjacent Head of Sinbad panel is far more complex and partially obscured by a layer of silt washed down from above. Two anthropomorphs with distinct attributes dominate the preserved scene, surrounded by representational elements such as birds, snakes, flying circles, and other motifs, all of which play a supportive role in this painting. Seven delicately detailed animal-like figures with white oval bodies that stand between the two figures are each about three inches high. These resemble pronghorn running away with white rumps on full display. The bug-eyed figure is the evident focal point of this scene, though at least one other anthropomorph to the left is faintly evident by legs. The snake-holding figure on the right has a plant-like headdress with swifts or swallows hovering around it. The plants are reminiscent of the one held by a probable shaman or medicine person at the Harvest Panel. Three concentric circles embellish the chest area; spalling makes these somewhat resemble a spiral.

Figure 2.21 Head of Sinbad.

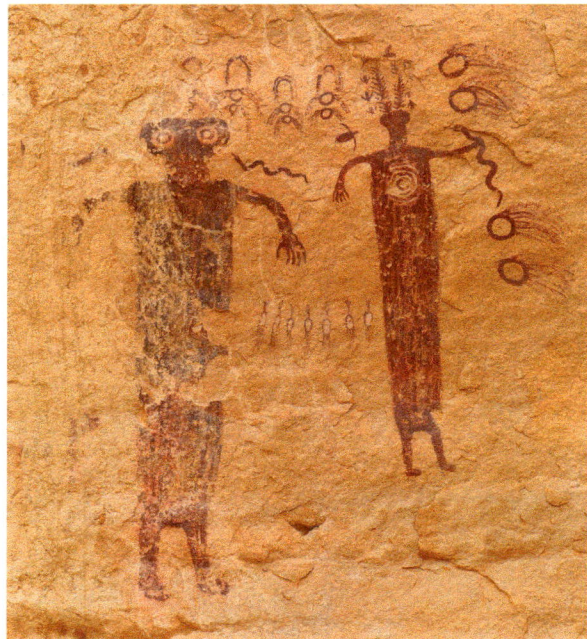

Figure 2.22 Head of Sinbad 2.

Ascending Sheep

The Ascending Sheep Panel is situated under a small sandstone overhang toward the western edge of the San Rafael Swell. Fremont pictographs occur on the left with the BCS images on the right and slightly higher. Much of the largest BCS anthropomorph has spalled off, though its head, shoulders, and one leg are present. The intact vertical BCS figures on the left are about ten inches high.

The figure in the center of the ascending lines of bighorn sheep is human in body form but has the head of a bighorn sheep and feet that end in claws or bird-of-prey talons. A serpent tongue lolls from its mouth for an excessive distance. This polymorph holds a sheep in its left hand along with a snake. In the right hand stands a small polymorph that somewhat resembles a human-bird fusion. Polymorphs are usually depicted along with spirit figures and do not provide the overall focus of a composition. This panel might seem an exception, but this misperception occurs because of natural spalling coupled with how the panel is usually photographed. A large, spalled spirit figure immediately right of these elements is commonly omitted since much is missing. By ignoring this entity, the composition seems centered on the polymorph interacting with two ascending lines of sheep approaching from opposite directions. Above the ascending sheep on the far left, and essentially at head level with the spalled spirit figure on the right, is another polymorph with a snake body and head of some ungulate, perhaps a pronghorn. This composite figure has a lizard-like front leg but none in back. Immediately above its undulating body are two more ungulates. This polymorph occurs above an obvious horizontal bedding plane in the sandstone that demarcates distinctly colored rock layers. This is unlikely to be a mere coincidence, since the horns of the polymorph just touch this bedding plane while the head of the spirit figure to the left extends above this horizon. The painter, perhaps purposefully, used this natural feature as a visual device to indicate separate planes of existence or distinct spiritual realms. There are other examples of BCS rock art where natural features were incorporated as key parts of a visual narrative.

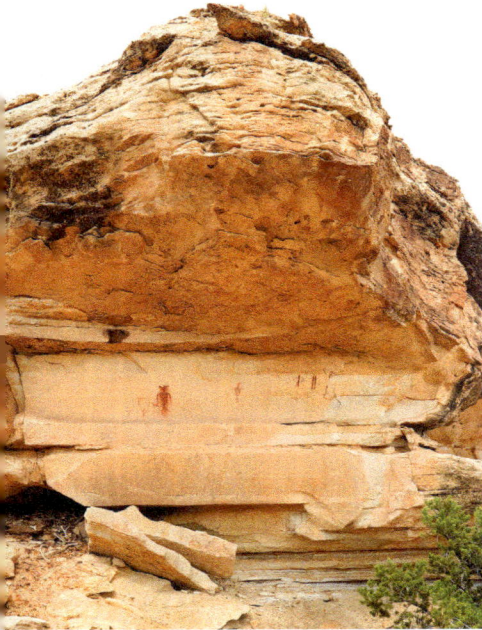

Figure 2.23 Ascending Sheep site.

Figure 2.24 Ascending Sheep panel.

Black Dragon

Figure 2.25a Black Dragon panel.

The Black Dragon site has three distinct scenes of BCS rock art, along with a fourth set of pictographs of a totally different style. The painted canyon wall receives considerable sunlight, which has unfortunately bleached out the red ocher and other pigment. Worse is that modern people damaged the art, especially by chalking figure outlines, something particularly difficult to remediate. One unique aspect is the natural ripples and color variations in the rock surface painted upon, which impart an impression of light rays coming from above. The most famous panel is the namesake, which consists of several distinct elements that an individual in the late 1940s chalked together as a single winged creature widely interpreted as an extinct pterosaur, a type of flying dinosaur that disappeared 66 million years ago. Researchers eventually demonstrated the hoax for what it was in a 2015 article titled "The Death of a Pterodactyl," published in the journal *Antiquity*.[4] A combination of DStretch and X-ray fluorescence revealed exactly where original pigments existed on the canyon wall. The drawing included here (figure 2.25b) comes from that article and shows the five BCS figures that actually exist. The separate image that made up one wing of the "pterosaur" is still remarkable,

Figure 2.25b Black Dragon artwork.

Figure 2.26 Black Dragon anthropomorph and dog.

consisting of a large-mouthed, serpent-like creature with cat-like ears. Its mouth is so wide that it could swallow the adjacent human figure, apparently a citizen suppli- cant. These polymorphs, like those at some other BCS sites, are of unusual form and not easily categorized. Adjacent to the "pterosaur" scene is another panel with several massive, larger-than-life-size BCS images. These too have been badly damaged by chalking, including the addition of facial features and interior body decorations, making it difficult to know for certain the exact nature of original details. A significant aspect of this panel is that it is one of the very few BCS paintings with a radiocar- bon date on pigment.[5]

The third BCS scene at Black Dragon (figure 2.26) depicts an anthropomorph and an unusual creature that appears something like a dog with human-like hands on the front limbs. It appears to howl toward the sky. The white outlining is chalk added in the 1940s.

Hog Springs

Figure 2.27 Hog Springs site.

The massive alcove pictured here, formed within Wingate Sandstone, lies on the west side of North Wash, a canyon that likely served as an important travel corridor in the distant past just as today. The wash dumps into the Colorado River at one of the few decent river fords, historically known as Dandy Crossing. Countless Native Americans likely crossed here. Travel up the wash heads toward a broad grassland and the conifer woodlands of the Henry Mountains. There are just two BCS paintings in the voluminous protected space of this amphitheater: an anthropomorph and an accompanying animal, or familiar. The back wall of this shelter is heavily spalled and eroded, such that either the painters purposefully selected the one stable location for the two figures or more images existed at one time but now no trace remains. Aside from proximity to a prominent travel corridor and an adjacent spring, the shelter amplifies sounds and demonstrates conspicuous echo effects. BCS artists may have envisioned settings with distinct acoustical properties as places of power that perhaps housed special spirits as well. A spacious level area clear of rocks and protected by the overhang below the panel could have provided excellent space for a group ceremony.

Figure 2.28 Hog Springs queen and dog.

This life-size anthropomorph stands well out of reach toward the center back of the Hog Springs alcove. The crown of white dots was created using a thumb dipped in white liquid pigment. These may represent bird feathers, one of the most common items used by native groups and other societies around the world for decorative purposes. Because of this feature and perhaps the earrings, some call this figure a "queen" or "princess," but gender distinctions are not obvious in BCS rock art and the creators lacked social hierarchies with royalty. The white dot and parallel line decorations of the torso match those at other BCS sites, including the Great Gallery. The pecked eyes and mouth are unusual, as is the large, pecked area in the chest, but these were not part of the original painting. The pecking likely represents modification by later Native Americans. The animal familiar originally lacked a head or legs, but at some point these features were added with an orange paint less durable or obvious than the red ocher used for the majority of the image. This animal is commonly interpreted as a dog, perhaps because of its tail posture and close human association. Deer tails stick upright like this when they flag them because of predator agitation. An animal skin of dog, deer, or other animal pulled inside out and turned into a bag also lacks head and legs, so that is another possible interpretation. Humans often secure important ritual items in animal skin bags (medicine bundles), so too perhaps spirits.

Perfect Panel

Figure 2.29 Perfect Panel site.

The perfection of this panel is in how well preserved the artwork is…truly amazing! The BCS paintings on this canyon wall of Cedar Mesa Sandstone include five anthropomorphs, a snake, and two small animals. The largest anthropomorphs are between four and five feet tall. The smooth, rain-protected sandstone canvas was an obvious reason artists chose this location. However, it does not lie along a route that would have been well traveled, as twenty feet down canyon beyond the panel is a 200-foot drop-off to the drainage bottom, which incises ever deeper as it flows toward Cataract Canyon of the Colorado River. The deep and sinuous canyon might have been a spiritual place, and once the BCS rock art was present, the art itself may have been a destination. That is the case today. Each anthropomorph is unique and carefully decorated using white dots and lines over the red ocher paint for the overall forms. Orange pigment was smeared over portions of these figures at a later time, partially obscuring some details. Three of the figures have white crowns similar to the Hog Springs anthropomorph. The dots on torsos are usually arranged in pairs that form undulating or straight columns and rows.

Figure 2.30a-b Perfect Panel Anthropomorph and snake.

The largest spirit figure has an arm extended with an enlarged hand pronated, palm away from the viewer. White is used to denote fingernails. The downward thumb serves as an attractant for a tiny quadruped. A larger quadruped stands on the shoulder of this figure, with front legs slightly raised and mouth open as though whispering to the spirit figure. Some interpret these two small animals as shaman's helpers for journeying into the spiritual realm, aiding the shaman while there and helping him to return safely to the terrestrial plane. Alternatively, the shoulder ungulate could be the shaman in animal guise relaying human requests to a spirit force that has reached out a hand of empathy. The white decorations on this animal mark it as special compared to ungulates when painted in groups such as at the Ascending Sheep Panel. One anthropomorph is distinct from the other four in having legs, fox- or coyote-like ears, and a narrow body. In addition to parallel rows of white dots, two vertical white snakes decorate the body. These serpents are similar in head form to the red vertical snake shadowed by white on the far-right side.

Dragonfly

Figure 2.31 Dragonfly Site.

This panel occurs in a rather small rockshelter of a Horseshoe Canyon tributary, well upstream from the Great Gallery. The main scene has four closely set red-and-white anthropomorphs, with a fifth just in white that is badly faded. Below the spirit figures is a small scene of tiny images with the main emphasis on a group of four red anthropomorphs with white feather headdresses. This group appears to be regular people involved in a ceremony but wearing regalia specific to the occasion.

On either side of the uppermost anthropomorph pair are insects that resemble dragonflies, including one more than twice as large as the rest—a possible dragonfly spirit. A small human grips one dragonfly by its tail. Another dragonfly at the far-right rests upon a vertical painted line such as a cattail stalk with a smaller bird flying overhead. The size comparison with the bird implies that these are not "normal" insects. Dragonflies are intimately connected with permanent water sources and spend their early life in pools, later to emerge and metamorphose into flying creatures. As such, they move between realms, imbued with spiritual significance and central to all life, that people cannot. Metamorphosis is also linked to specialists in the supernatural

Figure 2.32a Dragonfly Site detail.

Figure 2.32b Dragonfly Site detail.

Figure 2.32c Dragonfly Site detail.

when they enter spiritual realms and try to intercede or negotiate for humans.

Figure 2.32b contains the spirit figures on the right, one of which extends out an arm that a rabbit runs up much like at the Harvest Panel. The adjacent spirit figure is turned and facing toward the large dragonfly and its companions. It holds up a snake in that direction while a greatly elongated quadruped hovers near the back of the head with mouth open, perhaps in communication. This is perhaps another example of a shaman in animal disguise imploring a spirit figure for assistance. Figure 2.32c is the spirit figure below the large dragonfly that interacts with a bird and some unusual lifeforms.

Prickly Pear

Figure 2.33 Prickly Pear Complex.

The northern part of the San Rafael Swell has a broad tableland of grass-covered flats between low sandstone cliffs. This panel is located in a southwest-facing shallow alcove in one of these cliffs. No doubt this was a major BCS panel at one time, but natural spalling has reduced it to just a hint of its previous glory. What remains of the right scene is centered upon a large, canine-like animal that some have identified as a dog. However, it has fantastical features indicative of some otherworldly being. The tongue resembles a snake, and what remains of the front feet reveals ferociously long claws (the back feet are recent additions, perhaps modern). The ears are also those of a wild animal such as a coyote or wolf. The two large white spots on the animal were created after painting by pecking away the sandstone. A few additional markings on this animal were similarly created after painting and represent more recent modifications. The spotted canine occurs in the midst of a complex and intricately painted scene that is now mostly gone. Anthropomorphs of different sizes are crowded together on both sides with birds, ungulates, snakes, and other elements. The largest anthropomorph at the rear with antennae holds aloft a snake that is partially superimposed

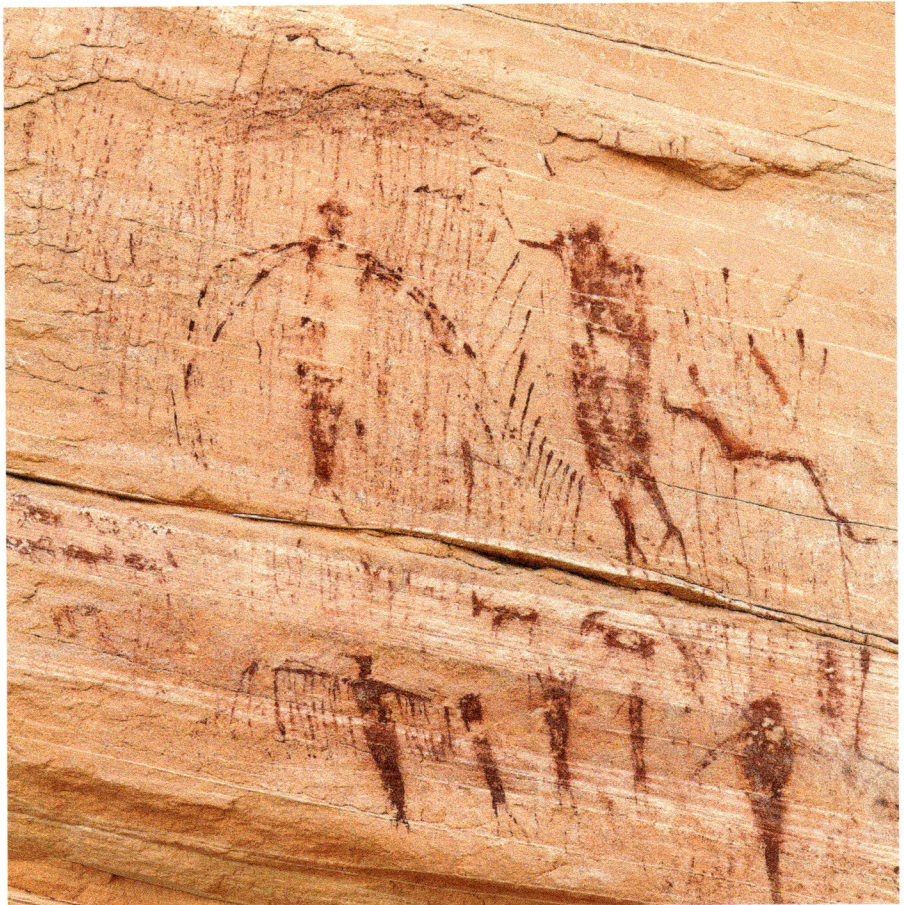

Figure 2.34 Prickly Pear rain.

by the vacant-eyed spirit figure immediately to the right. The latter figure appears to hold a flute; a later streak of purple pigment seems to turn this element into a serpent, whose head is between the two anthropomorphs. As is common in BCS rock art, birds flutter about the head of the largest spirit figure. The large anthropomorph at the head of the spotted animal also holds aloft a snake and other items. It is accompanied by four smaller and narrower anthropomorphs forming a line to the right, fronted by an alignment of birds flying above the deer ascending to the right.

The far-left side of the panel has numerous intriguing elements, many painted with fine lines and details. A major theme consists of rain clouds represented by wide red bands, with rain signified by vertical streaks of red that originate from the clouds. This theme is repeated at several BCS sites. The small rain cloud shown here showers down on human-bird polymorphs, two rows of bighorn sheep, and other figures. The red streaks on the far left originate at a larger rain cloud higher and to the left. Another interesting scene not shown here is an elongated centipede-like creature with an ungulate head spewing forth liquid from its mouth and midsection; it is beseeched by an individual wearing a horned and feathered headdress.

Barnes Panel

Figure 2.35 Barnes Panel Site.

This BCS Panel is named after Fran Barnes, who included a Steven Manning drawing of the main scene on the cover of his book *Canyon Country Prehistoric Rock Art*. The sandstone wall used as the canvas for this painting provides minimal protection from sun and moisture, such that the images are greatly degraded and difficult to see even in the best light. If you did not know that a rock art panel was located here, you might easily walk by without noticing. Many examples of BCS rock art are like this.

Past photographers have struggled to capture usable images of this panel, which is why Manning's life-size field drawing made decades ago by tracing on a clear plastic sheet rendered this scene comprehensible. Digital photography has now allowed various post-processing techniques, such as DStretch, to make subtle traces of badly faded pigment visible. Figure 2.36b was created by applying DStretch to the digital photo, then converting it to black-and-white. On the far-left side of the panel is a large, goggle-eyed spirit figure that is more than double the size of the other images (figure 2.36a). To the right are several other spirit figures of intermediate size, surrounded by dozens of small bighorn sheep, people, and other elements. Between the three similar anthropomorphs, all wearing deer antler headdresses, occurs a row of tiny human figures that may represent people gathered to witness a ceremony. Under a double rainbow walk somewhat larger human figures with arms outstretched, forming

Figure 2.36a Barnes Panel detail.

Figure 2.36b Barnes Panel detail.

a descending processional line. A director for this ceremony stands to the right in a headdress, with arms raised and rays emanating from hands. Above the double rainbow appears a cloud, with rain symbolized by vertical pigment streaks. The rain and resulting rainbows are important themes in BCS rock art, and the significance of moisture for plant, animal, and human life needs little comment. Ceremonies to ensure continued rainfall by appeasement and negotiation with supernatural forces are likely being portrayed, even if the specifics remain unknowable.

Molen Seep

Figure 2.37 Molen Seep Panel Crown.

Near Molen Seep at the far western edge of the San Rafael Swell occur several BCS pictograph panels grouped closely together. The Cretaceous sandstone in this area forms shallow shelters; hence the paintings are less well preserved, being both faded from sun, blurred from precipitation, and lightly coated with silt/clay from the local bedrock. Despite these circumstances, several of the scenes are beautiful and unusual, though some photo enhancement is useful for full appreciation of the art that remains.

The central and largest panel, shown here, depicts a tightly clustered group of BCS spirit figures, bookended by the headless anthropomorph on the left and the bison-like head on the right. The headless figure wears a crown-like headdress with antennae. This figure has an anthropomorph in the torso, suggesting a prior or important relationship with a particular spirit. The tightness of the figures is reminiscent of Archaic rock art paintings in the Grand Canyon. Occurring between the spirit figures are rows of tiny human forms much like those at the Barnes Panel. There are far more people here, suggestive of a much larger social gathering for a ceremony. As in that panel and many others, ungulates run vertically along the length of spirit figures and birds fly around heads.

The neatly composed scene of figure 2.38 occurs to the left of the previous one and seems to emphasize a rain spirit, in the form of the large central figure with

Figure 2.38 Molen Seep Panel Chorus.

outstretched arms and long claws for fingers on one hand. The dots along the top, made by fingers dipped in paint, represent big, heavy rain that the main figure appears to call forth and celebrate. Just a portion of the drops are shown here; by artful design, all the drops seem to emanate from the shelter ceiling. Seven elongated armless anthropomorphs with headdresses flank the central rain spirit. If not citizen figures in ritual dress, they could be supportive spirits of the central figure. Their variably sized crowns might signify thoughts or prayers flowing from their heads, nominally in support of the plea for big rain. The eyes on these figures are prominently drawn, suggesting they might all be witnessing a special event or taking a special journey together. A walking anthropomorph with a flowing white-and-red headdress approaches from the right. Numerous ungulates surround the main figure and face outward. Two pairs of horizontal snakes with open mouths beckon toward the rain spirit, and a vertical snake painted at a later time superimposes two of the narrow anthropomorphs. Moisture, along with rebirth or renewal, seems to be an overarching theme of this painting. The probable deer or pronghorn that flank the rain spirit might be helper animals, and species people yearned to see multiply.

Green Men

Figure 2.39 Green Men.

The central figure in this panel dominates viewer attention. While commonly referred to as "Intestine Man," the figure hardly appears human-like. Its serpentine form is suggestive of a snake spirit. A turtle such as the spiny softshell is a possibility consistent with the pointed head shape; a turtle also fits the leg forms and tail of the left figure. Green pigment is used in the curves of the torso area and the parallel vertical lines below. The more human-like spirit figure on the right has a set of wings and two plants within them. The headless left figure has three parallel lines arching over the torso with blue-green dots between the lines on both ends, with a plant-like termination on one side and four emanating birds on the other. A large bird approaches the plant and additional birds fly about the head of the right figure. These large figures are about four feet high. Over these spirit figures is a wide band of vertical streaks that seem like a clear representation of rain. This symbolic precipitation also occurs above a group of figures on the right not shown in this photo that includes a procession of eight delicately painted small human forms that approach along with a series of birds. An unusual undulating line above the humans is the most conspicuous part of this scene. Additional BCS rock art occurs on the cliff face of Wingate Sandstone at this location, but most of the other elements are faded and difficult to see. The south-facing canyon wall provides little protection from the sun and only somewhat better protection from precipitation. It is a testament to the longevity of the pigments selected by the artists that the images are as preserved as they are.

Snake Mouth

Figure 2.40 Snake Mouth.

At this panel most viewers focus on the striking blue-green eye pupils and snake in the mouth of the largest anthropomorph. This pigment is a rare one in BCS rock art compared to red ocher. It also makes a collar for the large snake extending toward the head of the main spirit figure. The bodies of both anthropomorphs were painted by dipping a hand in red paint and streaking it downward in short strokes to create broken vertical lines. The rain descending from the overhead cloud was painted the same way. The cloud appears to emerge from a crack in the sandstone face. This is just one example of BCS artists exploiting natural rock features to enhance the art. The head of the anthropomorph on the left appears odd because it is turned sideways and facing upward with the mouth open, as if singing or chanting to the overhead snake. The main anthropomorph holds aloft a human-bird polymorph in one hand that gestures toward the spirit figure. This could be a specialist in the supernatural, a shaman, who is relaying human requests to a spirit that might help to bring rain. The snake to the right is partially obscured by staining from water dripping down the rock face from above. At least one additional figure farther right is almost totally stained over.

BARRIER CANYON STYLE MOTIFS

Figure 3.1 The more complex panel at the Head of Sinbad site contains several BCS motifs, or recurring figurative elements: elongated anthropomorph bodies, large eyes, snakes, birds, quadrupeds, headdresses, and rainbows. The circles with emerging lines occur less frequently and what they represent is debatable. In this highly colorized image, two different color spaces were blended to make the many fine painted lines much easier to see. The delicately drawn horns and legs of seven pronghorns viewed from the rear are clearly visible with color contrasts added.

There are roughly a dozen representational motifs of note in BCS rock art. The painting of these motifs by BCS artists commonly reflects true talent in rendering form and action. Anthropomorphs are the most common, and many of them were probably artists' conceptions of what spirit forces might look like if they existed as visible entities. BCS rock art imparts a sense that its creators had an animistic conception of the world in which spirits were numerous and ubiquitous. More natural depictions of people and wildlife are generally much smaller in scale than the spirit figures, imparting a sense of the mundane world surrounded by large supernatural beings that hover over or around life. The spirit beings were likely those needing to be propitiated or acknowledged to help mortal humans in their struggles.

Barrier Canyon Style content was initially described by Polly Schaafsma in her 1971 monograph *The Rock Art of Utah*. This authority on southwestern rock art was in the early days of her career when the book appeared. Only a few dozen BCS sites were known at that time. Her tabulation of definable rock art figures at sixteen BCS sites listed 303 total elements, only one of which was abstract. The 302 representational elements consisted mostly of anthropomorphs, nearly 80 percent of all depictions. Other elements consisted of quadrupeds (four-footed animals) and forms such as birds and snakes. She also distinguished each element by specific attributes or traits, such as whether anthropomorph bodies were elongated and tapered or elongated and rectangular, whether quadrupeds were mountain sheep or dogs, and whether the other representational forms consisted of birds or plants.

Michael Firnhaber presented a much larger accounting of BCS content in his 2007 PhD dissertation (Anthropology Department, University College of London), tallying 1,179 elements, which he referred to as motifs, from 59 sites.[1] We tabulate his motif data here in order of numeric frequency, listing unidentified elements at the bottom and excluding these from the adjusted percentage column.

Anthropomorphs comprise 60 percent of all identifiable BCS motifs in Firnhaber's tally, likely a more realistic estimate than Schaafsma's due to the fact that he visited and documented four times the number of BCS sites. The proportion of anthropomorphs remains high, reinforcing a common conception of this motif being a dominant characteristic of this style. Anthropomorphs were present at all BCS panels he studied. Firnhaber embeds information about anthropomorph attributes in his detailed discussion of motifs. For example, he notes that 24 percent of the anthropomorphs have arms and 23 percent have legs, but with 61 percent lacking limbs entirely, consisting of elongated torsos with heads.

Animals are important motifs in BCS rock art and painted realistically enough that the general animal form intended is not in doubt. Some animals had significant survival value as food, such as bighorn sheep and other hoofed animals (ungulates) like pronghorn and deer. Ungulates are the second most common motif of BCS rock art on Firnhaber's list. Rabbits were also important food items but a rare BCS motif. When rabbits appear on a panel, they are often in a prominent role such as running down the arm of a spirit figure. Birds and snakes are both common depictions with insects more rarely painted.

Plant motifs appear less frequently in BCS rock art, but sometimes in a prominent way. The most iconic BCS plant motif is the probable grass appearing to sprout from the finger of a large spirit figure at the Harvest Panel. At other sites spirit figures appear to have roots extending from their feet. Ocher Alcove is one site with the roots-from-feet imagery and here there are plant-like people as well as what resembles a prickly pear cactus with buds. Plants were essential to human survival for Archaic period hunter-gatherers with the seeds of dropseed grass, sunflower, and goosefoot as staples during the Archaic period in this part of Utah. Spirits that ensured a bountiful harvest of these and any number of other key plant foods would have been important to local inhabitants.

Clouds and rain are other key elements at several BCS rock art panels. David Sucec, leader of the BCS PROJECT team, has long believed that the "Parallel-Line Motif" seen on many BCS panels represents rain and water, critical to human survival in the high desert of the Colorado Plateau. Connected to this theme are rainbows, another motif at some BCS sites.

We have chosen ten representational motifs, to view examples of what BCS artists drew, and to discuss what the motif might represent in a panel.

Table 3.1. Michael Firnhaber's tabulation of motifs or elements from 59 BCS sites.

Category	n	%	Adj. %
Anthropomorphs	591	50.1	59.6
Ungulates	123	10.4	12.4
Other Forms	100	8.5	10.1
Birds	72	6.1	7.3
Snakes	44	3.7	4.4
Zoomorphs	24	2.0	2.4
Polymorphs	14	1.2	1.4
Dogs	11	0.9	1.1
Plants	6	0.5	0.6
Rainclouds	6	0.5	0.6
Unidentified	188	15.9	
Total	1,179	100	100

Spirit Figures

Anthropomorphic spirit figures dominate BCS rock art. They provide the focal point of virtually all BCS rock art panels. They are usually the largest figures on BCS panels even if not the most frequent motif. All other elements surround them or support them in some way. Spirit figures were positive forces in people's lives, by showing a beneficial interaction with animals and plants. Powers that could ensure the flourishing of food resources took on great significance in the lives of hunter-gatherers.

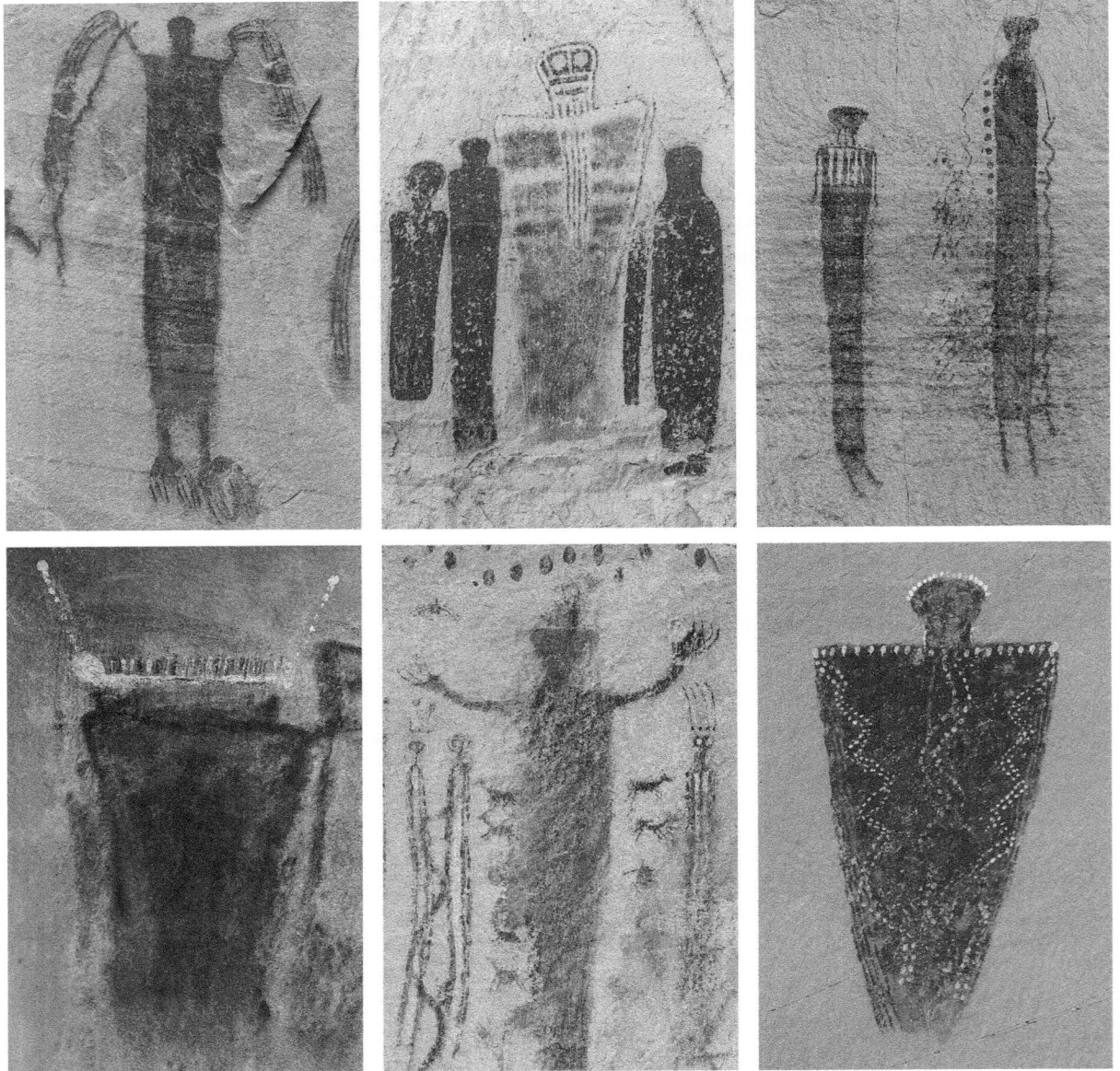

Figure 3.2 Top row, left to right: elongated anthropomorph motif (Buckhorn Wash); the "Holy Ghost" (Great Gallery); two elongated anthropomorphs (Harvest Panel). Bottom row, left to right: headless motif with headdress on top and another anthropomorph in the torso (Molen area); anthropomorph with rain above and many helpers (Molen area); well-preserved decorated anthropomorph (Perfect Panel).

BCS spirit figures vary in style, shape, and appendages. A torso is always present, and 95 percent have heads. Many spirit figures lack arms or legs, but when present, the torso always dominates these appendages. Torsos are usually greatly elongated, making the overall body appear narrow. Many spirit figures seem to float on the rock, and legless figures appear to have been intentionally drawn to fade out at the bottom, as if emerging from the rock.

Spirit figures can have vacant eyes, sometimes huge to demand attention. Sometimes the eyes and head shape are more insect-like, similar to those seen on damselflies. Some bodies are just a single uniform color. Some bodies and heads have elaborate decorations consisting of lines, dots, contrasting colors, and incisions for texture.

Spirit figures can be impressively large, as big as or bigger than humans in some cases. This is a frequently mentioned aspect of BCS rock art. The Great Gallery is a fine example of large scale, as most spirit figures within are life-size or larger and the tallest reach heights of ten feet. Yet, BCS artists also painted small spirit figures less than a quarter the size of large ones. A panel on the upper left of the Great Gallery has a grouping of three spirit figures about fourteen inches tall with their elongated bodies painted in detail. In association are realistic animals painted at tiny size relative to the spirit figures with some less than one inch in height. Tiny figures like this are common at BCS sites but are often lost or made indistinct by the ravages of time.

Several rock art experts suggest that BCS artists used anthropomorphs to represent spirits of different kinds. Societies with animistic beliefs maintain that spirits can reside in any phenomenon of the world, even rocks. Negotiating with these spirits is a critical part of survival and reproduction by bringing rain, helping plants to grow and fruits to ripen, and ensuring that game animals flourish. Making images on canyon walls likely played an important role in connecting to the spiritual world from the real world, a means to petition for assistance in life's travails.

Once painted on canyon walls, spirit figures might have been conceived as ancestral and in need of maintenance to continue propitiating the spirits. They also likely exerted an influence over subsequent artists, perhaps stimulating a desire to add more art while also constraining or channeling the nature of newly added images.

Citizen Figures

On some panels BCS artists depicted what appear to be real people. These anthropomorphs not only have arms and legs, but their body proportions are far closer to realistic than with spirit figures. "Citizen" is David Sucec's apropos label for this anthropomorphic category. They truly look like normal people involved in life's activities: walking, tussling, performing ceremonies.

A Great Gallery scene to the right of the Holy Ghost group provides an excellent example of citizen figures: two humans grapple over what is likely a spear or atlatl dart. The figure on the right is angled partially forward

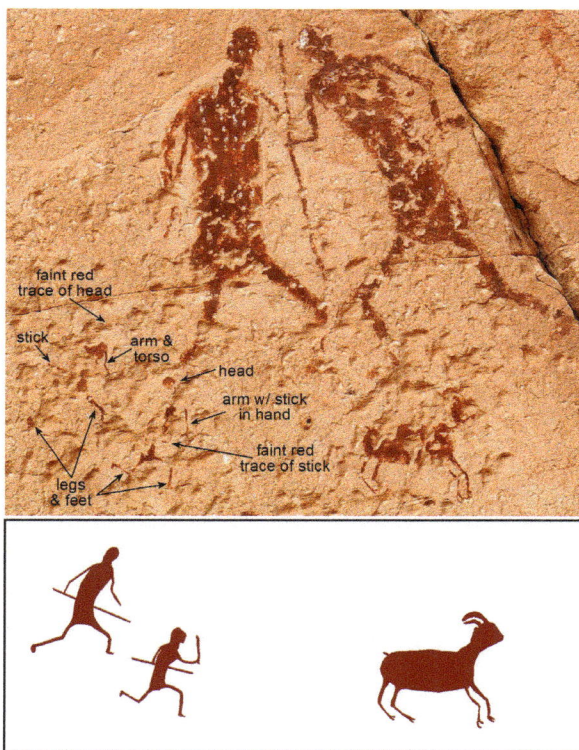

faint red trace of head
stick
arm & torso
head
arm w/ stick in hand
faint red trace of stick
legs & feet

Figure 3.4 Great Gallery scene with people grabbing a stick and the even smaller scene directly below that shows two people in hot pursuit of a bighorn sheep.

Figure 3.3 Top row, left to right: numerous citizen anthropomorphs with bighorn sheep and dog (Great Gallery); several anthropomorphs in procession that have both citizen and spirit characteristics (Ocher Alcove). Bottom row, left to right: eight citizen anthropomorphs engaged in a rain ceremony (Prickly Pear); four anthropomorphs with white headdresses under a rainbow engaged in a ceremony (Dragonfly).

and looking to the left whereas the figure opposite is angled partially backward and looking to the right, which means both clutch the stick in their right hand. Both hold other objects in their other hand, with the left figure grasping a short stick such as an atlatl.

Below them, two people a half-size smaller run in hot pursuit of a bighorn sheep in an evident hunt. Both hold linear objects in their hands, perhaps weapons. This is part of a larger scene involving ten additional bighorn sheep, a dog, and one other citizen figure.[2]

Whether a specific anthropomorph or group of anthropomorphs represents citizen figures or spirit figures is less clear in some cases. Ocher Alcove provides a good example with a scene that shows a spirit figure of red-and-white wide vertical strips beseeched by a polymorph of a snake body with mountain sheep head and human-like arms. The arms of this creature reach toward the spirit figure and its open mouth appears to drip, perhaps an indication of speech. A procession of characters approaches the spirit figure below the polymorph. These entities are much smaller, roughly one-fourth the size of the spirit figure. They are painted in red, and a large number have white accents. Many are anthropomorphs, but even the most human-like figures have overly elongated bodies, short legs, and arms that terminate in unnatural hands. Hovering in the midst of the first two pairs of anthropomorphs is a miniature spirit figure lacking legs or arms. In the procession are apparent walking plants, among other mysterious entities, though some of this lack of identifiable form is due to loss of detail through exfoliation. On this panel, distinguishing spirit figures from citizen figures based on body shape and attributes seems problematic. Relative size is likely an important indicator of whether a spirit essence or real human is portrayed.

The lower part of the Dragonfly Panel has a group of four red anthropomorphs with white feather headdresses that stand on what looks like a mesa or rock prominence under a double arc of red paint, similar to a rainbow motif seen at other panels. This group of four appear to be citizen figures involved in a ceremony.

Decoration

Nearly all BCS pictographs of anthropomorphs have their torsos painted a uniform dark red color using an ocher-based mineral paint. About one-quarter of these have some sort of decoration added to the torso or head. This is typically a white paint applied with a finger or a small brush. Paints of green, blue, black, grey, and yellow were also used on occasion, with most derived from different colored minerals.

If anthropomorphs are decorated, the adornment usually occurs on both torsos and heads, with torso decoration often appearing more elaborate, likely the result of having more surface area to work with. Some highly decorated spirit figures have a sort of crown or head gear created by short white lines or white dots.

Dots of white paint form lines and patterns, with vertical parallel and wavy lines common. Vertical lines attached to horizontal lines or bands might represent rain and water, a theme portrayed as separate elements in BCS art. Sufficient and periodic

Figure 3.5 Top row: three highly decorated spirit figures (all at Great Gallery); the middle figure has a variety of lines in the torso created using paints and incising; the figure on the right has two anthropomorphs contained in the torso and several animal spirit helpers in attendance. Bottom row: figure on left has pecked facial features and hole in heart area that occurred at some later point (North Wash); rare, decorated petroglyph with multiple parallel line motifs and pupils in eyes; digitally colorized to bring out decoration and panel details (Moab area); highly decorated spirit figure (Perfect Panel). All figures are life-sized except petroglyph (two feet high).

Figure 3.6 This image, from the "Unexpected Panel," depicts citizens in costumes under a rainbow and other rain motifs, suggesting a ceremony for rain and water.

amounts of water are central to renewal and rebirth in a desert, a common concern then as now.

Wavy and zig-zag lines often represent snakes in BCS art, which are commonly depicted beside or above anthropomorphs and sometimes in their hands. This theme was also carried over in body decoration. Lightning is perhaps metaphorically linked to snakes that might have served as messengers to rain spirits.

After applying paint, parts of some torsos were further decorated by incising wavy or parallel lines with a sharp, hard rock, likely a flaked stone tool. These additions add to a textile effect seen on some spirit figures. These embellishments were unlikely to be just decorative elements like those on a common dish or cup today, but rife with symbolic meaning and significance to the artists and their social group.

The highly decorated spirit anthropomorphs look like they are wearing ceremonial robes. Did participants in ceremonies paint their bodies and wear costumes? Many citizen figures of BCS panels appear to wear ceremonial regalia.

Eyes

Many BCS anthropomorphs lack eyes, but when present on spirit figures they are conspicuous. Eyes lack realism, appearing much larger than they should be, sometimes accounting for about half of the head. Often they are vacuous blank holes that were created by leaving circular or oval patches unpainted. This imparts an eerie feeling to many modern viewers.

In some cases, paint was added inside the blank areas, making it seem as though the figures have pupils. Sometimes eyes were painted directly onto solid red heads using white, but still retaining their disproportionately large size.

There is a tendency for spirit figures with horizontally elongated heads to have the largest eyes, making them look insect-like. This might be purposefully done to

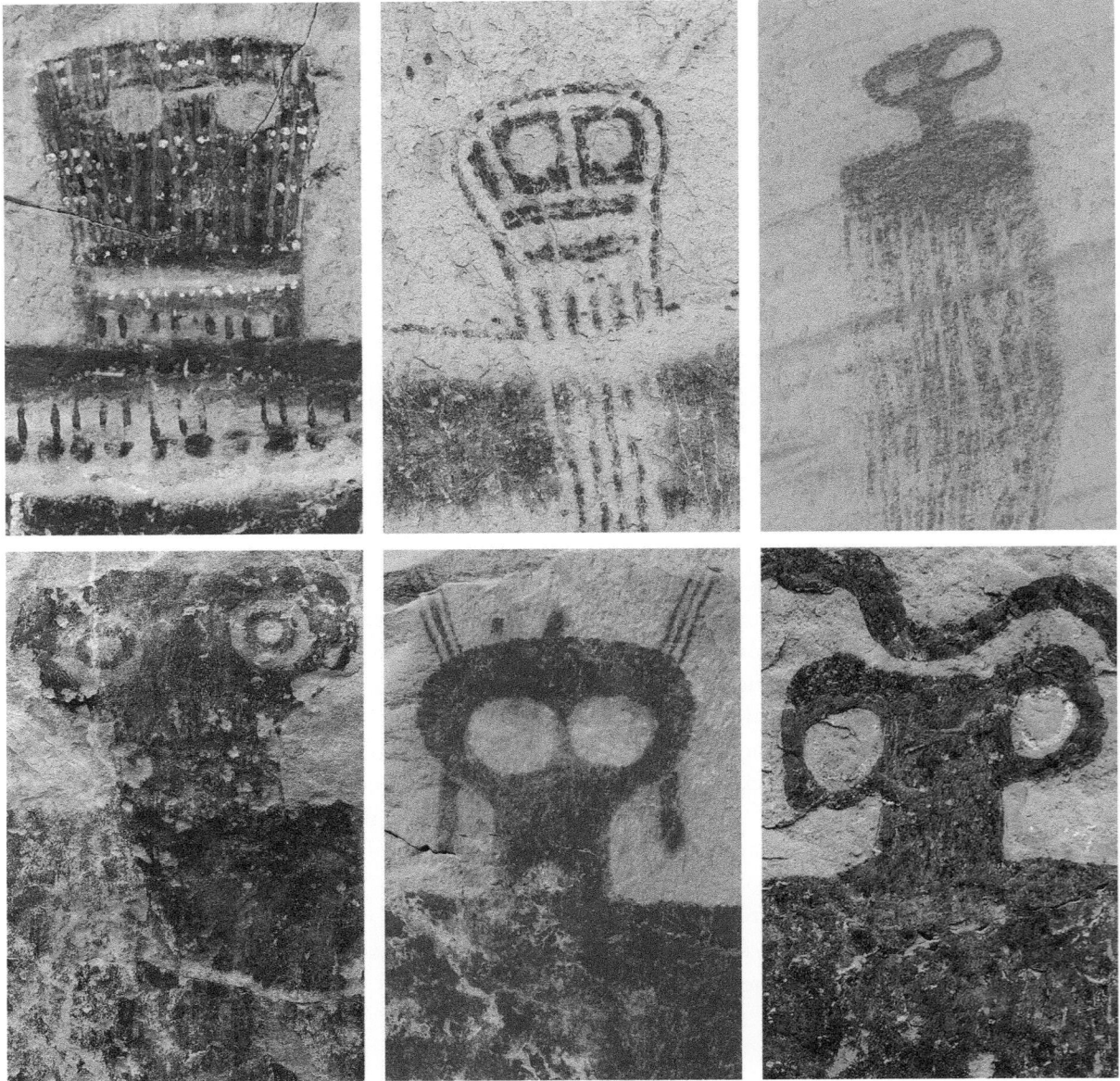

Figure 3.7 Top row: intricately decorated head and the head of the "Holy Ghost" (Great Gallery); only anthropomorph with eyes at Bartlett Panel. Bottom row: eyes drawn with pupils (Head of Sinbad); very large eyes (Sego/Thompson); eyes with eroding white paint inside them (Head of Sinbad).

mimic damselflies or dragonflies, insects intimately associated with water and perhaps the spirits of water. These insects hover around permanent water sources, where they hatch and develop later to emerge and undergo a metamorphosis to flying creatures. Water is central to all life, and sky is commonly conceived as a place where major forces of the world reside. Both usually have spiritual significance, as might beings that can move between these realms.

Polly Schaafsma thought that exaggerated eyes might signify a shamanic ability to see what others could not: "When a shaman is in a trance state, he is said to see with mystical eye—he can 'see' lost objects, the presence of evil spirits, the nature or cause of an illness, and into the past and future—things and places inaccessible to the uninitiated."[3]

Disproportionately large eyes could also be a feature of supernatural entities that likewise can perceive what mortal humans cannot. They can see the world better than humans whether or not they have pupils like ours, with otherworldly eyes perhaps especially useful.

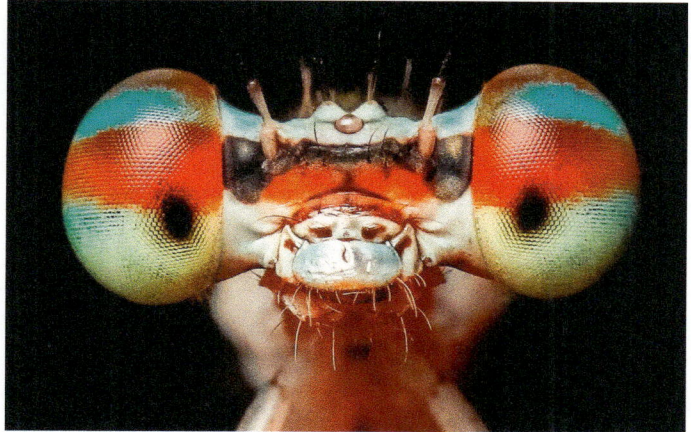

Figure 3.8 Damselfly head with typical large bulging eyes on the side.

Polymorphs

One common theme in BCS rock art is a fusion or melding of distinct life forms into single beings. Most polymorphs or composite figures have a mix of human and animal attributes, but there are a few with human and plant attributes. Some polymorphs have few if any human-like features, such as snakes with bighorn sheep heads. This horned serpent theme occurs on several BCS panels and continues in the later iconography of the Southwest and Mesoamerica.[4]

Another polymorph theme in BCS rock art is a fusion of obvious human and bird features. At the High Gallery, a human-bird composite appears to be released for flight by a possible citizen figure. This image is quite similar to one at Buckhorn Wash, and they appear at other BCS panels scattered throughout the region.[5] A similar one at the Prickly Pear Panel occurs under part of a rain cloud. Something more than a person in bird costume seems indicated. Perhaps it is a shaman or medicine person going into a trance state as some have suggested, taking flight to commune with supernatural forces.

At the Ascending Sheep Panel, a sheep-headed polymorph standing in partial profile interacts with two lines of bighorn sheep approaching from opposite directions. This figure seems to attract or direct the sheep and has captured one of them with its front legs. The polymorph has the feet of a predator, either claws or bird-of-prey talons, and a serpent's tongue. It holds aloft and looks at a small polymorph resembling a human-bird mix. Some interpret the sheep-headed polymorph as a shaman who directs the hunting of game animals. If a supernatural specialist is depicted here, it is more likely the human-bird hybrid held in the hand of this predatory spirit that might just turn over the bighorn sheep it holds firm.

While the winged anthropomorph is a common polymorphic figure, the panel at the Ocher Alcove (Figure 3.9c) has three snake-based polymorphs. Firnhaber's description is quite helpful in seeing what complex polymorphs look like.

The left-most polymorph bears the body and head of a snake, but has short arms which reach toward the anthropomorph to its left. The next creature is quite

Figure 3.9 Top row, left to right: polymorphs interacting (Ascending Sheep); a citizen releasing a polymorph (High Panel Horseshoe Canyon). Bottom row: polymorphs around a spirit figure (Ocher Alcove); polymorph with parallel line motifs (Prickly Pear).

bird-like, but its body transforms into a meandering, snake-like line, finally terminating with two legs bearing small feet at the bottom. The final polymorphic form is a horned serpent with a pair of outstretched, three-fingered hands.[6]

Humans in many cultures envision monsters and demons of all sorts that are thought to exist or that can be conjured or brought into being by various means or by actions or inactions. These creatures can be both dangerous and beneficial depending upon how they are "handled" spiritually. Such managing is usually the realm of specialists of the supernatural, authorities that occur in most human societies around the world studied by ethnographers. *Shaman* is the umbrella term applied to these specialists. To a shaman in a deep trance or an altered state of consciousness, the merging with animal spirit assistants into polymorphs seems not only possible, but likely.

Hoofed Animals

Hoofed mammals such as desert bighorn sheep, pronghorn, and deer are the most common animal motif in the BCS rock art tradition. *Ungulate* is a useful umbrella term for distinguishing these quadrupeds from ones lacking hooves that BCS artists also painted. A specific type of ungulate is sometimes unclear, perhaps purposefully so, when animals are quite stylized. In other cases, the images are blurred by moisture such that any specifying details once present are now indistinct.

Many ungulates have backward-curved horns, suggesting that bighorn sheep are the animals portrayed. Others lack these and may be female deer or pronghorn. At the Great Gallery, an ascending line of ungulates approaches a spirit figure. The animal outlines are less distinct than those of the Great Gallery hunt scene, but there is a notable lack of back-curving horns and the upward projections from the heads appear to be ears and perhaps the small straight horns on female pronghorn. A quadruped on the shoulder of the big-armed spirit figure at the Perfect Panel has white markings unrealistic for any ungulate species. In cases like this, the depictions likely signify something more than a common animal but rather a special interlocutor with the supernatural, perhaps a shaman in animal disguise.

Ungulates are most often depicted much smaller relative to spirit figures. Only when shown with citizen figures, such as at the Great Gallery hunt scene, are they proportioned correctly relative to anthropomorphs. Ungulates are sometimes depicted about the head and shoulders of spirit figures, just like birds, and usually at the same small scale. A crucial difference, however, is that, unlike birds, ungulates often touch spirit figures by standing on their heads or shoulders.

Another theme is for lines of ungulates to parade toward, away from, or alongside the bodies of spirit figures. One gets a sense that BCS artists believed that some spirit figures had an ability to call forth or multiply these animals and direct them.[7] Any supernatural force with such abilities requires special human attention.

At the Ascending Sheep Panel, the animals on the right side of the polymorph are painted as if climbing in switchback fashion directly up a steep slope. The intimate knowledge of bighorn sheep behavior on display here is that of a painter who observed animals closely as would a hunter. Farther right of the polymorph stands a pair of enigmatic figures, elongated and narrow with antennae at the top of their heads. Emanating from near the lower portions of these figures are two more ascending lines of animals that lack both horns and legs. The animals were depicted this way originally, and the lack of these features cannot be attributed to weathering or later damage. Other examples of legless animals occur in BCS rock art; perhaps they indicate animal

Figure 3.10 Top row: herd of bighorn sheep and a dog in a hunt scene (Great Gallery); sheep ascending toward a polymorph (not shown) and ungulates ascending away from two anthropomorphs (Ascending Sheep). Bottom row: a quadruped on the shoulder of an anthropomorph at the Perfect Panel and at the Pond Site.

spirits that do not need legs for movement. Such spirits might ultimately become real animals that run across the land on four legs and can be hunted for food.

Snakes

Some animals depicted by BCS artists likely had little if any food value, with snakes a prime example. It is possible that harming snakes, let alone eating them, was taboo. Snakes are one of most common animals depicted by BCS artists, occurring at approximately 30 percent of BCS sites.

Snakes are represented by undulating lines, usually with an obvious head and tapered tail. They are commonly held in the hands of spirit figures or otherwise interacting with them or in close proximity. Sometimes snakes appear to spit or have liquid dripping from gaping mouths. Vertical snakes also commonly occur adjacent to

Figure 3.11 Top row: anthropomorph holding a snake (Dragonfly); a green snake in the mouth of a life-sized anthropomorph (near Moab); anthropomorph holding a snake (Sinbad). Bottom row: life-sized anthropomorph holding a snake (Temple Mountain); a green snake inside a two-foot-tall anthropomorph (near Moab); snakes used to form a parallel line motif in the torso of a three-foot-tall anthropomorph (Canyonlands).

anthropomorphs or as body decoration. At the Head of Sinbad, a snake writhes just above a spirit figure's head. Greatly elongated horizontal serpents occur at a few panels such as along the bottom of the Horseshoe Canyon High Gallery or along the upper part of the Invisible Panel.

Many cultures around the world have revered and treated snakes with awe. The fact that some have killing venom might play a role, but likely more important is their shedding of skin (continual rebirth), their slithering movement between the earth's surface and underground, and a writhing body that some consider analogous to lightning. The Hopi have a special ceremony that involves snakes, which are thought to carry prayers back to supernatural forces that control rain. BCS artists likewise might have conceived of snakes as messengers or go-betweens with supernatural forces, especially those linked to rain.

Snakes are sometimes shown with tongues sticking out toward spirit figures or with drops and spray coming from their mouths similar to a snake–bighorn–human polymorph at Ocher Alcove. Some describe this as venom, but this seems a very western interpretation based on a learned fear of snakes. None of the depicted serpents exhibit rattles, the only kinds of snakes in Utah that are poisonous, a detail that some Native Americans depicted but not BCS artists. The red drips from snake mouths might be a visual means of representing sound and communication. Other animals in BCS rock art sometimes have what might represent depictions of vocalizations. Drops of red from a large snake in the hand of a spirit figure at Temple Mountain fall upon the shoulder of this figure and appear to create an alignment of dots like messages received (see figure 4.26).

Birds

BCS painters artfully rendered birds in active flight from a multitude of perspectives, similar to stop-action photography. They portrayed these animals in great detail, often using fine lines for wings and tail feathers. Beaks are regularly shown, as are toes, usually consisting of three lines. Despite the care and craft in depicting birds, few specific types are identifiable, save for some that appear like swifts or swallows, hummingbirds, a few like herons or cranes, and a possible duck. Bird bones at Archaic period archaeological sites are rare.

About 20 percent of the BCS panels have bird depictions. They are most commonly portrayed fluttering around the heads, shoulders, and bodies of spirit figures. There is an obvious close relationship between them, yet birds generally appear separate from the anthropomorphs they accompany and never in the hands of spirit figures like snakes often are.

Since spirit figures are not proportioned naturally, they provide no clear comparative scale for judging whether or not birds have a realistic size. Judging from other animals also depicted in specific scenes, such as a bighorn sheep or a rabbit, birds are depicted either larger or smaller than they exist proportionally in real life. A bird at the Dragonfly Panel is depicted smaller than an insect shown immediately adjacent, so natural proportions were often not adhered to in this art style. Relative size might have been indicative of significance in this world or the spiritual realm.

Given that birds appear small relative to spirit figures, they seem more like messengers or assistants to the anthropomorphs. The ability of flight into the heavens is a distinctive aspect that makes birds well suited as intermediaries between humans and supernatural entities. Birds also have metaphorical connections with a shaman's

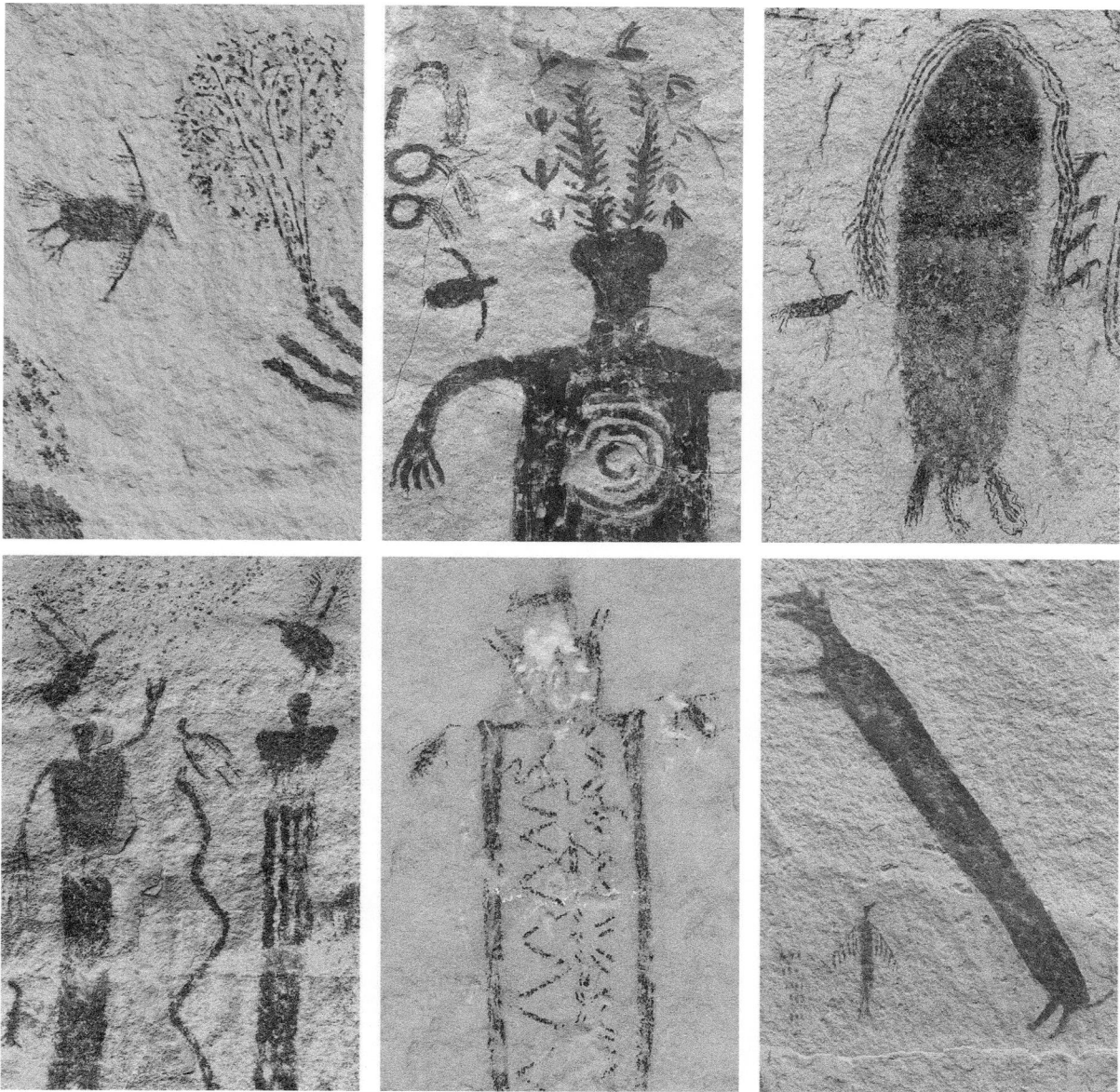

Figure 3.12 Top row: bird flying near hand of a key anthropomorph at the Harvest Panel; swift or swallow-like birds circling head appendages (Sinbad); several birds next to headless anthropomorph (near Moab); Bottom row: two anthropomorphs each with a bird overhead (Buckhorn Wash); delicately drawn "attendant" birds next to anthropomorph with crane on upper left chest (Great Gallery); small bird standing under elongated dog (Harvest Panel).

ability to leave their bodies and partake in magical flight. This association might be illustrated in BCS rock art by the winged anthropic polymorphs present at several sites. At the Ocher Panel of the San Rafael Swell, an odd-looking bird adjacent to a spirit figure has a long trailing line and human legs. Some suggest this signifies the transformation a shaman experiences when having an out-of-body flight of his spirit.

Dogs

Dogs appear at a few BCS sites and are identified as a boxy quadruped with upright ears and a short tail that is curved over the back. Domestication brought about this tail posture, a feature of dogs that differs from other canids such as wolves, coyotes, and foxes. The hunt scene with citizen figures and bighorn sheep at the Great Gallery has a dog appearing to "herd" the sheep. Another dog at the Great Gallery, the

Figure 3.13 Top row: dog and anthropomorph (Great Gallery); dog and 'Moqui Queen' (Hog Springs). Bottom row: dog and anthropomorph (Horseshoe Shelter); dog on BCS panel (Temple Mountain). Two dogs appear in the bottom left Great Gallery photo under Quadrupeds: one dog is at the bottom edge herding, and one dog is sitting at the top right edge next to a small anthropomorph.

last element at the farthest right side, barks down-canyon as if protecting this sacred space from any who approach. A similar dog-like animal at the Prickly Pear site, painted with some fantastic features such as a serpent for its tongue and horrendous claws, is more likely some special spirit than a dog per se. A third dog at the Great Gallery, on the upper panel to the far left, has been impacted by subsequent Native American visitors who removed paint from the head and feet. Similar sampling occurs at this and other BCS sites, part of later interaction with the rock art—removing minute portions, perhaps in an effort to obtain power from the images.

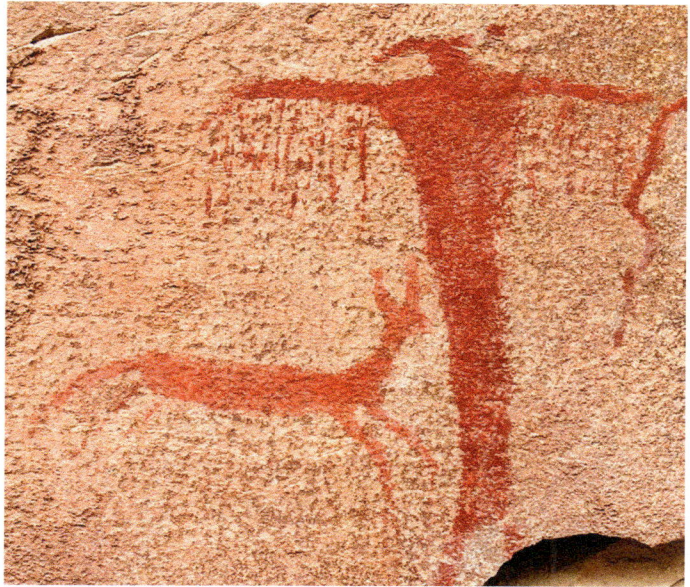

Figure 3.14 Probable fox in BCS rock art, San Rafael Area (photo by Brian Lee).

Dogs in the Americas date back at least 10,000 years and originated from northeast Asia, where domestication from wolves occurred.[8] Their utility to humans and the companionship they offer needs little elaboration: camp guards and cleaners, pack animals, food, help in hunting, warmth on cold nights. It is perhaps no wonder that dogs are sometimes shown as friendly companions to spirit figures. This does not mean that dogs had mundane roles when portrayed in BCS art, although this occurs at the Great Gallery. Schaafsma suggests that dogs perhaps served as guardians or guides for a shaman's journeying soul.[9] Certain spirit figures might also have had dog companions just like people; what we find useful could well have fulfilled the same role for supernatural entities.

BCS artists also depicted dog-like creatures on occasion, such as the example shown here that appears to be a fox or coyote. Its pointed upright ears, long tail that streams backward behind it, and lithe body form distinguish it from BCS dog images. A fox seems most likely for this depiction given the thin body and legs. It stands next to a spirit figure with outstretched arms and a "rain curtain." To the right of this figure stands a larger spirit figure with bug-shaped head.

Head Appendages

Head appendages occur on about 25 percent of BCS anthropomorphs. They can take the form of horns, antennae, ears, earrings, antlers, or simply dots or lines. Often there are only two or four very thinly drawn lines emerging from the top of the head that resemble feathers or insect antennae. Usually these lines are short, but some conspicuously long ones attract viewer attention. Ears vary in size, shape, and direction up or down with some wearing obvious earrings. At the Temple Mountain Panel, a spirit figure wears earrings of prickly pear cactus pads, an important food to Archaic period hunter-gatherers. Head appendages resembling horns and antlers appear to be drawn to resemble animals, while the antennae suggest insects as models for their delicate

Figure 3.15 Top row: insect-like antennae used on anthropomorph with several snakes adjacent to torso (Harvest Panel); lines and dots used to define appendages; horns, head, and torso all include parallel line motifs (Harvest Panel). Bottom row: similar horns on heads of six anthropomorphs of greatly varying size (Canyonlands); delicately drawn appendages (Molen).

renditions. Insects of various sorts occur in BCS rock art so the occurrence of insect features on spirit figures is not odd.

Horns are a common head appendage on display at some BCS sites, like the Harvest Panel, and according to Schaafsma are almost universally emblematic of shamanic and supernatural power.[10] Some ethnographically documented ceremonial headdresses of Native Americans and other societies included horns and feathers as natural adornments, so some BCS anthropomorphs with head appendages might be depictions of spiritually oriented occasions or rituals where special regalia was worn. Spirits with different powers or spheres of influence might be represented by the nature of the headgear as well as other embellishments.

4
BARRIER CANYON STYLE CONTEXTS

Figure 4.1 The Yellow Comet is unique among BCS panels in the amount of yellow paint used, in addition to the usual red ocher accented with white. The yellow is considerably faded, likely since this panel is exposed daily to direct sunlight for long periods. Digital photographic restoration of the yellow paint is now needed to see the panel as once drawn. The panel is located at the base of a 200-foot sheer rock face, a breathtaking BCS site. Access to the canyon floor where the panel resides is either lengthy and circuitous or dangerous down a cliff face.

Figure 4.2 Looking south from Dead Horse Point at the Colorado River as it winds its way south toward the Green River confluence and beyond.

Canyon Country

Barrier Canyon Style rock art is concentrated in an area geologists refer to as the Canyon Lands section of the Colorado Plateau. This dramatic and deeply dissected landscape is centered on the confluence of the Colorado and the Green Rivers. It is characterized by spectacular red-rock scenery of canyons, mesas, buttes, and rock monuments, some of memorable shape. Isolated mountains punctuate the landscape and ancient folds in the rock create striking hogbacks of upturned sandstone that stand in high relief.

It is in the desolate and remote reaches of this area that the creators of BCS rock art placed their work. The terms "desolate" and "remote" are from our present-day perspective, but this was not the perspective of those who created the rock art, as this setting was their place of residence. It was home. The landscape appears desolate and remote to us because of its challenges for an industrialized, food-producing society. There is the challenge of movement across a land of precipitous drops into deep canyons and blockage from towering sandstone walls. There is the challenge of making a living in a land bereft of water for farming and livestock. There is the challenge of excessive heat and sun in summer and the cold of winter. These and other difficulties have made the region remote from those places modern people occupy densely because they found them more favorable.

Horseshoe Canyon, the type of location for BCS rock art, is situated along the western edge of a wonderland of deeply incised canyons and cliffs centered on the Colorado and Green River confluence. Much of this broken country of precipitous drops is in Canyonlands and Arches National Parks, with some in the northern extension of the Glen Canyon National Recreation Area. Many BCS rock art panels are tucked away in the recesses of this scenic landscape, such as the Harvest Panel in the Maze and the nearby Perfect Panel.

To the north and west of Horseshoe Canyon stretches a vast, open plain covered with grass and shrubs, where opportunities for making rock art are virtually nonexistent. Beyond this plain occur sharply upfolded rock layers, the result of a large-scale geologic feature known as an anticline. Erosion has cut these layers to expose many sandstone cliff faces suitable for pictographs and petroglyphs. This San Rafael Swell area is another important location of BCS rock art, which extends westward to the foot of the Wasatch Plateau. Some truly spectacular BCS panels can be found here, including Temple Mountain Wash, Head of Sinbad, and the Ascending Sheep Panel.

Farther up the Green and Colorado Rivers to the north and northeast of the core zone, there is another concentration of BCS rock art in canyons draining the Tavaputs and Roan Plateaus. The Book Cliffs form a prominent scarp along the southern margin of these plateaus. The Cretaceous sandstones of this area are drab in color compared to the Jurassic and Triassic sandstones to the south, but there are some notable panels such as Thompson Wash/Sego Canyon. This zone of BCS rock art extends into the modern state of Colorado, though most imagery of this style occurs in Utah.

To the south of the core zone, BCS images quickly diminish in occurrence, but not for a lack of suitable rock surfaces. Much past where the Dirty Devil River and North Wash empty into the Colorado River and Glen Canyon begins, images resembling those of typical Barrier Canyon style are rare. Instead, another rock art style attributed to Archaic period foragers becomes predominant and covers many a canyon wall section and talus boulder. Whereas BCS largely consists of painted images, this Glen Canyon Linear style is almost universally pecked into the rock.

Experiencing the Environment

This country is no good anymore; everything is dry; the creeks are cut deep; the food plants are all gone.

—The words of a Southern Paiute woman to Isabel Kelly after seeing her old homeland along the Escalante River for the first time in forty years.

It is virtually impossible for people today to fully appreciate what life or the environment was like for the creators of BCS rock art. Modern visitors come to this region well

Figure 4.3 Example of historic period arroyo cutting in the Southwest that removed tons of alluvial sediment from canyons and valleys within the span of a hundred years. View of Dowozhiebito Canyon on Navajo tribal land in northeast Arizona. The people stand on the current floodplain but in the late 1800s they would have been on the surface of alluvial fill some forty to sixty feet higher than today. All of that sediment has eroded away. (Photo from Oxbow Ecological Engineering.)

equipped with conveniences, well fed, and packing a good supply of food and drink. Mechanized transportation often takes them directly to where they want to go. Even backpacking to out-of-the-way places occurs in limited time frames and is fully supplied. Such exploring provides a better experiential vantage point for contemplating what life might have been like for BCS artists, but one with real limitations.

The environment seen today is not what past people experienced. The large geologic features were certainly the same, but the density and distribution of plants and animals, along with the environs of canyons and grasslands, have changed substantially. Historic livestock overgrazing denuded the landscape and altered vegetation, resulting in a major loss of plant resources that Native Americans depended upon. This depletion, along with overhunting and extirpation of species like bighorn sheep, added to resource loss. Invasive plant species have replaced native ones, especially along riparian corridors. The historic loss and change in resources that Native Americans experienced from Euro-American settlement also occurred in the distant past, but from different causes: climate change, extinction of Pleistocene lifeforms, and slow shifts in the distribution and density of key plant and animal resources.

One aspect of environmental change with significant consequences for past people was dissection of canyon floodplains and the loss of alluvium. All canyons of the Southwest were variably filled and flushed of alluvium—sediment transported and deposited by flowing water. All have undergone times of sediment accumulation, when alluvium built up higher and higher (aggradation) followed by times of downcutting, when alluvium eroded and was flushed downstream (degradation).[1] During the last ice age, at the end of the Pleistocene, alluvium filled Southwestern canyons to a considerable height as a result of the increased moisture present at the time. This ancient sediment started to erode after the ice age ended and the climate both warmed and dried. Most of the ancient alluvium washed away, although high-terrace remnants preserved in some places provide a record of past presence. Cycles of canyon filling and flushing continued during the Holocene, although terraces never reached the heights of the Pleistocene and generally have decreased through time, such that more recent alluvial terraces are lowest in height above the stream bottom.

The most recent episode of massive downcutting in the Southwest started in the late 1800s and early 1900s, with various historical accounts documenting the location and timing of this event. The rapid pace of incision and widening of the arroyos made it memorable, especially due to the fact that it destroyed large swaths of farmland and irrigation systems and made travel in the region all the more difficult.[2] Ultimately, some Euro-American communities were abandoned and farming for Native American communities became more difficult. Vast amounts of alluvium got flushed from canyons and valleys of the Southwest within the span of 50 to 100 years.[3] In some cases it took just a few decades or less to wash away alluvium 100 feet or more thick down to gravel-strewn bedrock, sometimes leaving canyons bare of sediment from one wall to the other.

Floodplain dissection and loss of alluvium was disastrous for farmers, in both the historic and more distant past, but it was also tragic for preagricultural societies. Historical accounts describe pre-arroyo-cut floodplains as verdant swaths, dotted with marshes and ponds that supported birds such as ducks, geese, cranes, and herons, along with other wildlife. Canyons in this state were far more supportive of humans, such that loss of the habitat must have been as alarming in that earlier time as it was in recent history. Moreover, geologists have documented that cycles of downcutting were often correlated with periods of significant drought, perhaps a consequence of these drier-than-normal conditions. This, too, significantly impacted people trying to make a living from the land, since less moisture means fewer plant and animal resources.

Stephen Hall's[4] generalized reconstruction of climatic conditions of the Southwest for the past 14,000 years reveals oscillations in precipitation and temperature that are mirror reflections of one another: warmer conditions are generally correlated with dryer conditions and vice versa. The protracted cool and wet interval of the last ice age came to a close some 16,000 years ago as the climate warmed and precipitation decreased. There was a brief return to cold and wet conditions during the Younger Dryas, marking an end to the Pleistocene and the demise of Clovis culture. Afterward came the Holocene, with both increasing warmth and decreasing precipitation. Both trends culminated in an interval of aridity roughly 2,000 years long during the middle part of the Holocene, centered around 4000 BC.

The middle Holocene was a tough time for hunter-gatherers on the Colorado Plateau. Places where foragers had camped regularly for centuries or millennia stopped being used. Many sites reveal a long hiatus in human presence, with very little to no use prior to a return to cooler and wetter conditions of the late Holocene. Archaeologists have had difficulty locating sites in Utah's canyon lands that date to the middle Holocene despite finding both earlier and later sites. Alluvial deposits in many canyons are missing during this interval, suggesting that it was a time of floodplain dissection and erosion. Scientists who study packrat (*Neotoma* sp.) accumulations for clues to

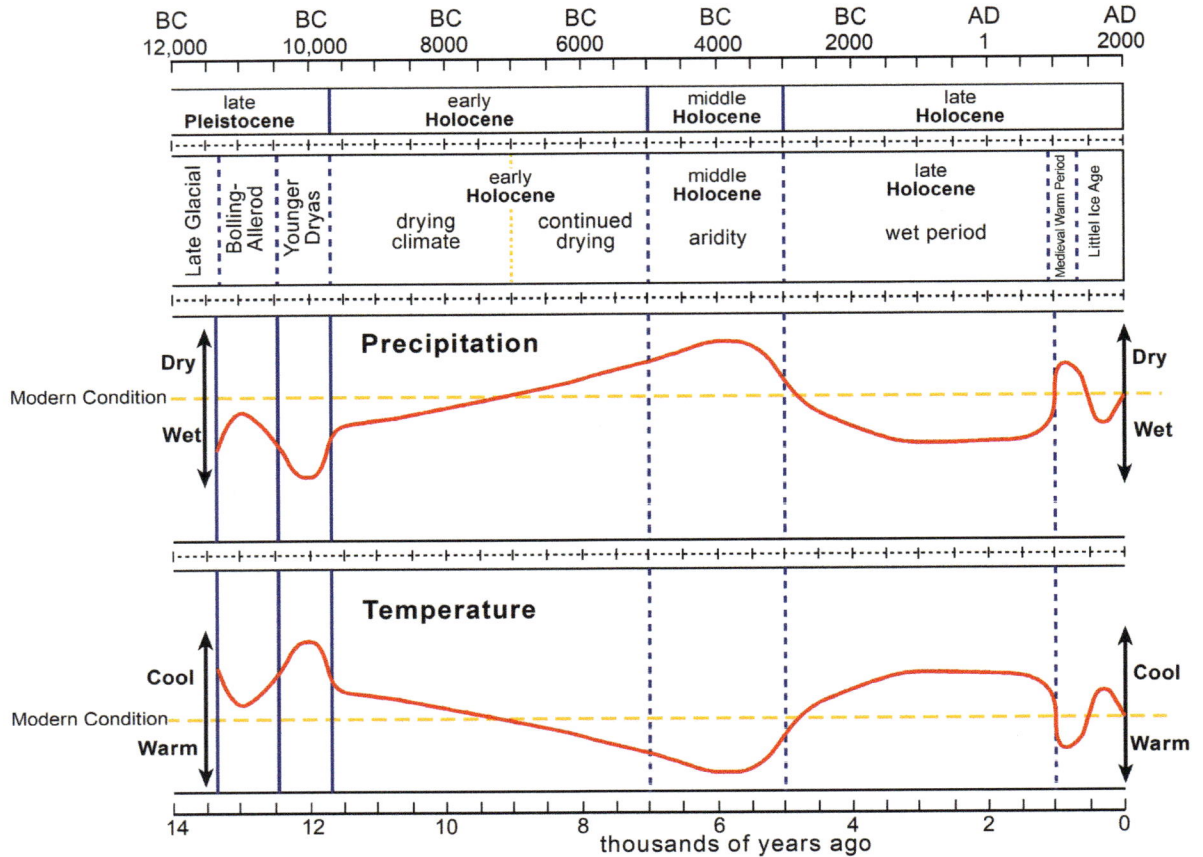

Figure 4.4 Generalized reconstruction of Paleoclimate during the past 14,000 years in the American Southwest as reconstructed by Stephen A. Hall. ("Paleoenvironments of the American Southwest," Figure 2.2, with modifications.)

past climate and plant distributions have also had trouble locating middle Holocene middens. If rodents well-adapted to eking out a life in deserts experienced difficulty, then all the more so for humans who might have trapped them for food.

The profound environmental changes experienced by Native American hunter-gatherers living in the Canyon Lands portion of the Colorado Plateau presented significant challenges for survival and reproductive success. This included a reduction in plant foods that humans depended on such as the seeds of grass and sunflowers, the tubers and bulbs like wild potato, onion, and lily, and the fruits and nuts of shrubs and trees like yucca, wolfberry, and pinyon. A reduction in forage for animals meant fewer of these to hunt and trap. Some loss of resources transpired across several generations. Still, increased frequencies of food shortages and outright famines were likely held within social group memories and the stories passed down from elders. Notable events occurring during rather brief intervals likely created a backdrop of insecurity and trauma for some individuals. Dissection of the canyon floodplains and the loss of resources as a result could have occurred within an individual's lifespan. Such occurrences surely would have registered on an emotional level as an existential threat.

Insecurity and evident threats to survival and reproductive success are aspects that all societies deal with one way or another. People face such challenges in a variety of ways sometimes dichotomized as practical and symbolic. One concerns strategies for obtaining more food, water, and protection from the environment and the other concerns strategies to obtain help from supernatural forces. From the perspective of those involved in a crisis, this is a false distinction and whatever practical steps taken are only short-term solutions that will not alleviate the envisioned root cause. The latter is what symbolic interventions are often directed at. Hunter-gatherers living in Utah's canyon country as the climate and environment transitioned to what we recognize as the middle Holocene had a crisis on their hands that likely prompted them to respond with some urgency in a number of ways. One may well have been various rituals and ceremonies directed at spirits that could bring more rain, that could make the canyons flourish again, that could help food plants to grow and game animals to multiply.

First People and Rock Markings

There was a time when the canyon walls and other rock surfaces of North and South America were unmarked by human hands. They were pristine. This was not all that long ago in the larger span of humanity, perhaps no more than 20,000 years. Humans evolved in the Old World, primarily Africa, and spread from there. The timing of rock art in the Americas is constrained by when the first people arrived on these continents. Well before this time humans had achieved a sophisticated sense of esthetics and were using rock surfaces as natural canvases for artistic expression. This practice dates back to at least 40,000 to 60,000 years ago in Asia and Europe and was esthetically well developed in portions of the Iberian Peninsula some 30,000 years ago.[5]

Archaeologists call the first Native Americans Paleoindians—the Old Ones.[6] To what extent these initial people marked their landscape remains unknown. A motivation for artistic expression was certainly present, given a universal human propensity for esthetic sensibilities and a common desire to imbue the world with symbolic meanings and creations.[7] Yet, the first Americans might have expressed their artistic inclinations in portable art more so than inscribing them onto the landscape.[8] One constraint on developing a cultural tradition behind landscape marking is the presence of suitable geologic features amenable to such a record. Another constraint is the movements and territorial ranges of social groups. Will I be back here again? Will my children ever come here? Will my group pass this way at some future time?

The first Native Americans originated from northeastern Siberia some 30,000 years ago. They lived as nomadic hunters and gatherers during the last ice age and followed the game animals that provided most of their food. They moved into a vast tundra landscape known as Beringia that connected the northeastern corner of Asia to the northwestern corner of North America. This "land bridge" was wider than

Figure 4.5 Mammoth petroglyph along the San Juan River near the modern town of Bluff, Utah. A mammoth is partially superimposed by another animal interpreted as a bison. Local Bluff artist Joe Pachak, who discovered these images, has suggested that the second beast might be a shrub-ox, an animal similar to but larger than the musk-ox; shrub-ox lived throughout the Colorado Plateau but went extinct at the end of the Pleistocene. (Image from Ekkhart Malotki.)

the state of Texas. A portion of this vast region lies in Alaska, though much is now submerged beneath the Bering Sea. The people that would become Native Americans lived in Beringia for thousands of years. They eventually penetrated farther southward either before the massive ice sheets stretching across northern North America prevented any movement or after they started to melt and allowed southward movement.[9]

We might never know with any certainty when humans started marking rocks in the Americas. Beringia as a whole might have been limited in geologic surfaces suitable for rock art, so the practice might have developed after people moved southward and settled into specific areas with exposures of durable rock surfaces. People may have started adding images to rock surfaces quite early in some areas, but most evidence is inconclusive. One spectacular set of ocher paintings, covering some eight miles of rock faces in the Colombian Amazon, includes animals interpreted as extinct mastodons, giant sloths, camelids, and horses. However, these interpretations are not universally accepted.[10]

As for North America, Clovis Paleoindians were evidently one of the earliest. The evidence for this comes from an important petroglyph panel in southeastern Utah near what is now the town of Bluff. Depicted on a cliff face near a place known as Sand Island is a line of pecked animals reasonably interpreted as Pleistocene mammoths.[11] The people who created this image apparently had firsthand knowledge of the animals portrayed, knowledge that provides a basis for general temporal assignment prior to around 13,000 years ago. The cultural meaning behind image creation is lost, but its general temporal placement is preserved, and Clovis hunters are known to have lived in the general area.[12] This panel of pecked animals started a long history of adding symbols to canyon walls of the San Juan River at this particular location.

Thousands of years later, well after mammoths had gone extinct, other Native Americans started to add images at this and other locations along the San Juan River as well as its master stream, the Colorado River, and other major tributaries thereto. The mammoth petroglyphs were chiseled into stone during the end of the Pleistocene. All subsequent petroglyphs and pictographs added here and elsewhere were executed during the Holocene. This current geological epoch began soon after 12,000 years ago with the end of the last ice age. Barrier Canyon Style rock art dates to the Holocene, not the Pleistocene, as it lacks any indication of such antiquity based on the animals portrayed—no mammoths or other extinct megafauna.

Subsequent People and Rock Marking

During most of the Holocene, people obtained their food from what nature provided. Societies surviving in this manner, by procuring wild foods, are known as hunter-gatherers or foragers. Archaeologists lack a commonly accepted name for Holocene hunter-gatherers, but the time period in which they thrived is called the Archaic period. Its temporal span varies across North America and according to the criteria used to define it, but on the Colorado Plateau in Utah it began around 10,000 years ago. The Archaic period came to a close with the introduction of a farming lifestyle based on corn and squash, two domesticates that originated in a portion of Meso-america that now belongs to southern Mexico. In much of Utah, where BCS rock art occurs, farming started after around 2,000 years ago.

Whereas Paleoindians seemed to have created few rock images, or few that have survived, Archaic foragers produced a vast repository of images of diverse styles and content across much of the Colorado Plateau and beyond.[13] Archaic period societies might seem less interesting than those ceramic-producing southwestern societies of the last 1,500 years that built the Chaco Canyon great houses and Mesa Verde cliff dwellings. Yet, Archaic age rock art suggests that life of early hunter-gatherers was rich with meaning and ceremonies. It is too bad we cannot interview any of those long-ago people to fully learn about their complex worldviews and conceptions of the supernatural. The closest that we can ever come is through their legacy of rock imagery. This rich corpus allows a glimpse into long-lost but fascinating traditions and belief systems.

The Barrier Canyon Style is but one type of rock art in the North American Southwest that is attributable to Archaic period hunter-gatherers. South of where Cataract Canyon of the Colorado River ends and Glen Canyon begins, images resembling those of typical Barrier Canyon style are rare. This decline is not for a lack of suitable rock surfaces. There are just as many sheltered canyon walls in Glen Canyon that would support painted images as occur to the north. Rather than BCS rock art, pecked depictions in another style attributed to Archaic foragers, Glen Canyon Linear, becomes predominant.

The name Glen Canyon Linear is appropriate, as it is prolific in this canyon system.

This location is also where the rock art was first officially studied and documented in any detail by archaeologists, during a large research effort of the late 1950s and early 1960s in advance of building the Glen Canyon Dam. Lake Powell, created behind this dam, submerged thousands of archaeological sites, including hundreds of rock art panels. Christy Turner, an archaeologist on this project, wrote a report about the rock art lost to flooding. He called the distinct early petroglyphs Glen Canyon Style 5, a name that proves confusing since Styles 1 through 4 are no longer used and his Style 5 predated the others.

Glen Canyon Linear is almost universally pecked into the rock. It shares the BCS predilection with anthropomorphs that have elongated bodies and minimal arms and legs. Pecked lines commonly outline the bodies with the interiors left unpecked or, more commonly, with a grid pattern of vertical or horizontal pecked lines. Images of blocky bighorn sheep executed with grid bodies or just with the contours pecked are another common theme. This style commonly occurs along drainages, especially the major rivers: the Colorado, San Juan, Escalante, Paria, and Little Colorado. It also occurs in selected upland locations, particularly along travel corridors and near water sources. Examples of Glen Canyon Linear well away from the core zone are somewhat different in character. For example, depictions along the Little Colorado River were assigned a separate style category called Palavayu Linear.[14] Closer to the core there is less pronounced subregional variation, such as between panels clustered along the San Juan River around Bluff, Utah, and in Glen Canyon proper. Glen Canyon Linear petroglyphs occur sporadically within the BCS style area and beyond, extending farther north up the Green River.

Well southwest from the core area of BCS rock art is a distinctive painted rock art tradition chiefly found in remote settings of Grand Canyon, especially on the prominent mid-elevation bench in the canyon known as the Esplanade Platform. Called Esplanade Polychrome (or Grand Canyon Polychrome), this style features paintings of very elongated anthropomorphs, often tightly bunched together.[15] Aspects of this style evoke BCS, which is why they are sometimes lumped together. Hence, some maps show the distribution of BCS rock art extending in a southward projection that encompasses Grand Canyon. The painted figures of Esplanade style are sufficiently distinctive as to suggest a different cultural tradition, including a heavy emphasis on pigments other than dark red. The panels also occur in places that are more secluded or secretive than is common for BCS. This, too, seems to reflect a different conception of what rock art is about or how to properly deploy this medium. This polychrome style was little known until recently, likely because it occurs in settings that, from the perspective of modern people, are remote, secluded, and difficult to access. Related pictographs found more on Grand Canyon's south side are distinguished as Tusayan style because less emphasis is placed on anthropomorphs.

Far to the south in the canyon country of the lower Rio Grande and Pecos Rivers occurs another rich assemblage of pictographs designated as the Lower Pecos Style. The rock art in this area has been extensively researched, in part because of flooding

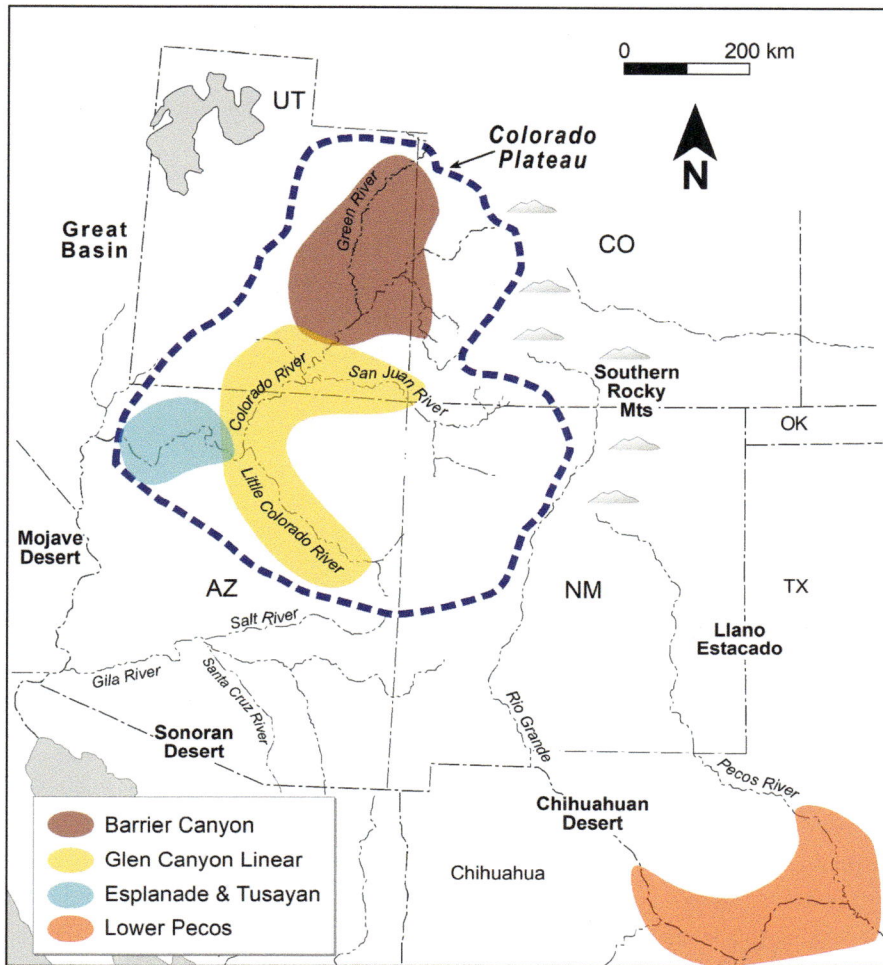

Figure 4.6 Core areas of Archaic period representational rock art styles in the North American Southwest that have anthropomorphs as a major focal element.

from the Amistad Reservoir. Even before then, the artist Forest Kirkland spent countless hours in the 1930s creating watercolor paintings of specific panels in an attempt to faithfully copy them. The rock paintings here tend to be even more complex and compositionally intricate than those of Esplanade Polychrome. Anthropomorphs are a major theme with many depicted larger than life and often associated with a myriad of artifacts, lifeforms, and more enigmatic elements. A wide range of paint colors was used and this polychrome aspect is more like that of Grand Canyon than the predominately red pigment of BCS.

Understanding Rock Marking

Rock art was created with meaning and intentionality. These works were not doodles executed idly out of boredom, as sometimes claimed, at least not BCS images and similar styles.[16] The specific meanings of past depictions are usually lost, but more recent viewers, even those in the present, can still find meaning.[17] Latter-day viewers of rock art assign their own interpretations and understandings, drawing upon their own cultural experiences and objectives. The inferred meanings at times include a belief that specific images can do harm in the present, causing injury that must be countered in some way.

As a form of artistic expression that encodes cultural meanings, rock images provide one of the best means for accessing or inferring the worldviews and paradigms of past cultures. This is true even if the specific meanings that images had for their creators are opaque. In Polly Schaafsma's words, "Above all else rock art is visual dialogue, and the dialogue takes many forms, actively conveying meaning and communicating, whether or not its intended significance defies interpretation. Even for its creators, it was multivocal, symbolically and metaphorically."[18]

The creators of rock art conveyed messages concerning beliefs, history, myths, and more in places on the landscape, images that long outlived their makers. Few are alive today who have insider knowledge about past meanings of images, and for truly ancient depictions, such as those of Barrier Canyon Style, there is no privy source of information. In lieu of interviews, archaeologists use knowledge and understandings gleaned from recent and contemporary foragers as an analog for interpreting what life was like in the distant past. Ethnographic analogy, as this practice is known, provides a means for making plausible conjectures about the behaviors of long-dead people based on the material remains that they left behind. Rock art is part of the material record of past societies. The motivations and intentions that historic foragers had and have for creating such art, and the contexts within which they did so, can serve as guides for inferring these aspects in the past. In the best of circumstances, this is based on direct analogy (homology), where there is known historical continuity between past and present people. In such cases, the information obtained about modern beliefs concerning image creation can be carefully applied to their distant ancestors based on the images that they created.

In the vast majority of cases, rock art from around the world lacks a good basis for direct analogy.[19] This is clearly the case for the BCS rock art of this book, which was made by hunter-gatherers thousands of years prior to any ethnographers being on the scene. Doubtless some Native Americans today carry the genes of the hunter-gatherers that painted BCS images, but a genetic link does not equate to cultural continuity. Likewise, some Europeans doubtless share genes with the painters of Lascaux and other Upper Paleolithic cave sites, but any claim for cultural continuity and inside knowledge of meaning is groundless. This does not mean there is no basis for understanding, which is what ethnographic analogy and comparative study can allow. Nonetheless, all modern people are ultimately limited in what they can know about past intentions and meanings of ancient imagery. Any such claims should be viewed as hypotheses with greatly varying degrees of plausibility.

In contemplating BCS rock art and what the people who made these images might have looked like, at least during certain special times when ceremonies were performed, Martin Gusinde's remarkable photographs of Tierra del Fuego tribes are

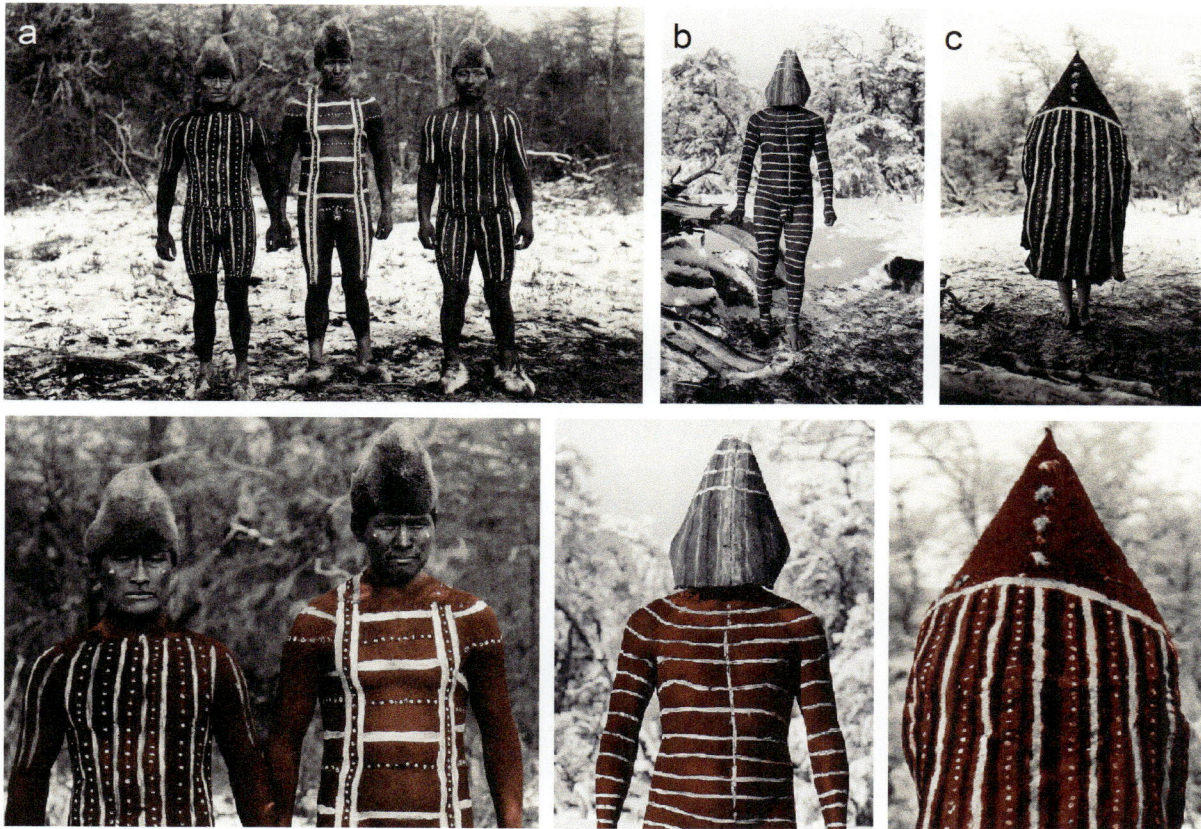

informative. Taken in the late 1910s and early 1920s, this record was largely forgotten until recently, when a large format book of the photographs was published.[20] During ceremonies, the people of this region commonly painted their bodies with red ocher then added white dots or lines, or even goose down, as well as donning various masks or body coverings of painted hide or bark.[21] These hunter-gatherers occupy a different environment than the Southwest, an extreme of a different kind, and the specifics of their ceremonies likely differed from those of the BCS artists. Nonetheless, their body decoration provides an interesting reference point when contemplating the human-like figures in BCS art.

An animistic conception of the world is common among many Native American societies and might provide a productive interpretive lens for rock art.[22] This remains to be seen, but some think that it holds promise. Shamanism once occupied such a position among archaeologists and rock art enthusiasts.[23] Animism actually subsumes, or can serve to integrate, some of the interpretive accounts grouped together under shamanism. With animism, virtually any phenomena, whether natural or cultural, can have agency or a spirit that gives them life. Just as two people can have social relations and reciprocal interactions to achieve pragmatic ends, so too can this happen with nonhuman agents or other-than-human persons.[24] Spiritual beings can be petitioned,

Figure 4.7 Selk'nam men of Tierra del Fuego in ritual costume consisting of red body paint with white-and-black accents for details and masks or coverings of similarly painted bark or hide. Masked figures represent various spirits in mythology. (a) Martin Gusinde, Kewanix Parade, 1923. The Hain ceremony, a Selk'nam rite. (b) Martin Gusinde, Ulen, the rebel, 1923. The Hain ceremony, a Selk'nam rite. (c) Martin Gusinde, West Tanu, 1923. The Hain ceremony, a Selk'nam rite. (From the book *L'esprit des hommes de la Terre de Feu, Selk'nam, Yamana, Kawésqar* [Atelier EXP, exb.fr]. © Martin Gusinde/Anthropos Institute/ Atelier EXB.)

cajoled, or reasoned or negotiated with, and these aspects are often essential in situations where some transgression might have offended them.

The content of BCS rock art strongly suggests that its creators likely had animistic beliefs. Having such beliefs does not mean that all members of a social group were prepared, able, or interested in trying to be intermediaries in the spiritual realm, especially for forces that might be malevolent and could do serious long-term damage. Most social groups have such intermediaries and the term shaman in a generic sense is often applied to such specialists. Some of these specialists in the supernatural may have been rock art creators but other group members probably were as well and BCS rock art relates to far more than shamanic vision quests.

There is considerable oral testimony from Aboriginal people of Australia emphasizing that the process of making rock art is the truly important part, rather than a final product.[25] It is the performance aspect that helps to ensure beneficial results. The re-marking of ancestral art by touching up the paint, or embellishing it by adding new decorations or other elements, even using new techniques, is a key part of achieving success. Rock art is analogous to a human tool but one applied to manipulate or control the spiritual realm rather than the physical world. When applied effectively it can generate positive consequences such as ensuring resource renewal, spiritual and physical health, and reproductive success—in short, the successful continuation of you and your kind.

Making Marks

People have marked rock surfaces using two basic strategies: reduction, where rock is removed to make an image, or application, where material is added to the rock to make an image. By convention, images made by reduction are commonly termed petroglyphs, with *petro* for rock and *glyph* for symbol. Images made by application are pictographs. *Picto* means a picture or drawing, but there is no linguistic reference that this drawing occurs upon a rock surface.[26] Regardless, pictographs are paintings on rock and are far less durable than symbols made by removing rock.

After this first order split, each general rock art production method has different decisions. This does not mean that they are utterly distinct ways of marking rock. Reduction and application techniques can be part of the same cultural tradition, indeed part of a single figure. There was no sole way of making Barrier Canyon Style rock art. BCS artists used about every technique ever employed by past people to make rock art. Nonetheless, they favored painting, the creation of pictographs, as a primary way of executing their images. Time after time, they carefully selected settings that could preserve painted depictions: sandstone faces sheltered by overhanging canyon walls.

Painting was the predominant technique BCS artists used to create their rock art, and in the vast majority of cases the pigment was red in color. Hematite or red ocher is an iron oxide mineral that likely served as a source of their red paint. Hematite nodules are readily available in the San Rafael Swell, an area well known for numerous BCS

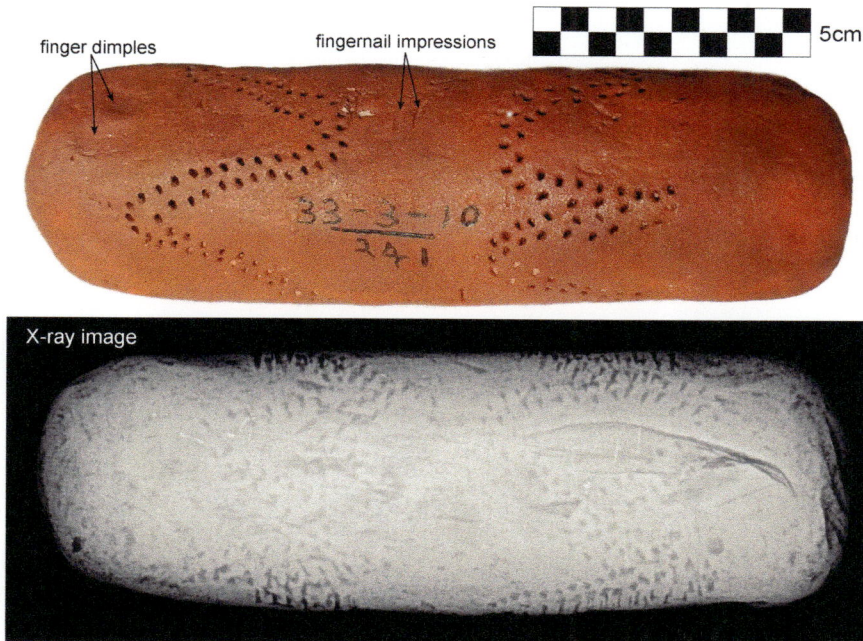

finger dimples

fingernail impressions

5cm

X-ray image

Figure 4.8 A prepared red ocher paint stick recovered in 1930 from Cottonwood Cave, an Archaic period camp near the Maze of Canyonlands National Park. The cave has BCS pictographs executed in a similar red pigment. (Accession 33-3-10. Photo and X-ray image courtesy of the Peabody Museum, Harvard University.)

art rock panels. Loose hematite nodules occur in many of the small and large drainages that flow eastward out of the swell. The deep red color of these nodules appears a good match for the red pigment of many BCS images.[27]

Abrading these hematite nodules creates a red pigment that is quite adherent to rock surfaces, even without added binder. Binders are usually some organic substance such as egg, blood, or fat; they serve both to make a pigment more easily applied and also to help ensure adhesion. Judging from the appearance of BCS red-painted images, the iron oxide was most commonly painted on as a slurry and seldom applied by abrading hematite nodules directly on rock faces. These nodules are hard, and abrading them directly also results in abrasion of most sandstone surfaces as the pigment is laid down. This is rarely in evidence on BCS pictographs. Rather, red paint was applied in ways that indicate the ocher had been rendered to powder first and then mixed with liquid and perhaps some sort of binder. A few specialized analyses of red paint from BCS images indicate several other colorless minerals occur with the hematite, such as clay known as kaolinite.[28]

A prepared red paint stick from a rockshelter with BCS rock art provides an example of what the artists likely prepared for use in painting. This artifact resembles a fat crayon and consists of a formed cylinder 4.5 inches long and 1.5 inches in diameter. It is made of dark red pigment similar to the color of most BCS pictographs, including those at the rockshelter of discovery. Recent X-ray imaging shows no foreign substance on the inside of the artifact. It is a solid pigment lump, but not a piece of hard hematite ground to shape. It consists of powdered red ocher that was mixed with some material that made for a malleable lump. Someone squeezed and rolled the red

Figure 4.9 Natural pigments obtained from Utah that BCS artists used. The powder produced by crushing or grinding such minerals can be mixed with water and a binder such as egg or blood to make a paint slurry. Paint application can include hands, mouth, and various sized and shaped brushes. Yucca leaves, whole or split, can be chewed to make broad-or fine-tipped brushes. The hematite nodules shown here came from a small wash of the San Rafael Swell near Wild Horse Window. Even without a binder, this mineral is impressively adherent to rock surfaces, hands, and more.

pigment into its current shape, as evidenced by the fingernail impressions and finger pressure dimples in a few places. Encircling the exterior are double rows of meandering punctations created with a sharp pointed tool. Paint sticks like this might sometimes have been used directly on rock surfaces much like a large crayon, but the nature of paint application at many panels indicates that pigment was turned into a slurry and applied that way, rather than dry.

Red is the predominant color of BCS rock art, but white, yellow, gray, black, and blue or green are also seen. Most of these were also probably made using minerals or mixtures thereof. White is more common than the other colors, at least in some areas, and is likely to be from an iron-free clay mineral that is usually bright white in color, such as kaolinite or halloysite. A clay would have the property of adherence without any need for a binder, although one could be added. Ground selenite or calcite crystals when mixed with some binder can also produce a white pigment and both of these occur with some abundance in the area.

The yellow color in BCS rock art is likely from limonite, which is a yellow ocher that mainly consists of the iron mineral goethite. This material is available from the Chinle Formation, which outcrops at various localities throughout the area of BCS rock art, such as the San Rafael Swell and around Moab. Limonite is often associated with mineralized chunks of wood, and in some cases it can be associated with uranium ore.[29] Earthy varieties of limonite might have needed a binder, but limonite-stained yellow clay could have been used as is or with more of the mineral added to intensify the color. Green and blue colors come from various copper minerals such as chryso-colla and malachite, and these too are available from the Chinle Formation. There are

Figure 4.10 Horseshoe Shelter anthropomorphs painted with clay showing how the pigment sits on the sandstone surface such that it can flake off, leaving little or no trace.

also other sources such as a localized deposit in the Navajo Sandstone at Coppermine in northeastern Arizona.

Although mineral-based pigments are most common, there are also some BCS pictographs painted with mud, with two examples in Horseshoe Canyon seen by many visitors. Unlike mineral pigments that were probably prepared ahead of time and brought to where they would be needed, the mud paints seem to be based on what was immediately at hand or quite close in a wash bottom or some exposed alluvial layer. Red ocher penetrates into the sandstone to which it is applied, making for a far more permanent bond than mud paint. The mud sits on the surface of the sandstone and is susceptible to flaking off. When mud paint flakes from a panel, little is left of where it once was except for perhaps a light stain.

BCS artists applied paint with a variety of techniques, including some means to cover broad areas, like hand smearing or using a pad or hide scrap. Narrower lines were created by finger painting or using brushes, such as the chewed end of a yucca leaf. The fine details seen at some BCS panels indicate well-prepared paint brushes capable of laying down precise lines. BCS artists also applied paint with a splatter technique on occasion, such as throwing or spraying it with their mouth or through a tube like a hollow reed or bird bone.

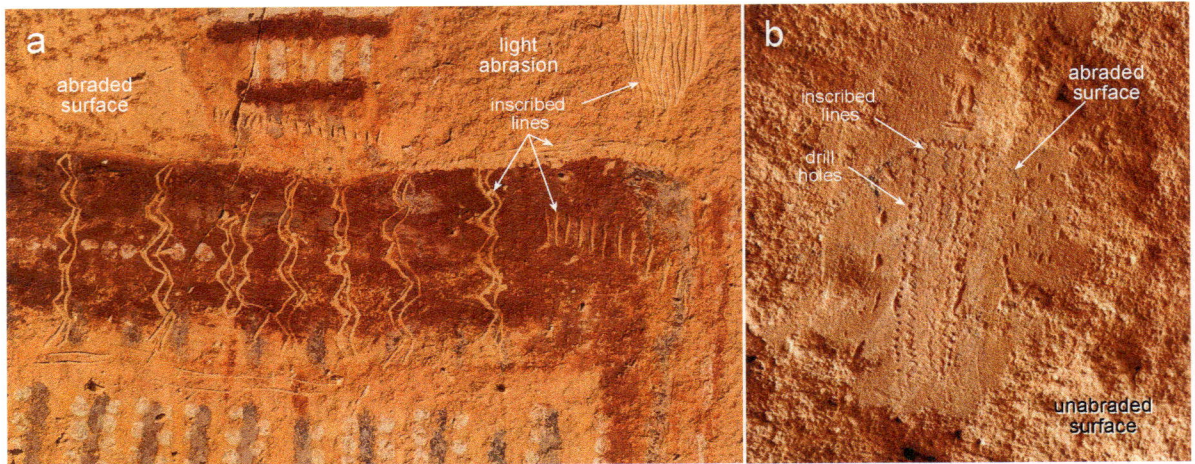

Figure 4.11 Rock art production techniques used by Barrier Canyon Style artists. (a) Great Gallery anthropomorph exhibiting abrasion to prepare the rock surface, followed by painting with red, white, and dark gray and then incision with sharp tools; (b) abrasion of rock surface prior to making an anthropomorph image by inscribing and drilling.

Removing rock to create an image was far less of a primary production technique for BCS artists than painting. Rock art creation by rock removal is achievable by abrading, inscribing, drilling, and pecking or dinting. Abrasion removes rock in a slow process of rubbing some object across a rock surface, often in a back-and-forth movement, to grind away grains. Rock is often used for this purpose, but it could include hard organic items such as bone or wood. Abrasion can occur as a preparatory step to ensure that a rock surface is optimal for creating images—smooth, and with scales or other defects removed. Such preparation is especially useful on ceilings or back walls of shelters when creating images with fine painted or incised lines. BCS artists sometimes readied rock surfaces for painting by abrading them first. This was also sometimes done prior to inscribing a figure and for removing or erasing previous figures or portions thereof.

When abrading to create an image, tool width controls how fine the lines can be: a very narrow abrading stone or bone tool can result in grooves that resemble inscribed lines. Inscribing differs from abrasion in that the artist uses a sharp-edged or pointed tool such as a stone flake. These cuts can be quite precise and produce lines either by engraving into the rock surface or into paint laid over that surface. BCS artists did both and did so primarily as a technique to accent or modify a painted image.

Drilling involves a rotational motion with either a sharp-tipped tool or one that is blunt but abrasive. A sharp-tipped stone hafted to a stick can be spun quite rapidly, the same motion that BCS artists likely used to create fire with a wooden base and fire drill. Drilling can also be done by simple hand-twisting with some pointed object; this is evidently the technique used for the holes shown on the right side in figure 4.11. If the drill bit is not sharp, the drilling is a form of abrasion.

Pecking involves striking a rock surface, usually with some sort of acute-edged or pointed tool that is hard enough to chisel out some of the stone being struck. In most cases the pecking tools were also made of rock, especially a hard stone that could be chipped or flaked to make sharp edges or projections. Quartzite is well suited for this approach, as are chert (flint) and some igneous rocks such as basalt or andesite. Pecking tools can be used to directly strike the rock, which is the simplest technique, but it takes good hand-eye coordination and an acutely pointed or chisel-edged rock to be precise. Much better control is achievable using indirect percussion, where the chisel is placed on the surface to be marked and then struck with another rock or something organic such as a wooden club. Judging from the degree of control for BCS petroglyphs, it seems that direct percussion, rather than indirect percussion, was the usual technique.

The BCS emphasis on painted images is also true of some other Archaic age rock art styles in the Southwest such as Esplanade Polychrome of the Grand Canyon area or the Lower Pecos Style seen in the canyon country of the lower Rio Grande along the U.S.-Mexico border. Yet, pecking was the almost-exclusive means of making rock art for Archaic artists living in a broad region immediately south of the core area of BCS art. The pecked images are reminiscent of BCS but distinct enough to be accorded a separate style category, known as Glen Canyon Linear. The people that made Glen Canyon Linear and Barrier Canyon Style rock art shared many aspects of material culture such as specific types of sandals, basketry, and projectile points. Despite this, their approach to rock art production was largely distinct. The reason why some hunter-gatherers favored pecking while their neighbors favored painting is not clear, but it has nothing to do with the natural distribution of protected alcoves suitable for painted art. The region where the Glen Canyon Linear rock art style predominates has plenty of protected alcoves suitable for pictographs. The technique of making images by removing rock allows far more surfaces to be rather permanently marked, but it's hard to say if this fact was a motivating reason for favoring pecking.

Rock Art Style

Barrier Canyon Style is but one of many distinct rock art styles that archaeologists and others recognize within the Colorado Plateau. But what is a rock art style in general, and what specifically is the Barrier Canyon Style? How do we identify styles, and what exactly does it mean to designate some image as part of a given style? Were these styles in the heads of the people that created them or are they just our creation, a means to help organize observations?[30]

The imagery that people created on rocks is a product of learning; it is part of their culture. The various decisions that go into creating rock art—from what, to where, to how—reflect learned behavior. Which locations to mark. How to make the marks. How one learns to transform thoughts into a visual record. And most significant of all, what subject matter to depict. Technique and substance both impact style, but rock art content is foremost.

The content of rock art is inextricably tied to socially acquired beliefs about the world, especially those that attempt to make meaning, that account for the unexplainable, and that help to sustain life. There are beliefs about the origin of the earth and heavens, beliefs about the creation of life and its destruction by sickness and death, beliefs about the causes of powerful natural forces such as lightning, tornadoes, volcanos, and earthquakes. Many societies have beliefs about the relationships among humans and those between humans and other beings of the world that are not human.[31] Especially important are beliefs about beings with supernatural powers, beings that control the forces of nature and the resources that humans depend upon, and beings that might cause or cure sickness.

Patterned social behavior is what leads to what we can recognize as *styles* in rock art. Contemporary people, archaeologists and others who study the medium, impose these styles on rock art. Our creation and naming of styles is not an arbitrary exercise, since it is based on perceptible properties of form and execution. But we should never delude ourselves into thinking that by doing this we have somehow captured some true essence of past reality. Style categories, such as BCS, might not equate with styles that rock art makers would recognize, the categories in the heads of those who created the images. It is possible that some styles are close approximations to those of the makers, but this can never be known with any certainty. The real question is, do the style categories have utility to answer specific questions? Style categories are only useful to the extent that they provide some understanding about past life. They can help but they can also become impediments and lead to arguments about what is or is not part of a given style.

A rock art style that seems specific to one region is rarely an isolate without connections or affinities to styles in neighboring areas. This is because rock art creators lived in a social landscape and maintained networks of relationships spread far and wide. Based on what ethnographers have learned from arid land foragers of North America and other desert regions around the world, survival for individuals and groups is enhanced by a vast web of social connections that one can draw upon. This means that people gain knowledge of the beliefs, traditions, and imagery of different areas. Moreover, a key reason for maintaining such networks is an ability for short-term movement to areas of resource abundance in other people's territories. Such movement not only exposes people to the beliefs and imagery of distant groups, but it might directly result in the addition of some foreign-looking images from distant places. Since any single style may well just reflect the local version of a widespread tradition of adding images to rocks, it is useful to consider that wider context, especially when trying to come to terms with the meaning or function behind images.

In trying to make sense of rock art, archaeologists and others have attempted to circumscribe it in space and time. The temporal issue is a difficult problem. Also tricky is attempting to bound a rock art style in space, defining its extent using lines on a map. Even a fuzzy line can prove difficult. Style itself is a slippery concept to grasp, and every individual brings a different set of eyes, conceptions, and biases to the issue. Some archaeologists and people in general are *splitters*, parsing out materials into fine categories. Others are *lumpers*, grouping things into several broad categories. Also variable between individuals are the attributes that receive emphasis, those elements or configurations thought to have the greatest salience for style classification.

It is also important to consider the extent to which a mapped style distribution is largely a byproduct of geology coupled with preservation. If hard rock surfaces suitable for images were equally distributed across a region, then spatial patterns for styles might be simpler to interpret. But that is not the case. The Southwest is well endowed with usable rock surfaces, especially when contrasted with areas such as the Great Plains, yet there are vast stretches of the Southwest lacking rock outcrops, or the surfaces are so friable that images do not last long. As with our paper billboards, an image once clear and readable soon becomes less so and ultimately not at all after a generation or two. Such a situation greatly complicates using the spatial distribution of rock art styles for making inferences about social aspects in the past.

Because style is an aspect of culture and culture is dynamic and always changing, rock art styles also change through time, even if the people making them are the direct descendants of those who executed the first images of a style in some distant past. There can be continuity in overall themes depicted—the subject matter—but subtle shifts in the nature of how the subjects are executed along with alterations of meaning. Cumulatively, across hundreds and thousands of years, the nature of a rock art tradition will evolve, even to the extent that connections seem less than clear cut, subject to debate.

There is good cause to believe that the BCS rock art tradition was one of long-term continuity that stretched back thousands of years. After around 2,000 years ago, the Fremont rock art tradition arose across much of the same portions of Utah. Fremont rock art is distinct from BCS and clearly postdates it, yet it does not take a stretch of the imagination to envision this tradition as something of a lineal descendant from BCS, at least in part.[32] Even when the original meanings of BCS imagery were lost in the mists of time, something doubtless true for the Fremont as well, the images themselves are powerful and can influence those who witness them. This power still holds today, as many visitors to the Great Gallery can claim such an experience. All humans bring meaning to the imagery they see, meanings that likely have little or nothing to do with the original inspirations behind them.

What Is the Barrier Canyon Style?

How would you describe the taste of peanut butter to someone who has never tried it before? Saying that it tastes sort of like peanuts assumes that they have eaten peanuts before. But if not, then what? Trying to describe a rock art style is similar in that there is no substitute for direct visual experience. Words invariably fail to accurately convey the essence of some style.

Reading that anthropomorphs are ubiquitous in BCS rock art provides some information, but this statement is also true of many other rock art styles of Utah and around the world. So, what makes BCS anthropomorphs distinctive from, say, Fremont anthropomorphs or Basketmaker II anthropomorphs? Adding "ghost-like" as an adjective to anthropomorph might help, although this too comes up short, since there are BCS panels that lack the supposed ghost-like figures common at the Great Gallery.

Barrier Canyon

Fremont

San Juan BMII

Figure 4.12 Anthropomorphs are a common theme in various rock art styles of Utah, but despite this commonality, specific details of how the human body shape was depicted are distinctive.

The preceding general style discussion should have made it clear that we impose styles on rock art and we can never know for sure how our categories, such as Barrier Canyon, match those of the rock art creators. What is or is not part of a named style category is a matter of opinion and social consensus among experts in the present. The panels and elements that get included in a style will constrain or expand the style definition. When categorizing handmade objects, whether artistic in nature or utilitarian, the more items that get included in a group, such as a style category, the greater the diversity there will be. This truism is greatly magnified when those objects are generated by numerous individuals living in different areas and across some lengthy span of time. Rock art styles strongly adhere to this maxim.

Considerable diversity was baked into the original naming of Barrier Canyon Style rock art, given the four key panels in Horseshoe Canyon (Barrier Creek) that formed a central basis for characterizing the style. From south to north, these four sites are the Great Gallery, Alcove Gallery, Horseshoe Shelter, and High Gallery. This is in the opposite order that people usually encounter the panels, since most visitors use a trail that enters the canyon to the north, then progress upstream to the south. Great Gallery is arguably the most important panel in the canyon, but the other three are lumped in as representatives. Each panel has distinctive qualities that add to the diversity of what constitutes the Barrier Canyon Style.

These four panels occur in the central part of Horseshoe Canyon where the walls are formed by Navajo Sandstone, a geologic formation well known for weathering into protective overhangs. The four panels in this stretch are the ones most visitors see. Preserving this rock art is why the National Park Service designated this canyon stretch as an extension of Canyonlands National Park. A seldom-visited place in the early 1980s, much change has occurred in the ensuing decades. Visitation has increased manifold,

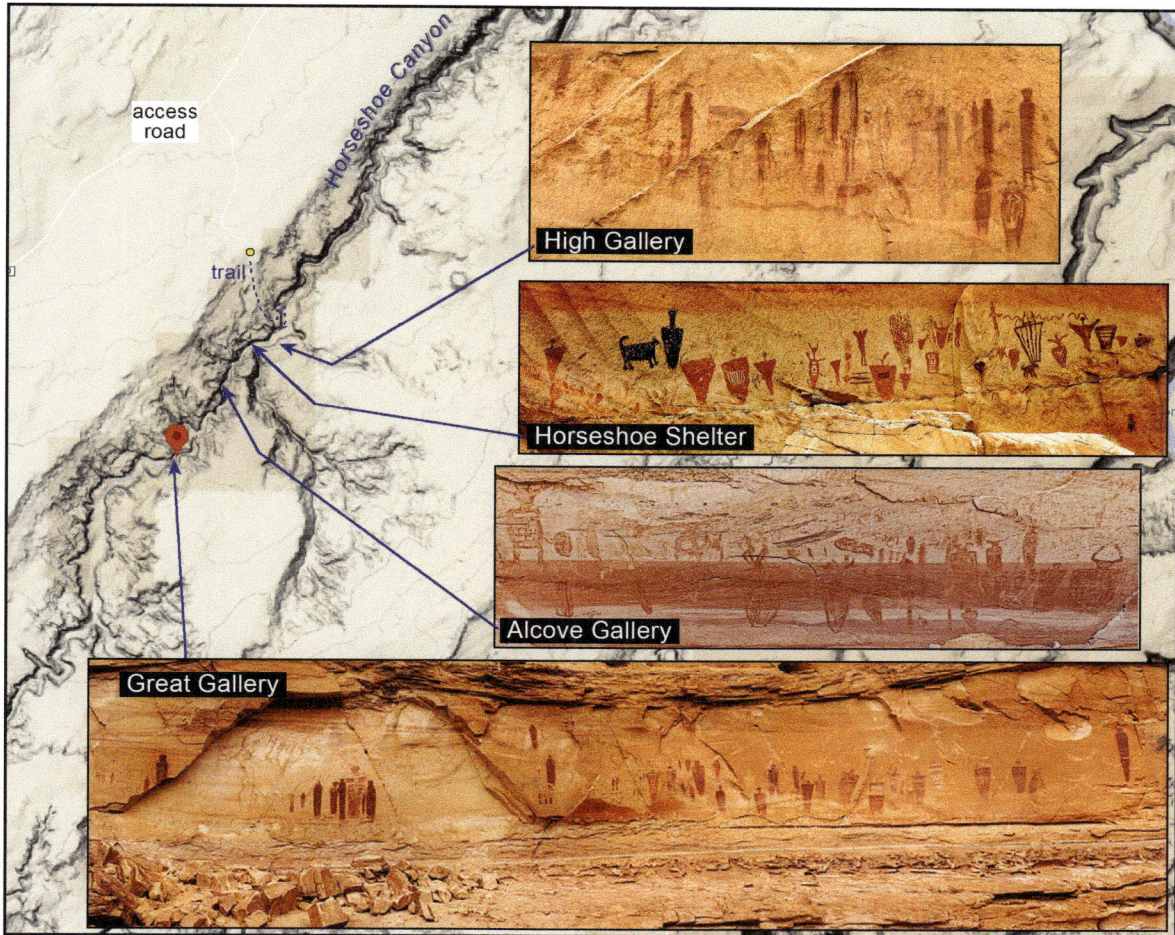

Figure 4.13 Horseshoe Canyon Map with photographic callouts of rock art panels in the Great Gallery, the Alcove Gallery, Horseshoe Shelter, and the High Gallery.

and along with it the necessary improvements to the trail, signage, and restraints to help protect the rock art from mindless vandals.

High Gallery

The High Gallery is the first panel visitors see upon heading upstream after descending the historic road that enters from the western rim. This is a significant panel for relative temporal placement, as discussed later. The rock art occurs high up on the canyon wall, eighty feet or more above the base. The artists evidently stood upon a rock ledge that collapsed in the distant past. The High Gallery exhibits many of the themes common to BCS rock art and is perhaps characteristic of this style in its early history. Dark red is the one obvious pigment used, the same dark red seen on many BCS panels. White accents might well have been present on many portions of this panel but nearly all are now lost to weathering.

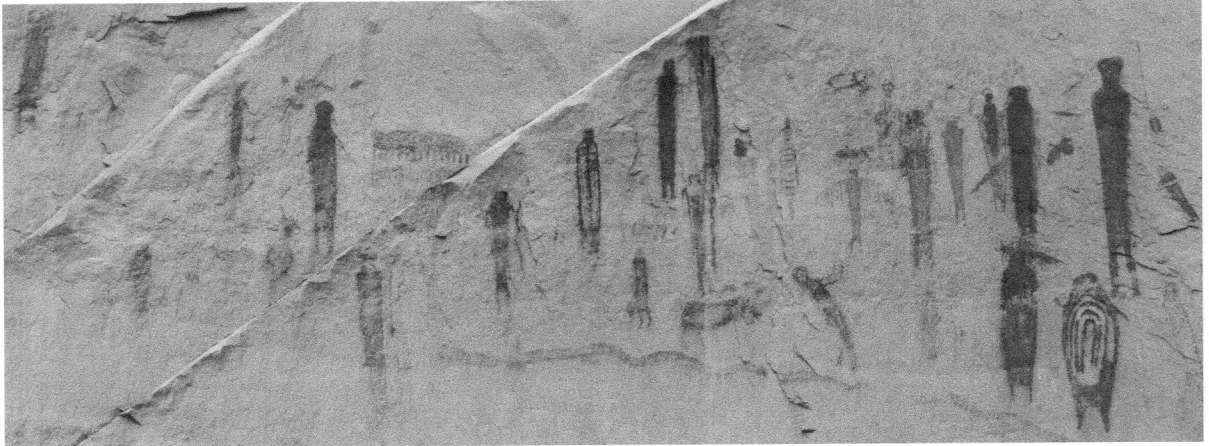

Figure 4.14 Overview shot of the High Gallery.

Figure 4.15 Closeup of a portion of the High Gallery near the right side showing characteristic fine details of BCS, although in this instance precipitation blowing onto the panel has blurred them and likely removed most of the white paint accents once present.

Two aspects make this panel less interesting to many visitors. One is simply how high up on the canyon wall the images occur, with no easy way to get close while also having a good vantage point. Climbing the slope brings you within about sixteen feet, but with a neck-craning, upward-viewing angle. Farther back is better, but then distance prevents the detection of small details. Compounding this issue is the "bleeding" of the red pigment into the underlying sandstone matrix, a likely consequence of moisture blowing onto this somewhat shallowly protected overhang. Fine details are now indistinct and the outlines of larger figures rather fuzzy. Moisture also mostly removed white paint accents on several figures. Bleeding or diffusion of pigment occurs at numerous BCS sites placed on rock faces less than adequately protected from blowing moisture, such as the panel at Molen Seep.

The High Gallery exhibits many motifs central to BCS rock art, yet this panel is distinct from the Great Gallery and even more so from Horseshoe Shelter almost directly across the canyon. Almost all anthropomorphs at the High Panel have legs, a few with distinct feet. This is not true for the Great Gallery. Arms are less apparent, though they occur on about half, with some carrying objects, including serpents. Most anthropomorphs appear to qualify as spirit figures rather than citizen figures. A human form appearing to release a bird-human blend might be a citizen figure, though one of larger-than-normal comparative scale. Zoomorphs (nonhuman animal forms) appear less numerous than anthropomorphs and many look rather unusual, with few resembling identifiable creatures. Some of this is likely a consequence of indistinct outlines caused by red pigment diffusing into the underlying sandstone matrix. Birds hover near heads and also fly along anthropomorph torsos. Some of the figures are insect-like, and one anthropomorph has distinct bug eyes on an elongated neck. There is a fringed horizontal band of red with trailing red lines below it that is a rain depiction like those at other BCS panels. A painted snake several meters long facing downstream seems to have served as a symbolic lower boundary for the BCS elements.

Horseshoe Shelter

The motifs and painting execution at the High Panel are common to BCS art throughout a large region. Yet, directly across the canyon on its west side, only a rough semblance of these motifs and technical skill are on display at Horseshoe Shelter. These pictographs are quite distinct from those of the High Panel. Had Horseshoe Shelter occurred elsewhere, rather than in the type locality, the rock art might have been omitted from the BCS oeuvre. Two aspects that strikingly diverge from the standard BCS style are immediately apparent: paint type and figure size/proportions. Clay and silt of several color varieties serves as the pigment, rather than the red ocher of the High Gallery, Great Gallery, and most BCS panels. Anthropomorphs remain a common motif at Horseshoe Shelter, but most have squat torsos rather than elongated ones, are small in scale (rarely exceeding twelve inches tall), and are highly pinched at the bottom. Also, a number of the anthropomorphs lack heads, and others have greatly exaggerated protruding shoulders or stubby upright arms that somewhat resemble extra heads. The rock art at

Figure 4.16 Overview shot of Horseshoe Shelter rock art.

this panel seems like an echo of the High Gallery and the Great Gallery, authored by painters temporally disconnected from those other panels.

The Horseshoe Shelter painters could gaze across the canyon at what was probably an early phase of BCS art on display at the High Gallery. It did not matter. This short spatial distance could not overcome a vast temporal difference between the authors of these panels. Life had moved on and changed, as had belief systems and their symbolic representations. The Horseshoe Shelter painters had different priorities and different conceptions about the world, all of which is evident in their art. A historical connection is present, even palpable, but the style had evolved. Descendant forms are rarely identical to those of their ancestral origin, though similarities exist and allow the tracing of historical connections.

Archaeologists excavated at Horseshoe Shelter in 1930 in hopes of finding an answer to the question about who created the magnificent rock art along Barrier Creek. This location was the only one they found in Horseshoe Canyon where a rock art panel was associated with evidence of occupation. Their hope did not pan out. Even if some dating evidence had been found, its relevance to the Great Gallery or the High Panel is doubtful based solely on the rock art distinctions. Whoever built structures in Horseshoe Shelter and left artifacts there might not have had any hand in painting most of the images on the back wall. The artifacts recovered in 1930 indicate a rather late temporal affiliation, perhaps as early as AD 800 and certainly by AD 1100. The ground surface during occupation was roughly what it is now, some ten feet or so below the rock art.

Alcove Gallery

Upstream from Horseshoe Shelter there is rock art within a massive alcove on the west wall of the canyon. A fifteen-foot-high alluvial terrace forms a level floor surface for much of the shelter interior, with a pile of large talus blocks along the back wall. Rock art occurs alongside and behind this talus pile in two general areas, one higher and one lower, with some stylistic distinctions between them. Most images are simple and painted with mud rather than red ocher. Weathering might have obscured some details of the oldest images, which are those in the upper right-hand side of the alcove. Many of these are so obscure that they are difficult to see and photograph.

The main figures of the upper panel are elongated anthropomorphs consisting of torsos and heads only. There are at least fifteen tightly grouped together in two main

Figure 4.17 Alcove Gallery in Horseshoe Canyon as viewed from upstream with rock art locations highlighted. (Photo by Eric Trenbeath, 2015.)

Figure 4.18 Alcove Gallery upper panel in Horseshoe Canyon; most of these images are difficult to see and photograph, progressively so moving upward to the right. Color levels were manipulated in this image for greatest contrast between pictographs and sandstone wall.

Figure 4.19 Lower panel of the Alcove Gallery in Horseshoe Canyon with insets showing specific details: (a) mudded-over figures; (b) a horned anthropomorph similar to those added later at the upper panel in the alcove.

rows. The tallest figure, measuring more than three feet tall, is on the right and spans both rows from head to bottom. A smaller figure immediately to the right is in the middle but the figures on the left occur in either the upper or lower row. The upper row heads are at roughly the same height as the tallest figure but have shorter torsos. Some of these are half or more the length of the largest, with two about one-third as long. Lower row figures are generally smaller and slotted between those of the upper row.

The outlines for these anthropomorphs are vague, so it is no surprise that details are not evident. Did they have eyes or body ornamentation? Were portions of the images painted with a pigment other than red? Fine details are common at many BCS sites, including those immediately upstream at the Great Gallery and downstream at the High Gallery. Were these present here as well?

Adjacent and below the elongated anthropomorphs on the left are several smaller anthropomorphs of a distinct style. All have arms and legs and two have markedly long horns that resemble those occurring on a prominent anthropomorph on the lower panel in the alcove. These anthropomorphs do not resemble the active citizen figures that occur at the Great Gallery and other BCS panels. They appear to be a later addition perhaps done at roughly the same time interval as when most of the lower panel figures were painted. Evidence for temporal priority of the elongated anthropomorphs is discussed later. The important point here is that the Alcove Gallery contains rock art that adds considerable diversity to the Barrier Canyon Style if all figures are included in the definition.

This is especially true for the lower panel on the left side of the talus pile. Here occurs an odd assortment of mostly anthropomorphs that are relatively crude by BCS standards, with sparse or no details. A few even seem like historical fakes.[33] Some figures are mudded over, including one that most resembles a BCS anthropomorph because it is painted in red ocher and has white added for details such as horizontal torso bands. The reddish yellow mud smeared over this figure in an evident crude attempt to obscure it is similar to that used on other figures of this panel. All in all, the elements of this lower panel have the same sort of derivative quality as seen at Horseshoe Shelter. Temporal placement late in the BCS rock art tradition is the likely reason for the nature of these depictions.

Great Gallery

The Great Gallery is the final rock art site seen by most visitors to Horseshoe Canyon, but the one that motivates people to make the hike. This panel was extensively illustrated earlier, so no additional images are provided here. Based on qualities of how images were made and their content, multiple individuals likely contributed to painting the gallery. There is also considerable evidence for subsequent enhancements, erasures, and other modifications, including some done much later in time by the Fremont. It seems clear that the Great Gallery was a temporal accretion across some span of time, perhaps a lengthy one.

Nearly all Great Gallery anthropomorphs lack legs, except for those small in scale that appear to be depictions of real humans. At the High Panel virtually all anthropomorphs have legs, yet nearly all seem like depictions of supernatural entities. Most of the Great Gallery anthropomorphs are much larger than those at the High Panel, often life-size or greater. Also, many have elaborate body and sometimes head decorations created by using other colors in addition to red ocher, as well as incised lines and other techniques. Larger scale certainly helps for the addition of subtle details, and the Great Gallery images are much larger than those at the High Gallery, but BCS artists also achieved fine details at rather small scale. Great Gallery's images are not crowded together like those on the High Panel, but this is perhaps because the accessible protected canyon wall at the Great Gallery was so extensive whereas the accessible portion of the High Gallery wall was limited. That aspect does not, however, explain the content differences between these panels.

The Great Gallery and High Gallery bookend the visitor experience of BCS rock art in Horseshoe Canyon and establish much of the basic subject matter of BCS rock art. Most of the subject matter and manner of execution on display at the Great Gallery and the High Gallery are seen at other BCS panels throughout the region. Spatially between are Horseshoe Shelter and Alcove Gallery, two sites that add to the variability in BCS rock art. Though there could be other factors at play, a temporal trend is a likely explanation for much of the diversity represented by these four panels.

The Age of BCS

Temporal assignment of rock art images is tricky. It has always been this way and might remain so even though clear progress has occurred. There have been missteps as well, such as the problems and controversies surrounding the dating of patina (the cation-ratio method) or the radiocarbon dating of carbon from under rock varnish layers.[34] Such missteps occur in science, but ultimately other scientists correct them and this can lead to improvements of technique or theory. That is why there is cumulative progress in our understanding of the physical world.

Relative temporal order of rock art is valuable, providing knowledge that style X is older than style Y or that some specific figure is older than another specific figure. Archaeologists have long used this approach to good effect and will continue to do so. The superimposition of other rock art styles, such as Fremont or Ancestral Puebloan, upon Barrier Canyon Style images indicates that they are clearly older, perhaps considerably older in some cases. At the Peekaboo Panel along Salt Creek in Canyonlands National Park, ancestral Puebloan pictographs painted white superimpose most red BCS pictographs that were considerably faded by the time Puebloans added their images. The same is seen at the White Bird Shelter, where Puebloan handprints of several different types are superimposed over BCS spirit figures.

Relative dating is important, but absolute dating is the gold standard in archaeology. Absolute dating techniques provide an estimate of chronological age, and most of these came into being since about 1960.[35] The absolute dating of rock art is a challenge worth solving since it could securely link rock images to the rest of the archaeological record, thus placing them within their proper historical context.

Knowing when rock art was produced is important in many ways, not the least of which is being able to understand the larger context of image creation. Such knowledge can go a long way toward correlating trends in art production with what was occurring in the natural and social environment. Events and processes of change at local and regional scales undoubtedly played an important role in people's lives. Such context can provide one avenue for understanding why people created images. Rock art might represent responses to environmental alterations, especially traumatic ones or those that otherwise resulted in profound social transformation. Temporal placement also matters for understanding who people were likely interacting with across a broad area. Since human populations varied in density and distribution through time, it is

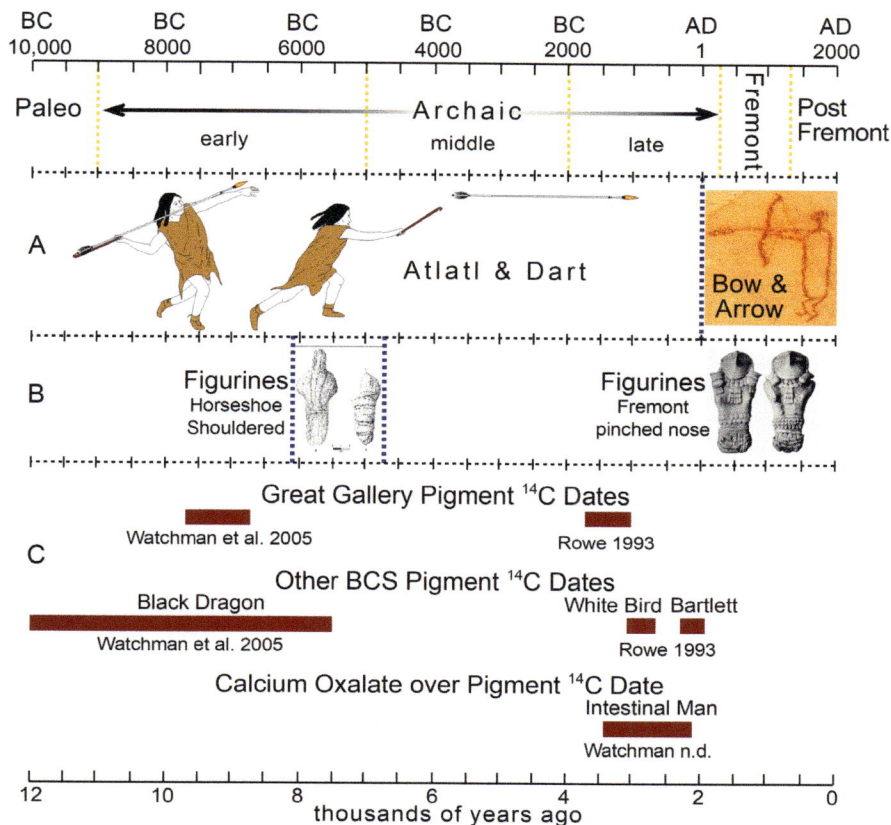

Figure 4.20 Timeline for the last 12,000 years, highlighting aspects relevant to the age of Barrier Canyon Style rock art: (A) age for the shift in weaponry from the atlatl-and-dart to bow-and-arrow, an event that occurred in Utah around 2,000 years ago. BCS rock art shows atlatl-and-dart technology and not the bow-and-arrow, while the opposite is true for Fremont rock art; (B) figurines that are portable art analogues for BCS spirit figures, with examples recovered from early Archaic layers at Cowboy and Walters Caves; (C) specific radiocarbon dates on pigment samples from specific BCS panels as well as one on calcium oxalate that covers pigment, with the rock art dating earlier.

useful to know about the existence of any population centers and important spheres of social and economic influence.

Temporal placement also matters for situating rock art within variable aspects of past lifeways such as the degree of residential permanence, the geographic scale of group movements, and whether social relationships among neighboring groups tended to be open and friendly or closed and hostile. Prior to the spread of farming in the Southwest, food was never in such abundance and concentration in any one area that people could survive in a small territory. The common pattern among arid-land hunter-gatherers is for family groups to range widely across vast areas and to have rather fluid social groups without territorial behavior such as defense and exclusion.[36] Introduction of corn and squash from Mesoamerica altered this calculus, as it resulted in localized concentrations of food created by the investment of human labor and seeds. Territorial marking and defense became important; conflict between groups increased.[37] The expansion of nonlocal farmers into new territories likely exacerbated social tensions.

Temporal knowledge also plays an important role in disentangling the diversity evident in a rock art style. What at first seems like a very diverse style might turn out to be a result of change through time. Space and time are key dimensions

Figure 4.21 Ancestral Puebloan pictographs in white (shield figures and dots) superimpose faded BCS pictographs painted red that include a large spirit figure with bird and citizen figure attendant on the right along with a smaller spirit figure farther right with vertical striped torso. Red has been intensified to make the BCS art more visible.

that underlie how varied a style will be, since increases in either dimension usually multiply the number of artists at work, which translates into greater diversity of expression. Some rock art traditions, such as Fremont, were in existence for a comparatively short time interval, a thousand years or less. BCS could have been in existence for at least six times this long, such that change over the ages is not only probable but highly likely. Modern people can gain some appreciation for stylistic shifts within relatively short spans of time by simply considering the repertoire of distinct art styles produced by single individuals, such as Picasso, during their lifetime. Consider, as well, the stylistic changes in Italian art that occurred during the last 500 years. BCS artists were perhaps more constrained by cultural tradition, but still there is good reason to expect that some of the variability in this rock art tradition is a consequence of temporal change.

Finally, any claims about the age of a rock art style depend on what images people classify as part of a rock art tradition. If the definition for the Barrier Canyon Style is so loose that it includes any red-painted anthropomorph, then there are essentially no temporal bounds—any time from the Pleistocene till yesterday could be included. If the definition is stricter, then more tightly drawn temporal bounds naturally follow. Since BCS rock art likely reflects a long tradition that persisted yet morphed through

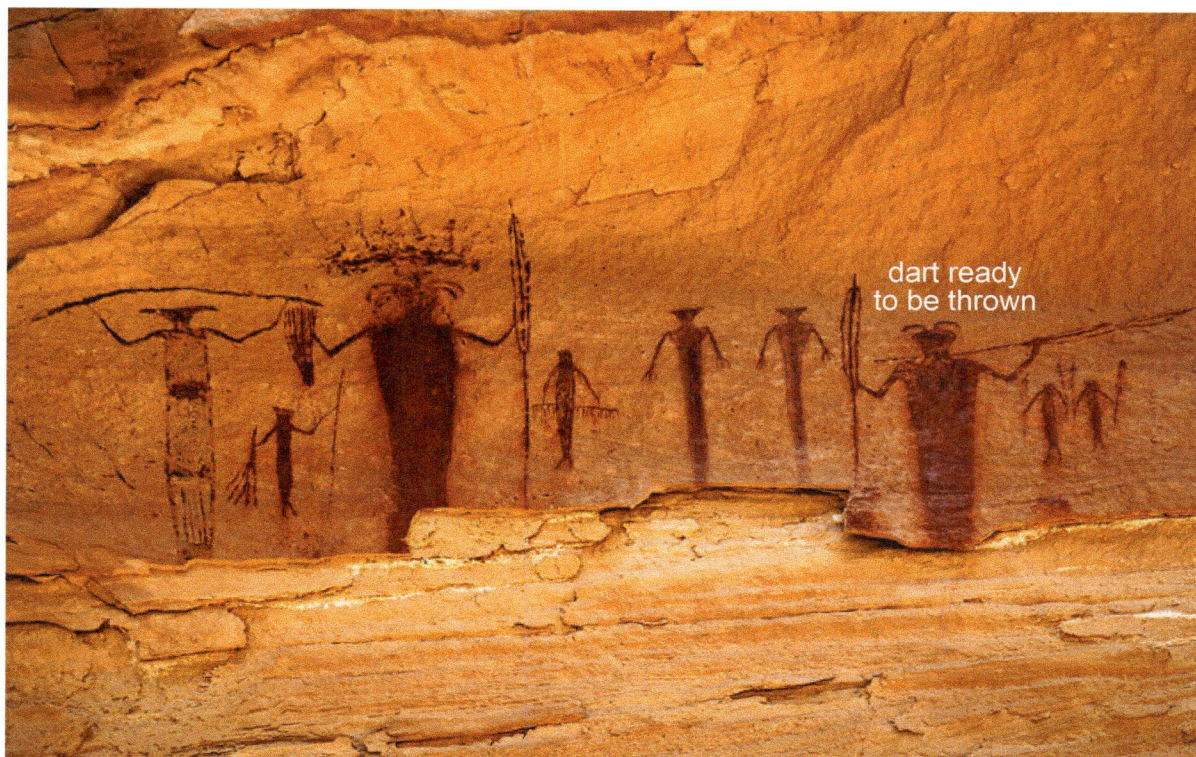

dart ready
to be thrown

Figure 4.22 Barrier Canyon Style pictographs showing anthropomorphs gripping atlatl darts, with one figure holding a dart in the customary throwing position. (Photo by Randy Langstraat, 2017.)

time, we might eventually be able to recognize early, middle, and late versions of BCS rock art, with the latter melding into Fremont.

Age Estimation by Art Content

Rock art content can provide important temporal clues, through both what is depicted and what is absent. Informative content includes natural lifeforms and human technology. For example, horses and riders are absent from Barrier Canyon Style rock art, but they occur on different style rock images of the local region attributable to the recent Ute and Paiute. At the other temporal end, BCS rock art lacks depictions of animals resembling mammoth, camel, ground sloth, or shrub-ox that went extinct at the end of the Pleistocene. As previously reviewed, BCS contains numerous depictions of Holocene-age animals, the kind that still exist today. These modern forms, however, provide no temporal resolution for the Holocene.

Material culture depictions can be more temporally significant, especially if technologies have well-known times of appearance and disappearance or disuse. The most prominent is bow-and-arrow technology, an innovation that spread into the Arctic region of North America from Asia rather late in prehistory, around 4,000 years ago. It was a slow southward spread, not reaching central Utah until roughly 2,000 years ago. At Cowboy Cave, just a day's walk upstream from the Great Gallery, arrow shaft fragments and arrow points occur in the upper layers dating no older than about

200 AD.[38] Other sites in the region also document an absence of bows and arrows until 2,000 years ago or shortly thereafter.

BCS rock art lacks bow-and-arrow depictions. The ranged weapons for killing animals from afar that BCS artists occasional illustrated are spears or the atlatl and dart. One particularly good panel showing probable atlatl darts occurs along the San Rafael River (figure 4.22); anthropomorphs with this technology occur at other panels as well, including the Great Gallery. Atlatls and darts were present in North American since Paleoindian times, and evidence of them occurs at archaeological sites throughout the Colorado Plateau and the Great Basin.[39]

Although BCS rock art lacks bow-and-arrow depictions, Fremont and later rock art styles display this technology, sometimes in a prominent way. A small panel at Horseshoe Shelter shows a hunter aiming a bow and arrow at a bison and two elk or deer. This particular image is likely to be Ute/Paiute because the bow is recurved, a weapon no older than about 1400 AD in Utah, but Fremont rock art of the region also commonly portrays bows and arrows in use hunting game animals.[40] In contradistinction, just like BCS rock art shows atlatls and darts but not bows and arrows, Fremont rock art shows bows and arrows but not atlatls and darts.

The temporal implication is that BCS rock art predates the bow and arrow, so is older than 2,000 years ago, whereas Fremont rock art postdates this technology, so is younger than 2,000 years ago. A rather rapid technological replacement is indicated by the lack of atlatls and darts in the upper layers of Cowboy Cave and similar sites. It is always possible that ancient weapons were held as heirlooms and even used on occasion such that atlatls and darts appearing in Fremont contexts might occur. But the converse is not true. When have pistols been found buried with Pharaohs or Vikings?

Age Estimation by Artifacts

Portable art analogues for the BCS spirit figures have significant implications for the age of the rock art. Archaeological excavations in 1975 at Cowboy and Walters Caves upstream from the Great Gallery recovered mummy-like clay figurines that strongly resemble many spirit figures in BCS rock art. An initial report on these finds appeared in the Cowboy Cave site description,[41] but an updated account and stratigraphic consideration by Nancy Coulam and Alan Schroedl is the reference to consult.[42] These anthropomorphic figurines are known as Horseshoe Shouldered after the main canyon of their discovery. Made from unfired clay, the figurines consist of heads and torsos that lack appendages. They have pronounced, rounded shoulders much like the BCS spirit figures, and many have torso decorations of incised lines or punctate dots arranged in lines, also just like many spirit figures.

Coulam and Schroedl found that this style of anthropomorphic figurine was restricted to the Early Archaic strata at Cowboy Cave and Walters Cave. The clay figurines occurred in deposits radiocarbon dated to between 5600 and 5000 BC.[43] The best example from both caves is a complete specimen over four inches long with incised and painted lines. This particular specimen came from an intact layer at Walters Cave

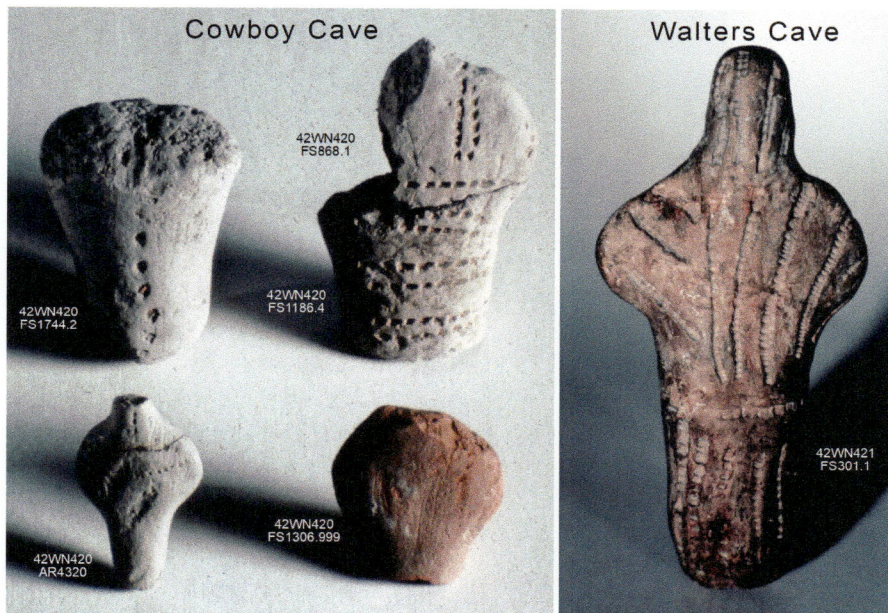

Figure 4.23 Horseshoe Shouldered clay figurines from Cowboy and Walters Caves that are portable art analogues for the BCS spirit figures. These figurines came from layers at the sites that are radiocarbon dated to between 5600 and 5100 BC. (Photos by David Crompton in the late 1970s provided by Alan Schroedl; courtesy of Natural History Museum of Utah and Bureau of Land Management.)

next to a plainweave sandal that has a direct radiocarbon date of between 5400 and 5100 BC.[44]

Anthropomorphic figurines stylistically distinct from the early Horseshoe Shouldered ones also came from Cowboy Cave. These "pinched nose specimens," as Coulam and Schroedl describe them, came from upper layers dating early in the Common Era. They represent Fremont artifacts that are stylistically distinct from the Horseshoe Shouldered figurines and temporally separated from them by thousands of years. Fremont anthropomorph figurines ultimately become quite elaborate as exemplified by a cache known as the Pilling Figurines.[45]

Sudden Shelter on the Wasatch Plateau also yielded a Horseshoe Shouldered figurine from Early Archaic deposits. This was a basal portion missing its head and shoulders, so Coulam and Schroedl were cautious about interpreting it as another good example of a BCS spirit figure analogue. Because preservation of unfired clay figurines was unlikely at this wet rockshelter, recovery of the one fragment was good fortune. BCS rock art is not documented in Sudden Shelter but appears in other locations close by.[46]

These portable art analogues for the BCS spirit figures are not easily discounted. Some who dismiss their temporal relevance for BCS rock art seem more than willing to accept split-twig figurines as a significant indicator for a late Archaic age of the Glen Canyon Linear rock art style. Another claim is that Cowboy and Walters Caves had mixed deposits that lacked stratigraphic integrity.[47] This is simply not true. Both caves contained well-differentiated layers that were excavated following the natural breaks. The Horseshoe Shouldered clay figurines that resemble BCS rock art were restricted to the Early Archaic strata at both caves. Contrary to the negative aspersions, this

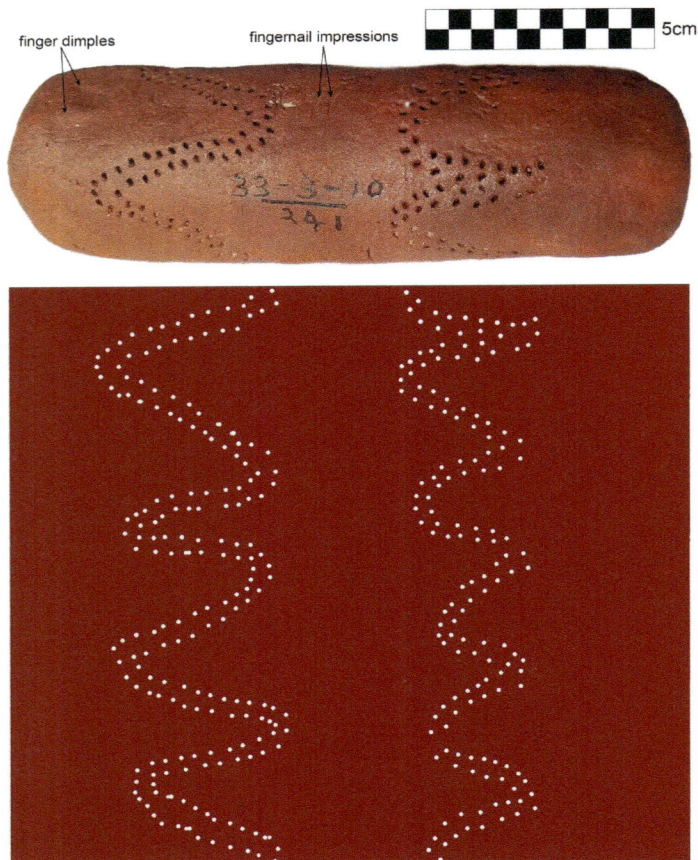

finger dimples
fingernail impressions
5cm

Figure 4.24 Prepared paint stick from Cottonwood Cave, an Archaic period campsite with BCS pictographs executed in similar colored red pigment. The wavy punctuation design is similar to the white dots painted on BCS anthropomorphs. Accession 33-3-10. (Photo courtesy of the Peabody Museum, Harvard University.)

artifact class was not mixed into later deposits at either site.[48]

Another significant indicator of Early Archaic age is a prepared stick of dark red pigment recovered from Cottonwood Cave near the Maze. The same Peabody Museum expedition from the 1920s that first documented the Great Gallery retrieved this interesting item. As described earlier, this paint stick is like a fat crayon, 4.5 inches long and 1.5 inches in diameter made of dark red ocher similar to the color of BCS pictographs. The cylinder was formed by mixing powdered hematite with some malleable material, then squeezing and rolling it into shape. Slight dimples from finger pressure along with fingernail impressions reveal how soft the material was. The probable period of production for this artifact is indicated by the double rows of meandering punctations created with a pointed tool that encircle the cylinder. Similar punctations occur on Horseshoe Shouldered clay figurines from the early Archaic layers at the three sites mentioned previously. This design feature provides a stylistic link between the paint stick and the Early Archaic figurines and also to the spirit figures of BCS rock art. It takes little imagination to see the punctate designs on the figurines and the paint stick as equivalent. Similarly little imagination is required to equate these to the white dots that occur on all pictograph images of Cottonwood Cave or other BCS sites.

This stylistic link is also a temporal link. Why create a red pigment paint stick? Because you plan to create pictographs with this crayon in the future. Why decorate it with punctate designs? Because this is the proper way to prepare such sacred paint for the purposes of illustrating supernatural entities. The creator of this valuable pigment preparation might have inadvertently lost it, or perhaps they purposefully set it aside for later use but never retrieved it.

Cottonwood Cave was one of the more rewarding sites these early archaeologists excavated in 1930. The site is a dry rockshelter with a well-protected but small living area containing slab-lined storage features. The paint stick was just one of dozens of recovered items that also included a split-twig figurine, a sandal, a wooden sickle, and a small hide pouch. These items span a long period of occupation history, likely from the early Archaic until around 800 years ago. Exposed on the upper wall of Cottonwood

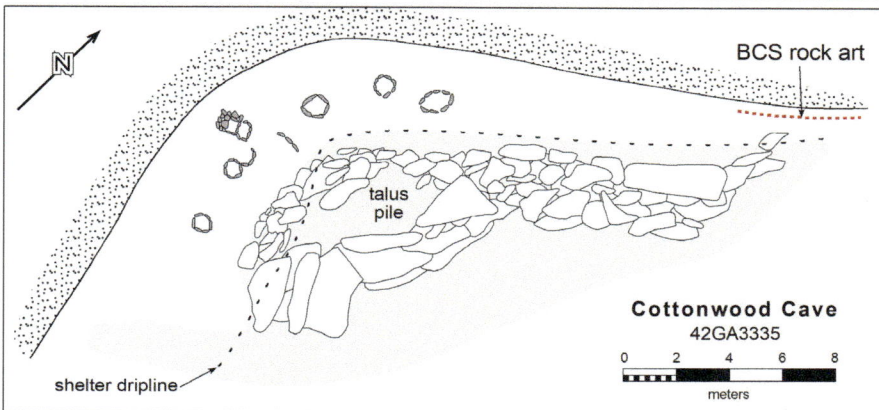

Figure 4.25 The badly spalled BCS pictograph panel at Cottonwood Cave (42GA3335), along with a map of the site prepared in 1930 by the Claflin-Emerson Expedition of the Peabody Museum. (Redrafted from Gunnerson, *The Fremont Culture*, Figure 7A.)

Cave is a BCS pictograph panel badly damaged by natural exfoliation of the sandstone cliff face. This painting was once of excellent quality and executed in a style similar to the nearby Perfect Panel, except that the Cottonwood Cave spirit figures have legs or once did. White dot decorations occur on the torsos of the figures similar to the punctations on the paint stick.

The large anthropomorph at Temple Mountain Wash that holds aloft a snake has a closely similar undulating set of white dots decorating the upper torso, even matching the count of five "peaks" on one end of the paint stick. Undulating paired white dots occur at several figures of the nearby Perfect Panel, and one of these figures has a pattern of undulations that matches that on the paint stick. It is worth pointing out that this undulating dot pattern replicates the snake theme that is so prevalent in BCS rock art.

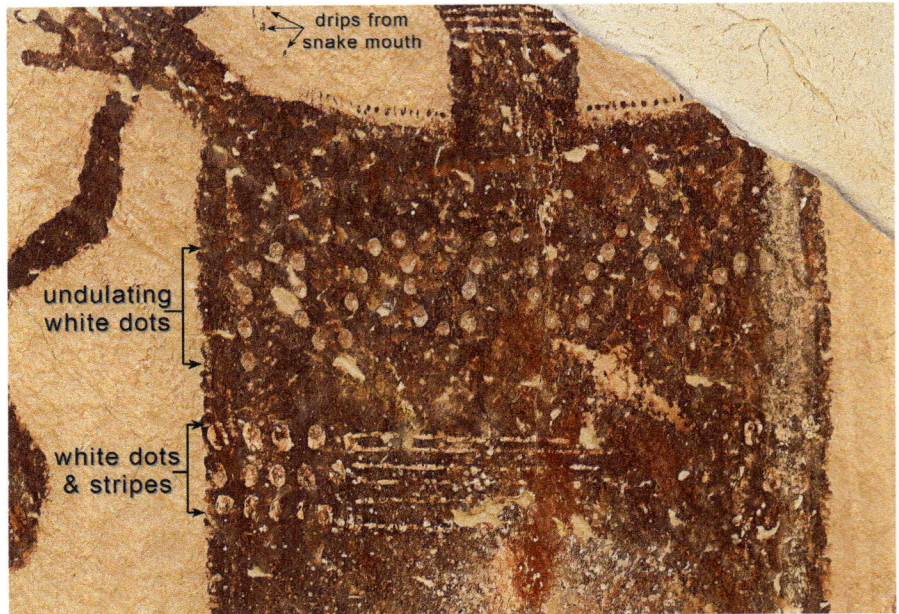

Figure 4.26 BCS spirit figure at the Temple Mountain Wash panel that exhibits a design of undulating white dots, similar to the design seen on the Cottonwood Cave paint stick.

Age Estimation by Superimposition

Superimposition refers to the placement of one thing over or above another. Rock art researchers have always relied upon this approach for judging relative temporal order, for both individual figures and images of distinct art styles. Examples of superimposition involving BCS rock art elements and those of different styles invariably show BCS to be older, perhaps considerably older in some cases. Puebloan images overlaying BCS images occur at several sites in Canyonlands National Park on the east side of the Colorado River. As discussed in greater detail below, there are many cases where later people could not easily superimpose their images upon BCS figures because they were inaccessible on account of erosion of ground surfaces or rock ledges used by BCS artists. In other cases, superimposition was possible based on ease of access but did not happen, perhaps out of respect for the ancient images.

A panel at Thompson Wash provides a good example of superimposition at a publicly interpreted BCS site that many people visit each year. Here, visitors can view multiple panels from different time periods, and a prominent one shows Fremont-style petroglyphs partially superimposed over BCS pictographs. The BCS paintings are somewhat faded and blurred on their lower portions from blowing moisture. The bulk of BCS images occur higher on this face than the Fremont petroglyphs, likely because of an intervening change in access between the time periods for the artists of these distinct styles. In this particular case, the change was likely a shifting of large talus blocks at the base of the cliff face. Fremont artists partially echoed or responded to the earlier BCS art, in that the largest pecked Fremont anthropomorphs occur below and centered upon the largest of the BCS anthropomorphs. This panel is just one example that illustrates BCS rock art dating earlier than Fremont rock.

Figure 4.27 One portion of Thompson Wash rock art panel that shows Fremont petroglyphs superimposed over Barrier Canyon Style pictographs. The latter are faded and occur higher on the rock face, indicative of a probable change in access between the time of BCS artists and the Fremont artists.

The well-known Temple Mountain pictograph panel provides another good indication of BCS rock art predating Fremont rock art. This panel largely consists of BCS images, with at least one obvious Fremont anthropomorph added a considerable time after the BCS paintings. There is also a superimposing anthropomorph whose authorship is debated by specialists, with some claiming it was a Fremont artist and others attributing it to a later BCS artist.

This panel occurs on a large, billboard-like sandstone face near the base of a high cliff that slopes upward from east to west on an angle. This area forms part of the collection of strongly folded rocks that make up the anticline known as the San Rafael Swell. Artists accessed the panel using a sloping, narrow bedrock ledge formed by somewhat more resistant sandstone along the base of the panel.[49] Talus blocks once present on this ledge provided higher access to the cliff face for painting BCS anthropomorphs and animals of massive scale, many larger than life.

The BCS images have suffered natural damage from both exfoliation of the rock surface and silt washing down the face from above. Silt staining occurs along the right side, with exfoliation also occurring here and extending in a broad swath to the left. Exfoliation both above and below the BCS images removed the heads or lower bodies of large anthropomorphs. To the left of the last BCS figures, exfoliation has removed

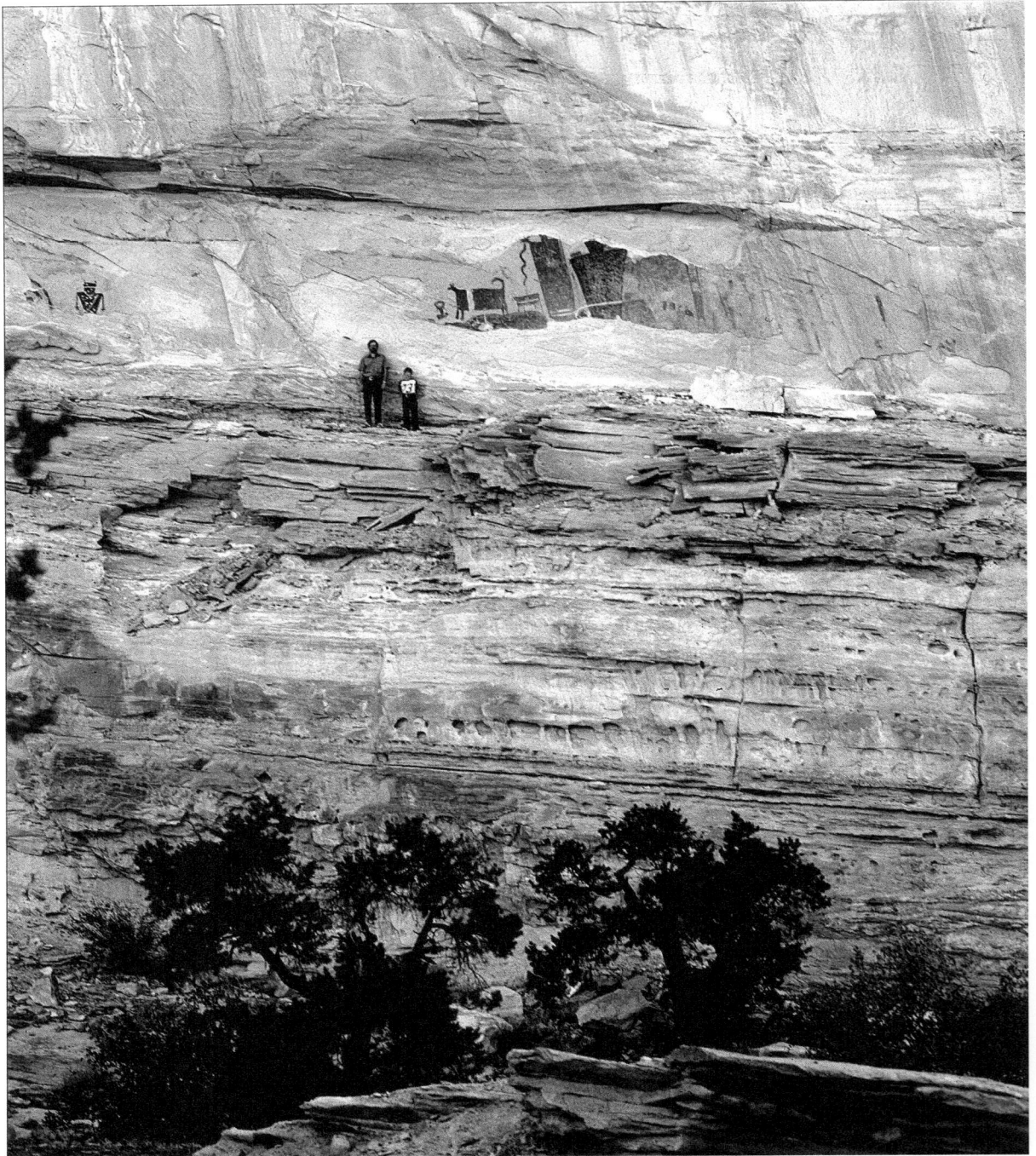

Figure 4.28 The Temple Mountain pictograph panel as seen in 1979. Steven Manning and son David stand on a bedrock shelf that artists used to create the images. This ledge is off limits to visitors to help conserve the irreplaceable paintings and for public safety, but Steven had permission from the Bureau of Land Management so he could record the images in great detail. Sometimes scientists are allowed in restricted places for research or conservation purposes. (Photograph taken by Elna Elizabeth Manning. Published courtesy of Steven Manning.)

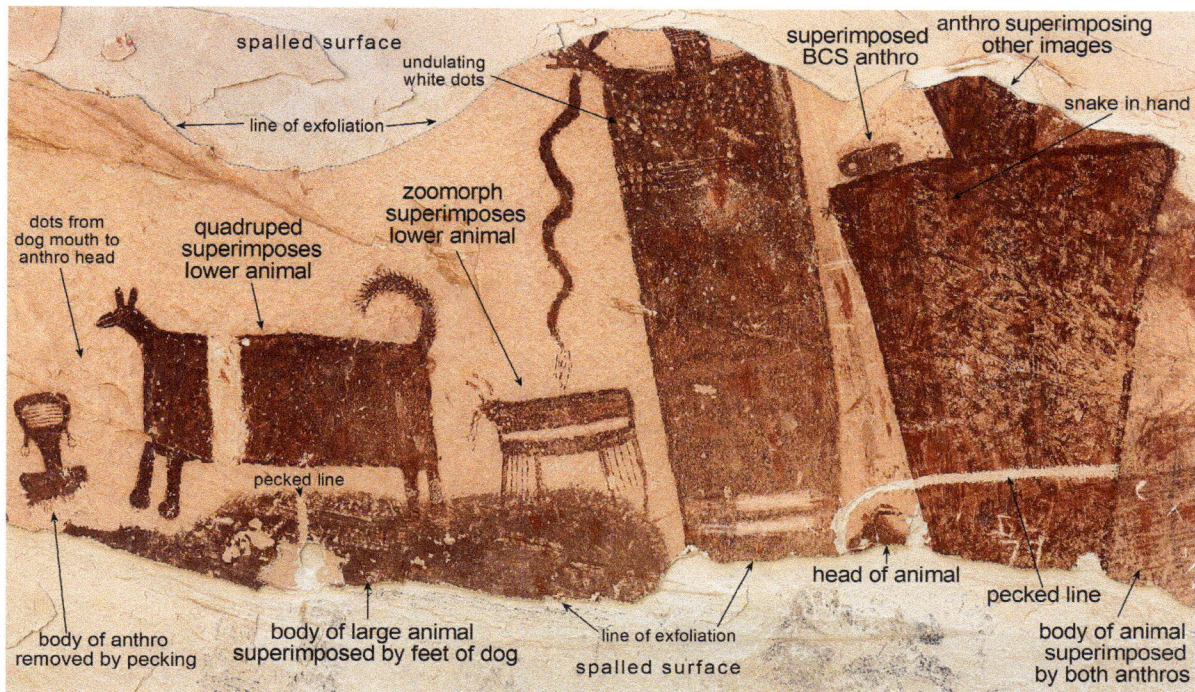

the entire old rock surface that these artists painted upon. It is difficult to estimate how far the BCS panel originally extended along this face, but perhaps thirty feet or more until a loss of overhanging protection. Some twenty feet to the left of the last BCS image, a Fremont anthropomorph occurs. It is painted upon a sandstone surface that became exposed after exfoliation of the rock surface that BCS artists had painted upon.

The extent of time between Fremont and BCS art remains unknown, but it would appear to be substantial based on two factors. One is the relative extent of weathering on the sandstone face upon which the Fremont art is painted compared to the BCS art. This judgment is possible because the rock face painted by the Fremont artist is also weathered and has itself started to exfoliate, exposing even fresher sandstone. A second factor is the superimposition of images evident on the intact portion of the BCS art, which indicates that some of these were painted across a span of time. The most obvious is a large, broad-shouldered anthropomorph painted over the top a smaller BCS anthropomorph.

The superimposed anthropomorph is about a quarter the width of the overpainted figure. Its head, with its bug-like eyes, projects just above the shoulder of the larger figure and its left arm, with an open hand occurs right at the shoulder of the larger figure. The overpainted right hand holds a serpent, although it is hard to see. The narrow figure is clearly a BCS spirit figure, similar to other examples, and was likely painted at about the same time as an adjacent larger spirit figure that also holds up a serpent. The large, superimposed anthropomorph is stylistically different than the earlier BCS images, but its more blocky body outline is seen in other BCS panels. Sally Cole and

Figure 4.29 Main portion of the Temple Mountain panel showing some of the superimpositions that occur here.

Polly Schaafsma argue that a Fremont artist painted the large anthropomorph, whereas Steve Manning claims that it was a later BCS artist.[50]

Both the narrow and wider anthropomorphs are painted over the top of a probable animal figure that is now largely gone; the head occurs to the left and the hind portion extends beyond the larger figure. A belt-like feature was eventually added to the large anthropomorph by pecking across the body and then encircling the superimposed animal's head.

The large BCS spirit figure that holds aloft a snake has decorations on its upper body consisting of white dots and fine horizontal white lines. Left of this figure is an unusual zoomorph of an unrecognizable animal form and a large quadruped that likely represents a dog.[51] Its back feet, and the lower fringed extremities of the zoomorph, are superimposed over the back of an even larger animal some eight feet in length. The back shape and size of this animal is similar to several large ungulates painted in a line at Fish Creek Cove near Grover, Utah.[52] Probable horns of this animal occur just to the left of the last anthropomorph.

The final BCS figure preserved on the left side consists of shoulders, neck, and head wearing earrings that resemble prickly pear pads. The lower portion of the torso was removed by pecking, and if this had not occurred then the neck of the large painted animal would have superimposed the anthropomorph. This evidence allows for a reconstruction of temporal priority, with the prickly pear anthropomorph first followed by the two large animals. Painted next were the two overlying and partially superimposed animals and the two spirit figures holding snakes, with the largest of these evidently painted between the two earlier large animals but the bug-eyed spirit figure superimposing the trailing animal. The larger broad-shouldered anthropomorph was the last major image addition, but smaller modifications continued, such as a pecked belt or sash across the lower body. Moreover, there are other additions and extensive modification to the panel immediately right of the broad-shouldered anthropomorph.[53]

The Temple Mountain panel demonstrates the temporal priority of BCS rock art over Fremont rock art, with a substantial difference in time represented between the two, and helps document that BCS was a long-lived tradition with subsequent BCS artists selectively adding elements and modifying, erasing, or editing earlier images. This is a common pattern in BCS rock art. Sally Cole makes a highly plausible argument, based on analogy to ethnographically documented practices among Aboriginal Australians, that BCS artists rejuvenated and amended portions of rock art panels during rituals when sacred "narratives were reillustrated, reinterpreted, or replaced."[54]

There are other examples of subsequent modification of BCS rock art, along with the superimposing of elements that might be late BCS or even early Fremont. One example is Alcove Gallery in Horseshoe Canyon, containing two main panels that are spatially distinct both horizontally and vertically and with some clear stylistic distinctions. The vertical separation is important since this aspect relates to differential accessibility and exposure of the canyon wall.

slight superimposition

underlying redder pigment

inset

Figure 4.30 Close-up images from upper panel of the Alcove Gallery in Horseshoe Canyon showing head of small, horned anthropomorph partially superimposed over a Barrier Canyon Style anthropomorph. The latter was originally painted with a redder pigment and then overcoated with a lighter pigment like that of the horned anthropomorph.

The upper panel main elements are difficult-to-see elongated spirit figures of torsos and heads that are so faded with age that the pigment provides little contrast with the underlying sandstone. Adjacent and below the spirit figures on the left are several smaller anthropomorphs with arms and legs, two of which also have markedly long horns. The horned anthropomorphs resemble a prominent human-like figure in the lower panel in this alcove. These distinct anthropomorphs appear to be a later addition, perhaps at roughly the same interval as when the lower panel was painted.

Support for temporal priority of the elongated anthropomorphs is the evident slight superimposition of their outlines with the same light-reddish mud used for the distinct small figures. This technique is most clearly seen with the two long-horned figures, especially the one on the left whose left horn and arm just touch the larger elongated anthropomorph. The larger figures were originally painted with a darker red pigment that was overcoated at some point with a lighter red clay. The small figures have similar light red clay without the underlying darker red of the elongated

Figure 4.31 A panel in Canyonlands National Park east of the Colorado River with multiple episodes of painting likely across widely different time periods. The carpet-like anthropomorph on the left was likely earliest. It is painted with red ocher with white dot accentuation. At a later point in time a rectangular outline was added around the torso of this figure with a lighter red pigment the same shade as used for the small bighorn sheep. The horns of this sheep partially superimpose the small red ocher painted anthropomorph. The pigment of this figure is distinct from that of the large anthropomorph. The smaller, horned anthropomorphs (lower right) with interior torso decorations seem painted with the same pigment as the bighorn sheep.

anthropomorphs. It appears that when the small anthropomorphs were added the painters also refurbished the lower portions of the older larger figures by applying the same clay used for painting the newer images.

Another form of subsequent interaction or engagement with the elongated spirit figures was by pecking a small area toward the upper central part of each torso, in the symbolic heart area. Virtually all of the faded spirit figures received this treatment; none of the smaller figures of distinct style were modified this way.[55]

Use of mud pigment rather than red ocher is characteristic of Horseshoe Shelter, a panel that likewise seems to date late in the BCS tradition. A few small anthropomorphs on the lower panel were painted with red ocher, but then mudded over with the same clay used to paint other pictographs in both the lower shelter and the stylistically distinct horned figures and small anthropomorphs of the upper panel. If the horned figures are not Fremont, although that is a possibility, then they likely date late in the BCS rock art tradition.

Age Estimation by Radiocarbon Dating

BCS as a living tradition spanning a lengthy interval of time is supported by the superimposition and modification of panels from subsequent artists of the tradition. It is also supported by the small handful of radiocarbon dates currently available on examples of BCS rock art from a few sites. The Great Gallery is one such site, in particular

Figure 4.32 Overview of the Great Gallery spalling section, with the lower image providing greater detail and more intense color. Radiocarbon-dated pigment came from the small BCS spirit figure at right, painted upon heavily abraded sandstone that partially obliterated a pecked bighorn sheep.

a spalled area immediately to the left of the Holy Ghost group that produced painted chunks of sandstone from BCS pictographs yielding two radiocarbon dates.[56] This part of the Great Gallery is of little interest to casual visitors, but it is temporally informative because of the complex arrangement of additions and superimposed elements made by both BCS artists and those of other and later styles.

The first pictograph fragment with a reliable age came from the lower portion of a small anthropomorph. Since the sandstone spall could be refitted to the rock face, we know exactly which image it came from: a small spirit figure without any body or head ornamentation. Marvin Rowe processed this sample in the early 1990s using his then newly established low-temperature plasma extraction technique.[57] Organic carbon from the pigment produced an age estimate of about 1600–1700 BC.[58] Rowe considered this age an upper limit for the painting, since organic carbon in the underlying sandstone likely contaminated the sample to an unknown degree.

As is true for any directly dated object, the age estimate only applies to the sample processed. It is a matter of inference how well a sample represents the rest of an item. In this case, as with most directly dated artifacts, it is probably a close approximation. Yet the age on one artifact is unlikely to represent the age for an entire artifact collection from a site. Nor is it likely that the date on this one anthropomorph is representative of the entire Great Gallery. Was the Sistine Chapel painted by one individual in a short span of time? The dated Great Gallery image seems like a late addition. Extending the age of this sample to the overall panel is highly questionable and its relevance for adjacent figures is even doubtful, except perhaps the small BCS anthropomorphs to the left and the partially spalled and stylistically similar but larger anthropomorph just to the right.

Immediately left of the dated anthropomorph is a horned Fremont figure, now almost gone save for a white painted headband, inscribed horns, abraded surface for the head and upper torso, and a red painted necklace. Perhaps this image was never finished, but the sandstone was prepared by abrading it smooth for the head and upper torso. Left of the Fremont figure is a large, angled anthropomorph with the bottom portion also lost to exfoliation. This figure was painted upon a heavily abraded sandstone surface, one so thoroughly abraded that deeply pecked bighorn sheep were nearly obliterated. These pecked sheep are of a distinctive style with greatly exaggerated horns that curve back over much of the body length. The sheep petroglyphs were there first, known to predate the directly dated pictograph as the latter was painted on an abraded surface and the pecked horns immediately alongside the lower left have been removed to varying degrees by this abrasion.

The angled red painted anthropomorph had much of its pigment removed by additional abrasion, as though someone tried to erase it. This figure has white outlining the head and extending across portions of the upper torso, although most is now gone. There is also a white anthropomorphic element immediately left of the head and above the three small anthropomorphs resembling small spirit figures. The white here matches that used for the headband of the horned Fremont figure. Abrasion has removed portions of the three small spirit figures, especially within the lower body of the one on the far left. A tangential line, something like a belt, was added by incision to the far-right small red figure. Farther left there is a white anthropomorph with some red outlining of the upper torso and perhaps head. It appears that abrasion removed much of the lower part of this figure. Abrasion also removed what was likely another anthropomorph or other element at the far left. Here, there is red pigment that occurs in dimples of the sandstone surrounded by an abraded surface.

The canyon wall for this part of the Great Gallery moving left from the medium-sized, radiocarbon-dated anthropomorph is still in reach of modern humans. Fremont people made one obvious addition to this portion of the gallery wall.[59] They could well

Figure 4.33 Alan Watchman sampling a large, fallen pictograph block at the Great Gallery to the left of the Holy Ghost group, with a close-up of the block prior to sampling. Gary Cox, NPS ranger, looks on with Carol Paterson examining the rock art. (Photos by Richard Reed.)

have made other modifications and additions, such as the incised belt to the small anthropomorph. The BCS artists who created the dated figure, as well as three small figures farther left and likely also the angled figure, did so after the pecked sheep. Were these BCS artists in the same temporal period as those artists who painted the figures on the Great Gallery wall to the right? The answer seems to be no, based on even casual inspection of the images. If the prior radiocarbon date is a close approximation of a late Archaic maximum age for the medium-sized figure, then larger anthropomorphs to the right might be older. Such antiquity is coincident with other evidence such as the clay figurines and paint stick reviewed previously.

A second radiocarbon sample from the Great Gallery consists of pigment removed from a large painted block that lay to the right of where the previously dated sample came from. Alan Watchman, a rock art dating expert from Australia, obtained this sample and performed a series of exhaustive tests and preparation protocols to be certain the correct material was dated. He analyzed both the paint and the underlying rock to identify and eliminate potential contaminants.[60] After pretreatment, two different AMS labs obtained independent age estimates on acid-treated paint residue. These dates were almost contemporaneous, which allowed them to be averaged and thereby provide the best estimate of age: 8655 ± 210 BP.[61] BCS artists therefore painted a large figure, presumably an anthropomorph, sometime between about 8300 and 7300 BC, in the Early Archaic period. Given that Marvin Rowe demonstrated that natural organic carbon occurs in sandstone at the Great Gallery, it is possible that the 8655 BP estimate is somewhat too old. Even so, it certainly provides rather strong evidence for early Archaic authorship of this painted image.

Additional radiocarbon dates are available from four other BCS rock art panels: Black Dragon, Bartlett, Intestinal Man, and White Bird. Little information is available for the Black Dragon and Intestinal Man dates, which Alan Watchman obtained in early 2000. The Black Dragon sample produced an age estimate of just over 8,500 radiocarbon years before present.[62] Watchman provides this result at the very end of his Great Gallery dating paper as support for an early Archaic age. The Intestinal Man date is on an oxalate layer that overlies the paint on the foot of the anthropomorph on the far-left side. This sample produced an age of just over 2,600 radiocarbon years before present. Since this image occurs on an overlying mineral accretion, the date means that the art is older than ~1000 BC, but how much older is unknown.[63]

Archaeologist Betsy Tipps reported details about the White Bird and Bartlett Panel dates.[64] The White Bird site is mostly an open camp focused around the east side of a sandstone outcrop that forms slight shelters. This location has abundant archaeological evidence of occupation that began about 4000 BC during the Middle Archaic period (or mid-Holocene), with sporadic use extending up until about AD 1000. The shelter walls contain a series of BCS anthropomorphs and some zoomorphs, including the White Bird site namesake, along with numerous Puebloan handprints in white and red. Some of these handprints superimpose BCS figures, and a white painted Puebloan sheep also superimposes a BCS anthropomorph. Most BCS anthropomorphs are painted with red ocher, as is customary, with some having white accents, but three are painted with an "orange" (reddish yellow) clay or mud similar to the mud paint used at Horseshoe Shelter. These figures appear to lack any accents or features except for horns. They also have more squat torsos. Tipps reports that Marvin Rowe processed exfoliated clay paint from two anthropomorphs to obtain CO_2, with both gas samples submitted for radiocarbon dating. One was unfortunately ruined at the dating lab, but the other returned an age of 2710 ± 75 BP, or roughly 1000–800 BC.[65] Unlike paint samples from other BCS sites, this one was pure pigment without any of the underlying sandstone matrix, so contamination from older carbon is unlikely.

A late Archaic age for the mud-painted BCS anthropomorph at White Bird Shelter is a believable result for what looks like a figure from relatively late in the BCS tradition. The ocher-painted BCS figures at this site are stylistically somewhat distinct and

Figure 4.34 Two panels at the White Bird site. Upper image shows BCS spirit figures superimposed by negative and positive Puebloan handprints; a Puebloan white bighorn sheep also superimposes a BCS anthropomorph (third one in on the upper right). Lower image shows BCS spirit figures in faded red ocher with some white accentuation; one of these is partially coated with clay added at a later time.

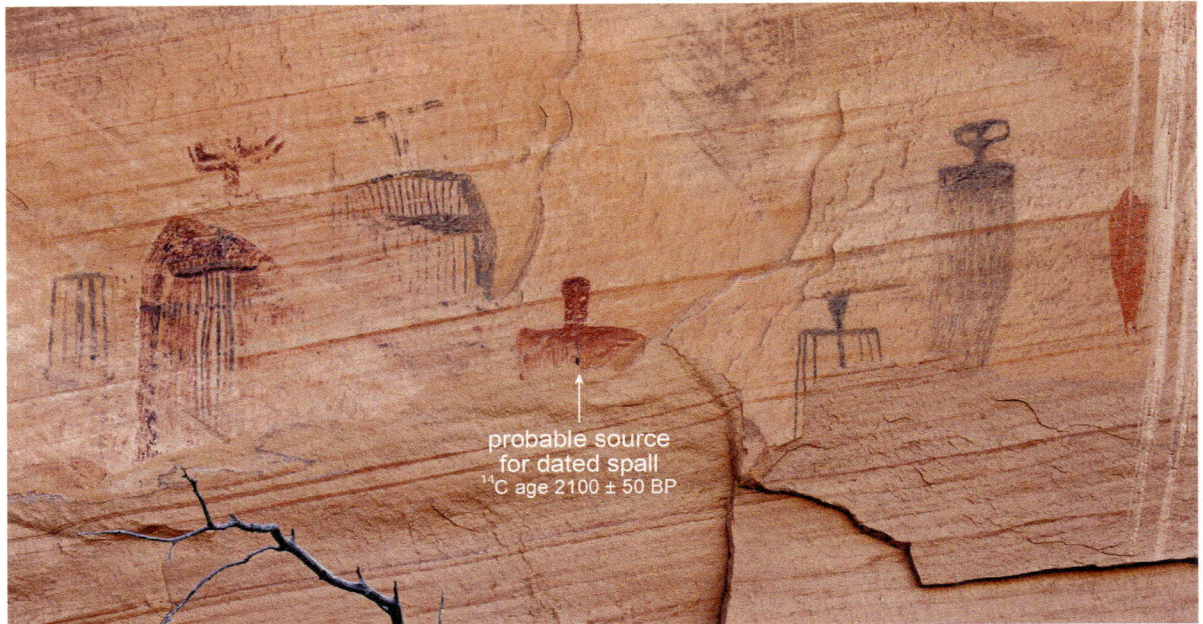

probable source
for dated spall
^{14}C age 2100 ± 50 BP

Figure 4.35 Bartlett Panel near Moab. A painted spall with red strips found below this rock art was radiocarbon dated to 2100 ± 50 BP.

likely earlier in age. They have more elongated bodies and white paint accents as well as designs both inside and alongside, especially snake-like wavy lines. A further indication of temporal priority for the ocher-painted figures are splotches of orange clay that occur on and around the head of at least one of these figures, clay that appears similar to that used for the dated anthropomorph.

The Bartlett Panel date was on a large sandstone spall with red parallel strips, which matches just a single spirit figure at the panel, centrally located and now largely gone except for its head and shoulders. Marvin Rowe also processed this sample, extracting two different components: one consisting of paint mixed with sandstone, and the other consisting of just sandstone. Organic carbon from the pigment produced an age estimate of roughly 350 BC–50 AD. However, as at the Great Gallery, the underlying sandstone here also contains organic carbon, meaning that the painting is likely younger to some unknown extent.

Age Estimation by Condition

Significant antiquity is also indicated by the often-weathered, faded, exfoliated, or otherwise naturally damaged condition of the BCS art. A few BCS rock art panels are well-preserved, but the vast majority are not. The Perfect Panel is so named because its degree of preservation stands out as notable when compared to most other BCS sites. Even some panels that are relatively well preserved, such as Head of Sinbad, have lost images to one degree or another. At Sinbad, silt washing down the sandstone face from above across an extended span of time has almost totally obscured some images along the left-hand side of the panel. Similar silt wash has recently started a slow creep across the attendant to the "skeleton" spirit figure, with just a single jagged trickle extending

across the hand on the left. Similar overwashing occurs at other panels, such as the previously discussed Temple Mountain.

A fine example of both fading and inaccessibility is the Invisible Panel, discovered in 2017 within a canyon of the Robbers Roost area south of the Great Gallery.[66] This panel is large, approaching the Great Gallery in horizontal extent, yet it went undetected until recently because the pictographs are so incredibly faded. It is virtually impossible to appreciate the designs on this panel in the field. Digital images had to be processed using the computer-processing algorithm called DStretch to begin seeing the painted figures. Many BCS panels benefit from this technique, since faded red ocher paint can start to match the color of the background sandstone, rendering

Figure 4.36 BCS rock art panel along the San Rafael River that shows extensive damage from spalling of the rockface along sandstone sheeting joints. The lower-left images are almost completely gone, while those on the upper right are partially exfoliated. (Photos by Brian Lee.)

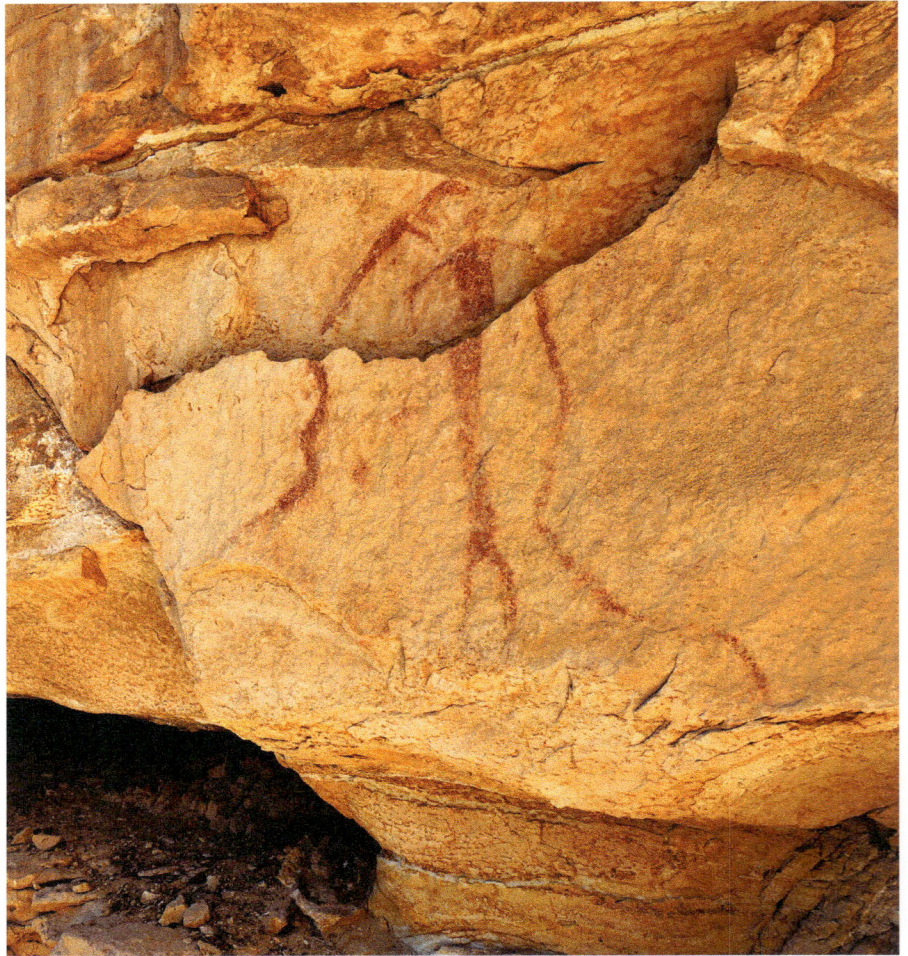

Figure 4.37 BCS images cracked and separated by slow erosional processes. San Rafael Swell. (Photo by Randy Langstraat.)

figures almost invisible. There are many examples where previously hidden or muddy BCS content has been revealed using this technique. Does rock art look better when well preserved and in real colors? Yes! But to counteract the effects of time and sustained UV exposure, DStretch and other image post-processing can prove a real asset.

No image enhancement technique can help with another aspect related to the length of time since some BCS panels were painted: loss through exfoliation. This form of image decay has already been illustrated at several sites, including Temple Mountain and the Great Gallery. Much of the painted rock face at Temple Mountain has sloughed off, reducing a panel that once might have rivaled the Great Gallery in its significance. In this case there is a minimum age for when BCS art was lost, since Fremont art was added to the new surface exposed by rockfall. The sheeting joint at Temple Mountain that resulted in loss of BCS rock art was just an inch or two behind the painted rock face, meaning that the spalls that separated were thin and fragile. The case is different at the Great Gallery, where a deep sheeting joint resulted in spalls up to a foot thick or more.

Some of the spalled BCS rock art panels are now close to being lost, which serves as a reminder that several might have disappeared already. A broken panel along the San Rafael River provides a good example of this, since it is difficult to estimate the number of figures once present. Two separate, partially preserved portions occur at this location, with the scene on the right seemingly more intact. The left-hand scene has little that remains except for small portions of at least three figures. A large expanse of rockface both above and to the left of the pictograph remnants is exfoliated to a depth of an inch or two. The sloughed rockface extends some twenty feet left of the painting fragments, so plenty of protected wall was once present here. Erosion has occurred along relatively narrow, horizontal bedding planes in the sandstone and then perpendicular cross joints, resulting in elongated blocks falling away from the cliff and removing art.

The scene on the right is more intact and has exfoliated by a thin rind of sandstone "peeling" away from the cliff face. The old rock face that was painted upon is intact to the left, so no images have been lost in this direction. A foxlike animal and portions of three spirit figures occur here, with one anthropomorph nearly gone except for a head, one shoulder, and an arm holding a snake. At some point, someone peppered these images with pellets of a white substance, which must have occurred after much exfoliation had already happened, since these blotches also occur on the newer surface.

The erosional process exhibited here and at many other panels are gradual ones that occurred across hundreds, if not several thousands, of years. The implication is that some BCS rock art has significant antiquity, which is consistent with other evidence.

Age Estimation by Context

Significant antiquity is also implied by the inaccessible, elevated positions for some Barrier Canyon Style rock art panels, which were painted from ground surfaces or rock ledges that no longer exist. One retort to this observation is that painters could have accessed impossible-to-reach cliff walls with scaffolds, ladders, or timbers from below or ropes from above. Ropes would not work for pictographs since the overhanging cliff faces used for paintings cannot be reached with them. A painter suspended in this manner would be left dangling in the air far from the cliff face. Although use of some ascension device is technically possible, it runs counter to what ethnographers have documented for mobile hunter-gatherers. Such an approach is also incongruous with the horizontal layout of BCS panels. Had BCS artists regularly used climbing aids, then why didn't they stack figures vertically in protected shelters like the Great Gallery, since there is so much prime wall space available that way? Also, there is a large difference between leaning up a short timber to get a slight boost now and then from a convenient ground surface at the base of a panel versus needing to use a long timber just to reach the base of a panel, let alone its full height.

The High Gallery in Horseshoe Canyon is just one example of a BCS rock art panel that awes visitors with its inaccessibility. The images of this panel occur so high

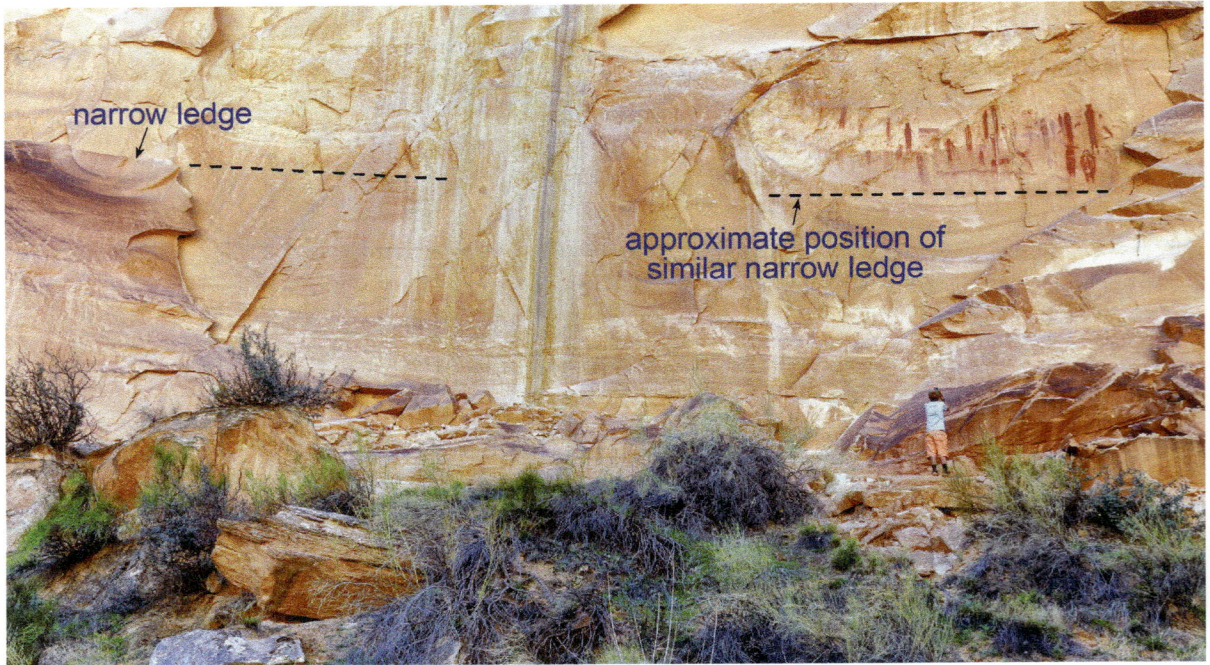

Figure 4.38 High Panel with person standing where easy access ends. The rock ledge on the left side is formed on a sheeting joint in the sandstone. A counterpart on the right side once provided access but collapsed a thousand or more years ago. (Photo by Alan Cressier, March 2014.)

up on the canyon wall, some eighty feet or more above the creek bottom, that it boggles the mind. How did people paint those images way up there? Climbing the talus slope below the panel brings you within about sixteen feet, but well short of the rock art. This panel occurs so high on the wall that any ancient alluvium once filling the canyon never obscured the rock surface, nor did it provide a useful surface to stand upon for painting purposes. The inaccessible nature of this panel has limited senseless modern vandalism and also restricted the artistic efforts of later people to make additions or modifications to the BCS images.

Painters of the High Gallery likely used a rock ledge that no longer exists. An analogous ledge occurs to the left (downstream) of the panel. Access via talus slope boulders is improbable given the steep slope at the base and lack of evidence for such an accumulation that could account for this route. Use of log ladders or other scaffolding to reach the rock surface is a poor fit for the horizontal layout of the overall panel. There is also subtle evidence on the rock face itself suggesting that a narrow ledge (or ledges) once existed along the base of the panel. It was likely never an easy ledge to get to and was both narrow and somewhat precarious even when the ledges were intact upon the wall.

Later rock art additions and vandalism at the High Panel are limited to the bottom portion, with the latter restricted to the far-right edge. A series of pecked images added to the lower part of the panel in a later rock art style strongly suggests that subsequent artists stood upon a surface largely the same as that used by the BCS artists. It is possible that they could not reach as high without some sort of assistance, since the pecked elements do not extend more than half the way up the panel and appear

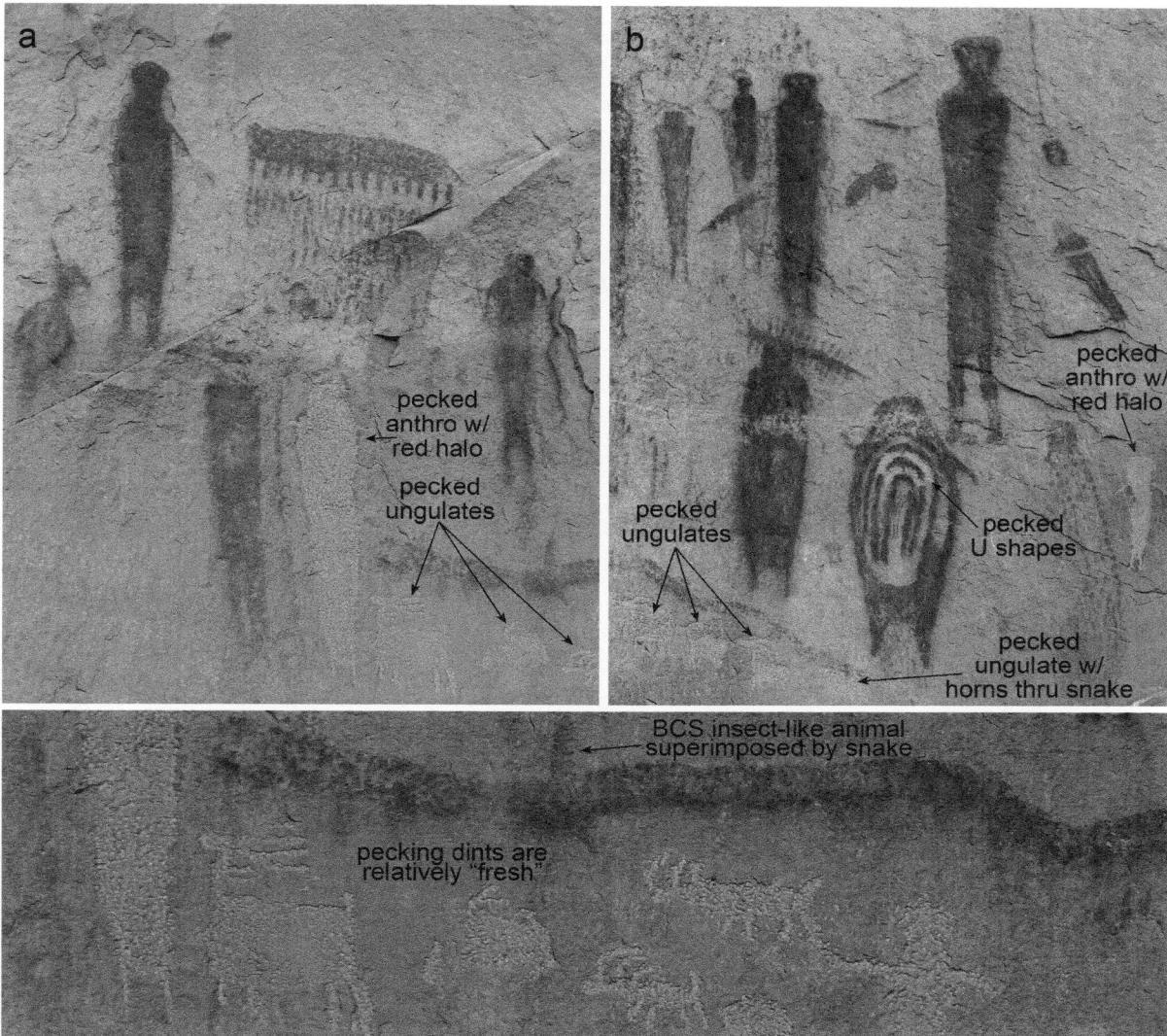

Labels on image:
a

pecked
anthro w/
red halo

pecked
ungulates

b

pecked
anthro w/
red halo

pecked
ungulates

pecked
U shapes

pecked
ungulate w/
horns thru snake

BCS insect-like animal
superimposed by snake

pecking dints are
relatively "fresh"

in just two limited spots. The pecked images consist of solid pecked anthropomorphs and quadrupeds that generally occur below a BCS painted snake several meters long. Temporal priority for the BCS images is established by a few instances where the petroglyphs disrupt the painted snake. In two cases red-painted anthropomorphs were pecked away, leaving a halo of red pigment around the pecked area. This halo represents diffusion of the hematite paint into the sandstone matrix, something readily apparent with all the BCS images on this panel. This evidence supports a lengthy interval of time separating painting from pecking.

BCS artists painted some rock art panels in canyon settings while standing upon old alluvial terraces that no longer exist. The Harvest Scene in the Maze portion of Canyonlands National Park is one such panel, although the presence of a narrow bedrock ledge here makes this less obvious. The Great Gallery in Horseshoe Canyon

Figure 4.39 High Gallery in Horseshoe canyon with insets of specific details, especially the pecked images along the bottom that superimpose BCS pictographs in a few instances. Pecking totally removed two painted anthropomorphs, except for a red halo that remains around each figure.

provides a better example. When standing in the wash bottom, Great Gallery's images loom above you, far out of reach. The bedrock bench immediately under the panel gets you closer, but the art remains inaccessible.

Horseshoe Canyon was variably filled and flushed of alluvium just like all canyons of the Southwest. Alluvium up to forty feet high once filled Horseshoe Canyon wall to wall in the stretch from the Great Gallery downstream to the High Panel. This high terrace, which geologists designate as T2 (terrace 2), formed during the late Pleistocene and early Holocene, starting more than 16,000 years ago and ending shortly before 8,000 years ago.[67] This Pleistocene alluvium eroded from the canyon long ago except for a few remaining traces. One remnant occurs at the Great Gallery, protected by a massive rock pile that accumulated from partial collapse of the overhanging sandstone sheltering this area.

Horseshoe Canyon rock art panels occurring above this alluvium include the High Panel, the upper portion of Alcove Gallery, and the upstream portion of the Great Gallery. Painting images at the upstream part of the Great Gallery likely required the T2 terrace to have reached maximal height or close. The painted figures in this portion are typical for the Barrier Canyon Style and closely resemble other BCS pictographs such as at the Perfect Panel, Harvest Scene, Hog Spring, and Temple Mountain Wash. A Pleistocene alluvial terrace was not required for BCS artists to access the High Gallery, nor did this terrace impede them from painting this wall since it is above maximum T2 terrace height. High Gallery rock art is typical Barrier Canyon Style.

Other central Horseshoe Canyon panels occur below the Pleistocene alluvium and could not have been painted until after that sediment had eroded from the canyon wall at those locations: Horseshoe Shelter, the lower portion of Alcove Gallery, and much of the Great Gallery. The timing of erosion is an obvious key constraint for when these galleries could be painted.[68] When these walls became exposed is debatable.

One argument is that it took some 4,000 years or more before the sandstone cliff face at the Great Gallery was cleared of ancient alluvium and capable of being painted.[69] If true, this glacial pace for T2 erosion would stand in marked contrast to what we know occurred in other canyon systems of the Colorado Plateau, both historically and in the past, where much greater heights and volumes of alluvial sediment eroded in brief intervals. The history of arroyo cutting throughout the Southwest in the last 100 to 120 years is well documented and stark testament to the rapidity of this process.[70]

Alluvium obstructing the Great Gallery canyon wall until after the middle Holocene is also contradicted by the radiocarbon date of 8300–7300 BC on pigment from a large red painted figure, likely an anthropomorph, once present to the left of the Holy Ghost group. This pigment date suggests that the ancient alluvium had eroded from the canyon wall before 8,000 years ago.[71] Given the 1,130-year counting error on the OSL (optically stimulated luminescence) date for the end of T2 deposition, there is no necessary conflict with the pigment radiocarbon age since their ranges overlap. In short, alluvial deposition might well have stopped more than 9,000 years ago, leaving hundreds of years of incision, sufficient exposure time of the Great Gallery cliff face to allow for the radiocarbon date range.

The pigment sample dated by Watchman might be somewhat too old because of old carbon in the rock, so it should perhaps best be treated as an estimate for the time after which the image was painted. Assuming, for argument's sake, that T2 alluvium did not start eroding till after 8,000 years ago (~6000 BC), there remains ample time for the wall to be cleared of sediment so that early Archaic foragers could paint images. People occupied Cowboy and Walters Caves upstream from the Great Gallery until about 5200 BC, with rather intensive use starting at around 5600 BC. This date range is some 400 to 800 years or more after the end of T2 deposition as estimated by the mean OSL age, more than enough time for stream erosion to have cleared T2 sediment from the canyon wall at the Great Gallery. This fact would remain true even if alluvial incision occurred at a rate less than half that of historic-period arroyo cutting.

Dissection of this floodplain, and the larger environmental trends that caused it to happen, likely alarmed the forager societies that called Horseshoe Canyon home. This event was a harbinger of disaster for their traditional lifeway. Aside from loss of the fertile floodplain in Horseshoe and other canyons of the region, the drying and warming trend that led to such dissection diminished both plant and animal resources on a broad scale. Existential threats require action. Rock art might have been one form to appease angry spirits and rebalance evident chaos in the world.

The ground surface that BCS artists likely stood upon to paint the downstream side of the Great Gallery consists of a partially eroded portion of the Pleistocene alluvial terrace. A remnant of this old surface remains to the left of the Holy Ghost group as the horizontally bedded alluvium plastered against the canyon wall next to the spalling portion of the Great Gallery panel. This T2 remnant has a horizontal surface that extends for several meters upstream before becoming buried and obscured by talus. Talus also covers the T2 alluvial remnant next to the rock art panel, consisting of rocks that fell onto this eroded portion of the terrace. The horizontal surface in the T2 alluvium evidently extended all along the entire base of the Great Gallery and represented the bottom of an erosional channel created by the downcutting Barrier Creek. This event occurred during the end of the early Holocene when the stream channel, downcutting through the Pleistocene alluvium, ran right along the canyon wall. The massive rockfall in the Great Gallery alcove that preserved the T2 terrace forced the stream away from the canyon wall and the channel shifted toward where the modern wash now flows. Incision continued and left a terrace remnant along the canyon wall that became the painter's work surface for executing the art.

The T2 terrace remnant once plastered along the base of Great Gallery alcove eventually eroded away, leaving the rock art in its isolated perched position where subsequent Native American visitors could not easily add their own marks. The only exception to this is at the far-left upstream side, next to the talus pile where even now people can reach the rock surface, with some unfortunately vandalizing it. This location is the only one where a few non-BCS additions occur, as well as some that might

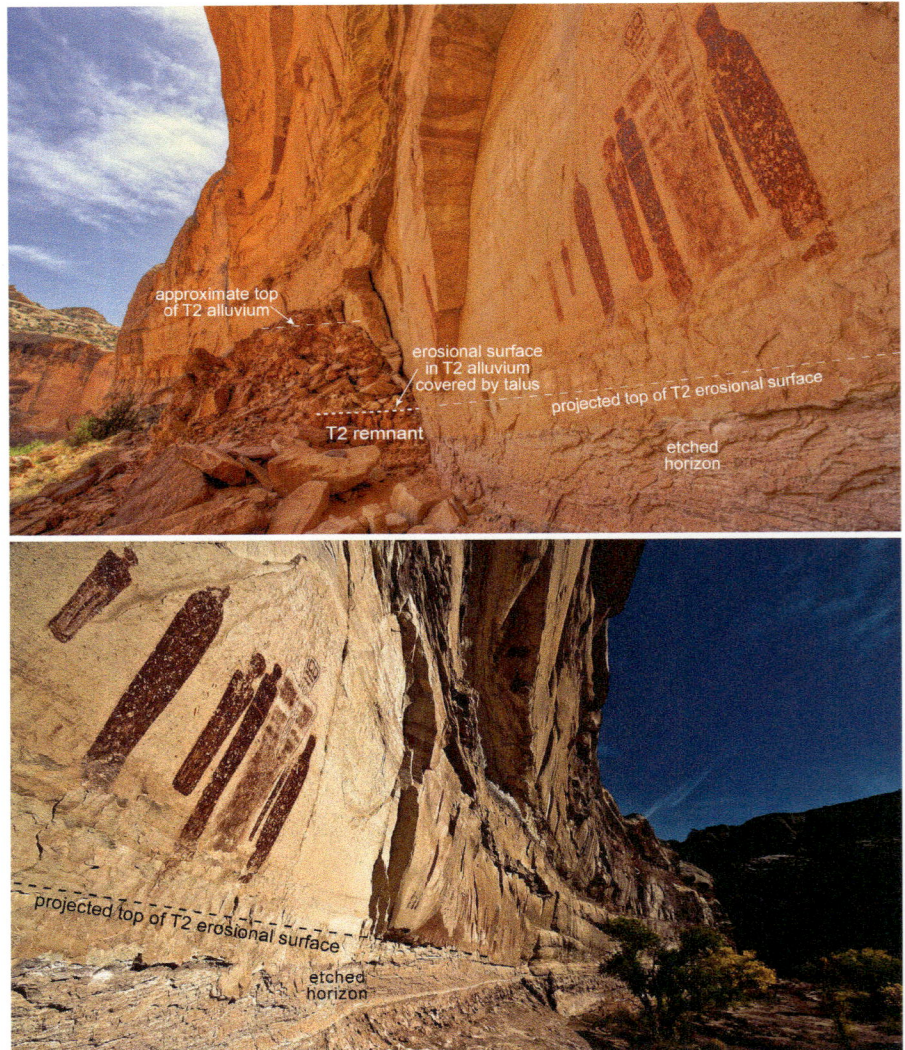

Figure 4.40 Great Gallery "Holy Ghost" group from different angles. Upper image looks upstream at the old alluvial terrace remnant covered by talus. A horizontal erosional surface about midway down in this alluvium coincides with a conspicuous etched horizon on the rock face. Lower image looks downstream, showing how the etched horizon extends the full length of the Great Gallery. The erosional surface of the old alluvium formed the probable original ground surface used to paint this portion of the Great Gallery. (Top photo by Richard Ansley [richardansleyphotography.com]. Bottom photo by Jason Pavalonis [Warm Desert Wind Photography].)

be attributed to a late part of the style. This portion of the Great Gallery is the previously discussed actively spalling part to the left of the Holy Ghost group.

BCS rock art outside of canyon contexts can also occur in out-of-reach places that are indicative of a loss of ground surface over some length of time. The pictographs at Head of Sinbad are just one example. This setting is not one that should suffer from excessive erosion, yet several feet of sediment have been lost since the images were painted. The probable original ground surface used by the artists seems to have been eroded by strong winds blowing away sand and silt from the base of the sandstone outcrop, a process known as deflation, as the overhang faces the prevailing winds out of the southwest. The interesting aspect of this particular panel, and some others like it, is that the out-of-reach aspect is also coupled with aspects of rock art condition such as weathering and other time-related natural damage. For the Head of Sinbad, this process is marked by the slow accretion of silt washing down the sandstone face from high above, gradually entombing the rock surface and images. An adjacent panel to the east along the base of the same sandstone prominence has extensive exfoliation of the painted rock surface, with just the lower parts of most images remaining. Given the loss, some have taken to calling this panel the "Feet of Sinbad."

What About BCS Antiquity?

When Polly Schaafsma penned her first major report on Utah rock art and tried to pin down the antiquity of the Barrier Canyon Style, little was actually known about Archaic period foragers on the Colorado Plateau. This situation was somewhat improved when her more general book, *Indian Rock Art of the Southwest*, appeared in 1980. However, if Schaafsma had waited just another year or two, her knowledge base would have been much greater, at least for Utah, as coincidentally 1980 was also the publication year for descriptive reports on two key Colorado Plateau Archaic sites: Sudden Shelter and Cowboy Cave.[72] Schaafsma briefly mentioned Cowboy Cave in her 1980 book, stating that this site's findings indicated that Barrier Canyon Style rock art was from late in the Archaic period.[73] She soon sided with Alan Schroedl and Nancy Coulam, who argued that the anthropomorphic clay figurines found at Cowboy and Walters Caves could support a much earlier inception date for BCS.[74]

When all the various strands of evidence are interwoven, it seems clear that the Barrier Canyon Style was a long-lived rock art tradition. Its origins can be traced back perhaps as early as 8000 BC, and certainly by around 6000 BC. It evidently continued to be produced until less than 3,000 years ago and perhaps right up to the Common Era, although by then it had started its transformation into Fremont-style rock art. The bulk of images classifiable as BCS were made prior to the Common Era. Such antiquity would accord with all the aforementioned archaeological and geological evidence, which are overwhelmingly indicative of considerable age. Based on the archaeological temporal scheme for Utah, BCS rock art is a product of Archaic period foragers, as long suspected, with an origin likely in the early belief systems of this period. But it was the traumatic climatic events that transpired as the early Holocene ended and the middle Holocene began that caused a proliferation of BCS rock art. Dissection of the Horseshoe Canyon floodplain was just one small part of a larger explanatory whole.

Lifeways of the BCS Creators

Archaeologists today understand far more about the context of BCS rock art than back in the early 1970s when the style was first described, yet much remains to be learned about the Archaic period foragers of the Colorado Plateau. It is a general truism that archaeologists know far less about societies of the distant past than more recent ones. This is especially true of those ancient societies who survived by hunting and gathering what nature provided and lived in arid environments like the Canyon Lands country of Utah, where wild foods rarely occur in abundance and are quickly used up in any one locale.

Figure 4.41 Cowboy and Walters Caves, upper tributary drainage of Horseshoe Canyon. These two sites have provided a wealth of information about Archaic period foragers.

Most arid-land hunter-gatherers could rarely stay put for long in any one place, tending to move often and sometimes over great distances. Home was not as most experience it these days—a place where you stay for years on end, if not generations. Rather, home was a temporary camp, lived in for a week or a month but seldom longer. As such, living shelters were usually hasty constructions that did not last long. Natural shelters of rock overhangs or caves were often favored when available. Frequent movement put a premium on not being burdened with lots of extra weight to carry. Consequently, they did not make or accumulate many material objects, limiting most gear to survival essentials. Ethnographers have documented this pattern worldwide among arid-land foragers. Essentials should not be equated with tools or other utilitarian objects for acquiring food. The paint stick and clay figurines described earlier were just as essential to survival as projectile points and seed-grinding equipment. From a perspective inside a society, ritual symbolic items and their related practices could be more significant than these other tools, as they help to ensure there will be plants and animals to harvest at all.

Because Archaic foragers tended to carry little and resided in no one place for long, they rarely created localized concentrations of living debris. Having large territorial ranges, the meager remains tossed away or lost in a given year were widely dispersed. With low population densities, any particular chunk of territory saw infrequent use. Because many artifacts were perishable, consisting of wood, fiber, and hide, only a fraction of an already-meager material trace is usually available for archaeologists to find. Organic decay is just one of time's ravages resulting in a loss of early archaeological material. Thousands of years of erosion and disturbance by rodents, roots, and other causes all take their toll. Stream erosion can remove archaeological sites utterly. Deflation of the ground surface exposes artifacts, allowing archaeological discovery but usually at a cost: hundreds or thousands of years of accumulation mixed together on a single surface without any datable features or subsistence remains. Burial by eolian sand or stream deposits helps to preserve occupation layers and provides stratigraphic separation of discrete temporal intervals, but with a different penalty: remains are lost from view and therefore rarely encountered, and costly to study if they are found.

Although home was always temporary and moves from one camp to another were frequent, foragers returned to some camps repeatedly. These places persisted as important locations for centuries and millennia. Sites like this usually had some amenities that favored reuse, such as nearby permanent water, abundant firewood, and natural shelter from the elements. The latter was a key benefit for the past users and is also a boon for archaeologists. Naturally sheltered sites often preserve organic artifacts and other materials seldom recovered from open settings because of a lack of moisture.

Much of what archaeologists know about Archaic period foragers on the Colorado Plateau comes from a small handful of sheltered sites such as Cowboy Cave and Walters Cave, two adjoining shelters that produced a large amount of information. These sites are located in an upper tributary of Horseshoe Canyon a mere nine miles from the Great Gallery. Excavations by Jesse Jennings and students in the mid-1970s produced a wealth of materials and information that are still being studied to gain new insights.[75] Yet, even at these data-rich and rewarding sites, the record of the earliest occupants is more impoverished than that of the later occupants. The people responsible for the final depositional layers left far more materials behind, in a more diverse assortment, than those responsible for the lower and earlier depositional layers. The descriptive artifact tables of the site report bear this out.[76]

These caves are undeniably important to archaeologists, but their significance to Archaic period foragers fluctuated through time. Sometimes they served as important nodes in annual movements, but other times not at all, since shelter deposits reveal major time intervals when few if any people visited, at times extending for thousands of years. The decline in use and subsequent outright abandonment of Cowboy and Walters during the middle Holocene indicates a major shift in settlement. During this interval, these caves evidently lay outside the normal seasonal movement for hunter-gatherers, perhaps because so few resources were available close at hand. The land had become like a Southern Paiute woman once lamented about the Escalante area: "no good anymore; everything is dry; the creeks are cut deep; the food plants are all gone."[77] The cessation of regular use of Cowboy and Walters Caves seems unlikely to

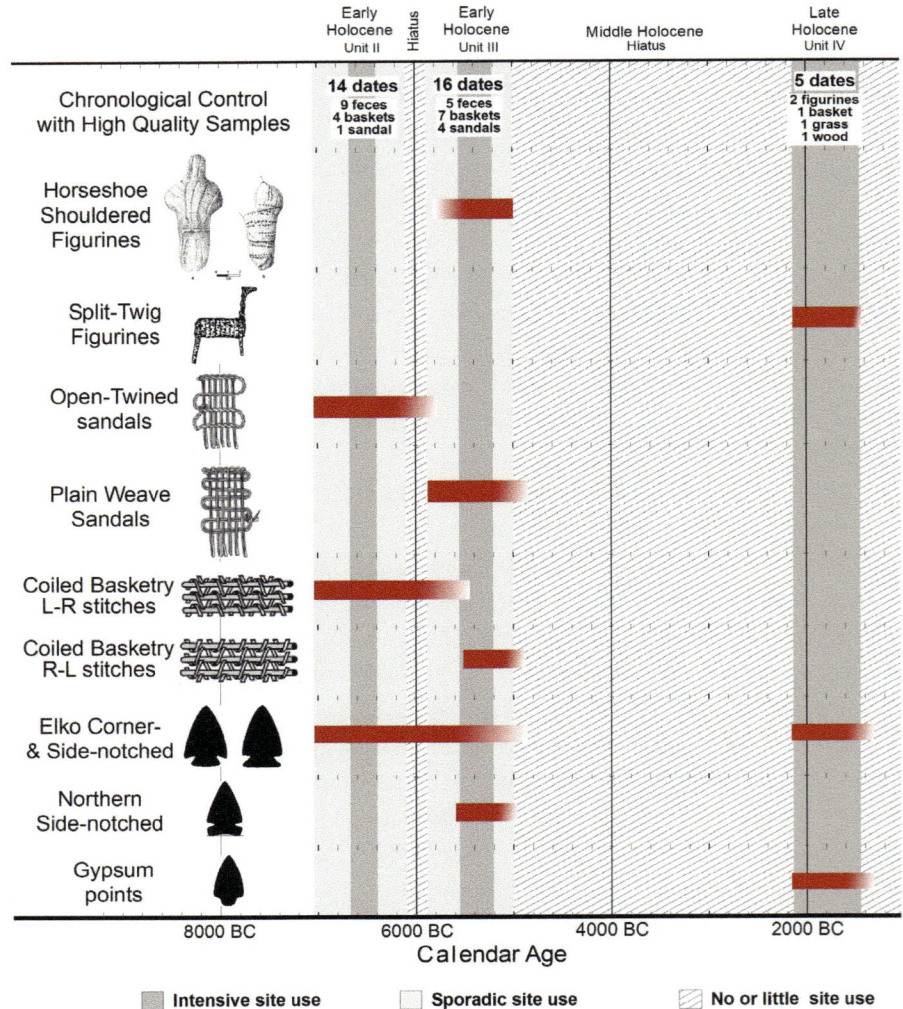

Figure 4.42 Periods of human occupation at Cowboy Cave and Walters Cave during the Archaic period, based on radiocarbon dates of high-quality samples such as human feces and artifacts. Foragers used the shelters intensively, sporadically, or not at all (or at least, minimally), resulting in large differences in the quantities and types of materials recovered from depositional layers. Different types of remains also reflect temporal change in cultural preferences for various reasons, with several such shifts noted here.

have lessened the significance of the Great Gallery, less than a day's saunter down a level and usually dry streambed from these sites. But if much of the entire region had been vacated, then visitation to this panel might have become less common, more of an out-of-the-way trek.

Many other archaeological sites have added to our knowledge about Archaic foragers. Some of these are wet shelters that lack organic preservation, such as Sudden Shelter and North Creek Shelter. Both sites occupy settings quite distinct from that of Cowboy/Walters Cave, and this is important for gaining a more complete picture of forager lifestyles. Some of the informative sites occur south of the main area of BCS rock art in the region where the Archaic period Glen Canyon Linear rock art style predominates. These include Dust Devil Cave, Benchmark Cave, Broken Arrow Cave, and Old Man Cave.

Sandals and human feces are some of the more informative materials that Archaic hunter-gatherers left behind in dry shelters. Feces provide a detailed glimpse of what ancient people ate. The pads of prickly pear cactus were commonly consumed. Native Americans reported to ethnographers that pads tended to be starvation food, but the frequency of occurrence in feces suggests that they functioned as Archaic period staples, at least during some times of the year. When all else fails you can usually find prickly pear cacti, even in the dead of winter, and beyond filling bellies they are nutritious and a good source of fiber. The fruits of prickly pear cactus were also consumed, but they have a limited season of harvest and are smaller and less abundant than the pads.

Archaic period feces are also full of the small seeds of several different plants, especially dropseed grass, sunflower, and goosefoot. Basketry was essential to effectively harvest, winnow, and parch small seeds. Parching was done by stirring or shaking seeds with hot coals in a basket tray, thereby toasting the grains and making their nutrition more available. The parched hard seeds then got crushed to flour on stone slabs with hand stones. All of this effort is quite labor intensive, but it was a critical part of how Archaic foragers survived year to year.

This reliance on plant resources is a key point of differentiation from earlier hunter-gatherers of the Pleistocene, who could rely more on animal resources that provided lots of energy for the time spent in acquiring and processing them. The first people of North American originated in and near the Arctic region, where survival hinged on animal protein and fat. As people spread southward, a diversity of plant resources became available, ones that afforded new subsistence opportunities. The attractiveness or necessity of plant foods increased during the Holocene after the extinction of megafauna, such as the mammoth, and the retraction of bison to the extensive grasslands of the Great Plains. Hunting continued to play an important role for Holocene foragers, but the gathering of plant foods became central to forager survival in the Southwest and many parts of the world. A dependence on plants generally required considerable effort in harvesting and processing, along with new technologies to assist in the effort.

Aside from dietary information, well-preserved feces contain a wealth of information pertaining to health, gut microbiomes, and genetics, with the likelihood that further scientific techniques will be developed in the near and distant future to extract additional information.[78] DNA recovery from feces is one of the more significant new techniques, providing a powerful means of tracing how early forager populations are related to those that came before and after. DNA also allows identification of consumed plant and animal species, including those that might not leave remains that standard techniques can recover or identify.

Archaic foragers made sandals of whole yucca leaves, plucked from a plant and woven together in particular ways.[79] The earliest footwear has folded leaves running the length of the foot, with the fold occurring at the toe. Other leaves were twisted around each other and then each of the folded leaves in turn, holding them together, with the twisted leaves also providing side loops for strapping sandals to feet. This

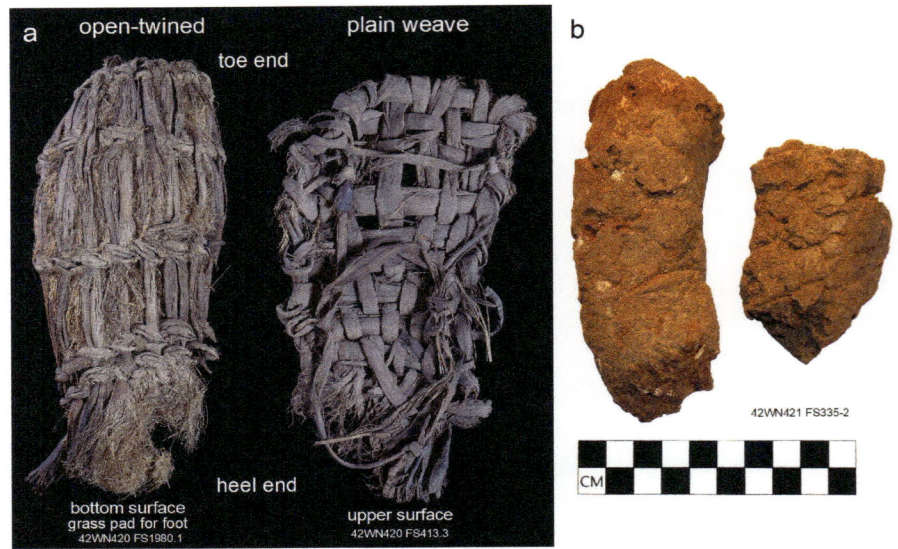

Figure 4.43 Two of the common material remains recovered from Early Archaic depositional layers at sites in Utah: sandals made of whole yucca leaves (a) and human feces (b). (Sandals photo by Alyson Wilkins and feces photo by Phil Geib; courtesy of Natural History Museum of Utah and Bureau of Land Management.)

twisting around the folded leaves is known as twining and represents a way of making not just sandals but other perishable artifacts such as basketry. The technique dates back to at least the early Holocene in the Great Basin.[80] The earliest sandals of this style found in Utah are at least 9,000 years old, with one from Walters Cave dated to around 6800 BC.[81]

Several thousand years later, as the early Archaic period was coming to an end, foragers made sandals in a different way. The foundation was the same: yucca leaves folded in half for foot length, with the fold at the toe. Now, though, the folded leaves were cross-woven with other yucca leaves in a simple over-one, under-one pattern. Examples of this plain-weave sandal occurred in the same layer as the large Horseshoe Shouldered clay figurine from Walters Cave. The people that wove these sandals also made spirit figures of clay. They also likely painted at least some of the BCS imagery.

Archaic open-twined and plain-weave sandals like those from Cowboy and Walters Caves occur at a few dozen sites widely scattered across southeast Utah, extending as well into southwest Colorado and northeast Arizona. The sandal distribution does not match the spatial extent of BCS rock art, although there is major overlap. Notably, the sandals were also common in locations containing pecked Glen Canyon Linear rock art.

The sharing of some traits but not others is not a surprise. Contemporaneous hunter-gatherers living across a vast region are likely to share similar aspects of technology, such as footwear and projectile point styles, as well as some basic conceptions about life. This sharing of cultural traits can occur while still maintaining mostly distinct artistic traditions for marking rock surfaces. Yet these traditions were not foreign to each other. Various rock art specialists have noted certain commonalities shared between Barrier Canyon and Glen Canyon Linear rock art, suggesting some degree of social interaction.[82]

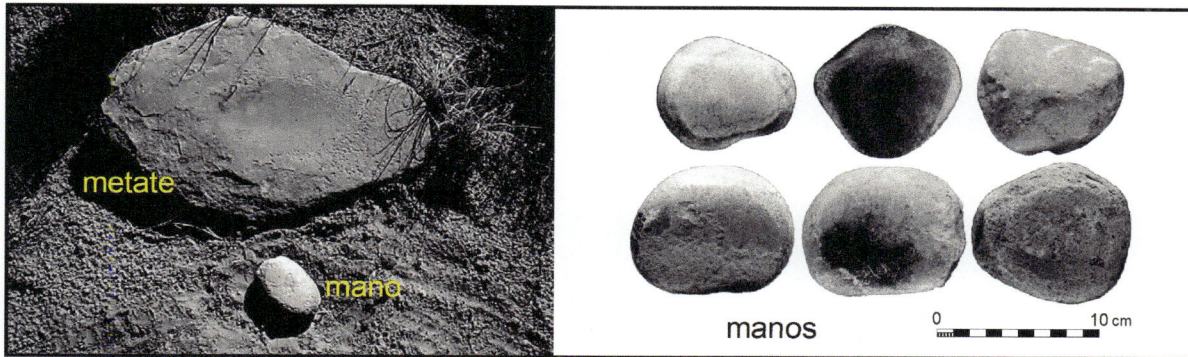

Figure 4.44 Grinding tools were essential for Archaic period hunter-gatherers in the canyon country of the Colorado Plateau, used almost daily for crushing small seeds and other resources.

Figure 4.45 Burden basket in use as modeled by an Apache girl and as depicted by BCS painters at the Harvest Scene. (Apache Photo by Carl Werntz, ca. 1902, Library of Congress, https://www.loc.gov/item/91481170/.)

Seed-grinding tools called manos and metates are also common artifacts at Archaic period sites. Their rather sudden appearance in the archaeological record during the early Holocene is a strong indication of how forager survival strategies changed with the warming climate after about 10,000 years ago. These tools were not only essential for crushing the small seeds that became staples of the Archaic period diet, but also for processing the tubers and bulbs of wild potatoes, onions, lilies, and other plants and for crushing up rodents and other small game. Metates are flat slabs of stone that can weigh twenty pounds or more, not an object that people generally like to carry far. Hence, archaeologists commonly find these tools at Archaic period campsites where foragers left them for reuse whenever the site was again visited. Flat sandstone exposures in some favored locales, such as next to a spring or plunge pool, also got used for seed processing,

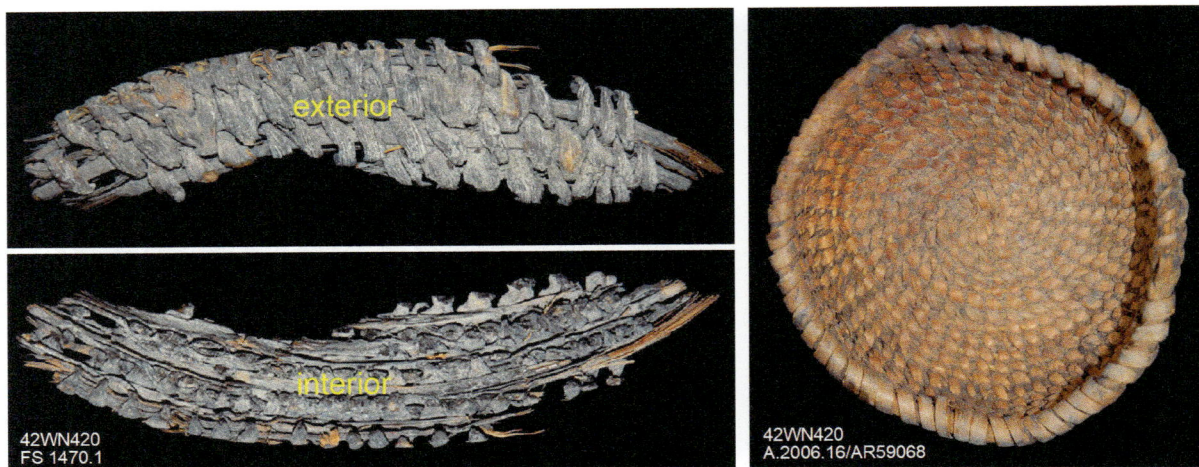

Figure 4.46 Baskets were essential tools for Archaic period hunter-gatherers in the canyon country of the Colorado Plateau, used almost daily for collecting, winnowing, and parching small seeds. They were also used to collect, transport, and store other resources. The fragment on the left comes from a large parching tray, as indicated by the carbonized interior. The whole basket is about the size of a cup measure, and therefore is too small for seed processing. Both come from Cowboy Cave, with the complete basket dated to about 6800 BC. (Photos by Edward Jolie; courtesy of Natural History Museum of Utah and Bureau of Land Management.)

as evidenced by open bedrock grinding slicks. The much smaller and lighter manos were perhaps sometimes cached as well, although some of these probably formed part of the mobile tool kits carried by foragers on their moves.

Baskets were important tools for harvesting and processing the small seeds that foragers relied upon. They used large, shallow baskets to gather, winnow, and parch the seeds. They also used large, conical baskets to carry burdens such as seeds, nuts, or other foods that were harvested. Burden baskets, as they are known, were commonly carried on the back, attached to a strap that ran over the forehead. BCS artists depicted such baskets in use at a few sites, with the most notable being the Harvest Scene, where the burden bearers walk under the outstretched arm of a spirit figure that holds aloft a plant commonly interpreted as ricegrass, just the sort of resource harvested and processed with basketry.

Baskets only preserve at dry shelters, and even then rarely occur as whole items or even large fragments. Still, the small fragments usually found can be highly informative about cultural differences. Baskets have many subtle manufacturing details that reflect the learning traditions of small social groups. They can also be woven in utterly distinct ways that reflect distinct learning traditions of large social units such as ethnolinguistic groups.[83] Twining and coiling were the two main ways that Archaic foragers of Utah produced basketry, with coiling by far the most common. Coiling is basically a form of sewing, where a foundation of horizontally coiled sticks or fiber bundles are held together by using stitches that encircle each successive pair of foundation coils. They are time consuming to produce but light and durable, and can even be made watertight if needed.

Debris from the plants and animals that Archaic foragers processed and consumed comprises a significant proportion of the accumulation at residential camps. The depositional layers at Cowboy and Walters Caves, alongside other sites, contain an abundance of plant material, especially the chaff, stems, and other inedible debris from the plants harvested for their seeds, bulbs, and other portions. Stems and chaff

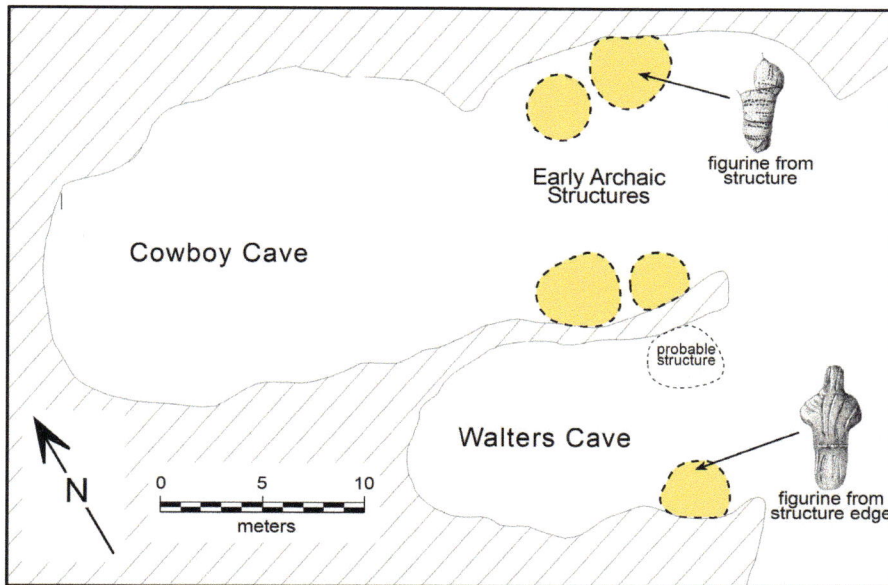

Figure 4.47 Hunter-gatherers during the end of the early Archaic period built structures within the protected space of Cowboy and Walters Caves by excavating shallow basins down to a soft bedding material of Pleistocene herbivore dung. Schroedl and Coulam ("Cowboy Cave Revisited") provide information about these structures, except for the one in Walters Cave, which likely had at least one other structure on the north side.

from dropseed grass are especially prolific and account for a large proportion of human accumulation at sheltered sites. Shelters provide handy places to escape the sun and wind when winnowing, parching, and grinding grass and other seeds.

Foragers acquired animal protein by hunting with weapons, nets, and snares. The atlatl, or spear thrower, was the chief weapon to bring down large game. It was used to fling darts resembling extra-large arrows. The atlatl allows greater leverage force than hurling a spear by hand. The bow and arrow ultimately replaced the atlatl and dart, but this technological transition did not occur until the Archaic period had ended. The first arrow points at Cowboy Cave and other sites occur in deposits dating no older than about AD 200. This temporally significant change provides evidence for the relative antiquity of Barrier Canyon Style rock art, which lacks depictions of bows and arrows.

Archaic period hunter-gatherers lived in societies thought to be small in scale and low in population density. This dynamic follows from what is known about the ecology of the Colorado Plateau, where wild foods rarely occur in abundance and are quickly used up in any one locale. Hunter-gatherers in such environments live dispersed and in small social groups most of the time, although they do come together at intervals of seasonal abundance or on special occasions. Small social groupings imply that just a few to several families live together.

It is quite difficult for archaeologists to estimate how many people lived together at any one time for the Archaic period. Some of the best evidence on this matter comes from Cowboy Cave, where early Archaic foragers scooped out basins in the deposits for living purposes.[84] There were at least five of these, four in Cowboy Cave and one in the adjoining Walters Cave. There is ample space in Walters Cave for an additional structure. Assuming that all living basins were in use at the same time, with one family per structure as is common for ethnographically documented hunter-gatherers, then

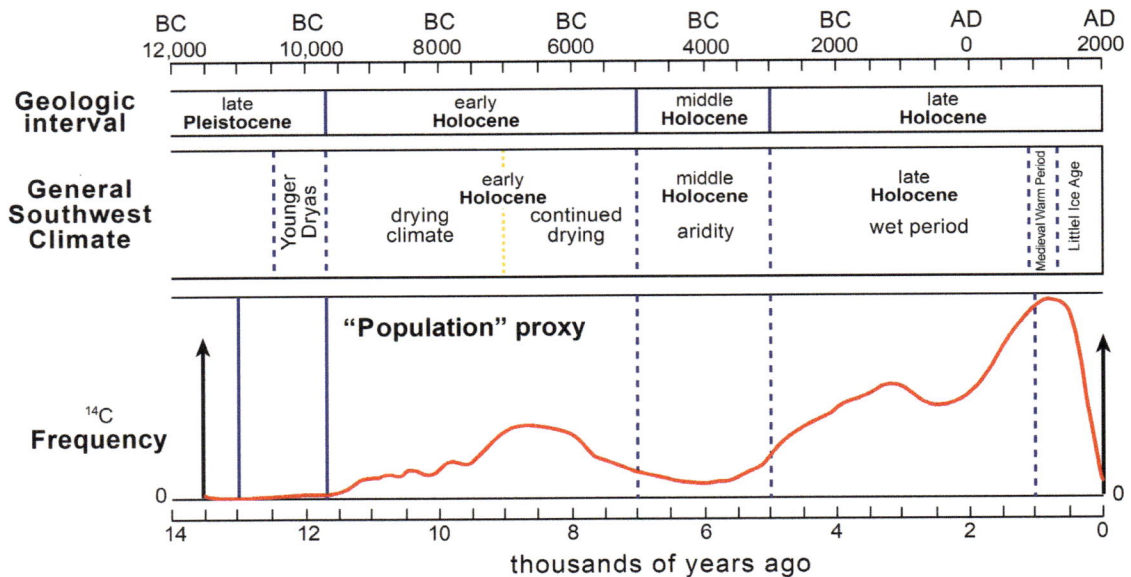

Figure 4.48 General reconstruction of human population in the Canyon Lands section of the Colorado Plateau, as indicated by the proxy of radiocarbon date frequency. The proxy assumes that fluctuations in dated materials roughly equates to differences in the number of people generating such samples, which is to say, more samples correlates to more people present and vice versa.

just five or six families at most occupied the caves simultaneously. Thus, the residential group here was likely no more than about thirty people. Schroedl and Coulam's interpretation is that the early Archaic foragers who built the structures used the site as a winter base camp, living off food reserves stored from fall harvests and supplemented by whatever could be obtained during the lean season, such as prickly pear pads and game animals.

Two of the clay figurines that are analogues of BCS spirit figures occurred in these structural basins. Such items were perhaps left in locations like these for anticipated return at some future time. These structural basins are also contexts where items are likely to get lost in loose sand and living debris, inadvertently preserving them for archaeological discovery.

Population trends through time and across a region are also difficult for archaeologists to estimate, especially regarding mobile hunter-gatherers. One approach that archaeologists have used effectively is counts of radiocarbon dates on cultural material such as artifacts, hearth charcoal, human feces, and plant debris, or bone food scraps from occupation layers.[85] The logic behind this approach is the simple notion that more people result in more datable material and vice versa. The patterning in dates shows that forager populations were stable and evidently growing during the Early Archaic until after about 6000 BC. Populations evidently crashed for the next few thousand years during the middle Holocene, a period more arid than before and since. The time of transition leading to the middle Holocene was likely stressful for hunter-gatherers. Food resources, though never abundant, became harder to find, and some previously favored places were no longer used because the distribution of plants and animals had shifted. Environmental conditions improved after around 3000 BC. Correlated with this climatic shift was an evident increase in human population to levels perhaps higher than they were during the early Archaic period. Places little-used for hundreds or even thousands of years, such as Cowboy Cave, saw renewed occupation. This trend continued up through the introduction of farming, which greatly accelerated population growth.

Why Here?

The Colorado Plateau contains vast stretches of grasslands, forestlands, and badlands that lack geologic outcrops suitable for rock art. Yet, surfaces that could serve as canvases for images seem nearly ubiquitous when compared, for example, to the Great Plains of North America. By comparison, the Southwest as a whole is rich in opportunities for creating rock art. The Canyon Lands section of the Colorado Plateau, where BCS imagery is concentrated, is especially well-endowed with suitable rock surfaces, with sandstone layers uplifted and exposed by erosion resulting in long cliff faces and large talus blocks. Such exposures are often well-suited and highly attractive for marking by humans.

Sandstone is relatively soft and yielding compared to most igneous and metamorphic rocks, and thus easily modified by the mechanical means of dinting or incising. Despite the relative ease of making petroglyphs upon them, many sandstones on the Colorado Plateau are resistant to weathering such that images tend to last. Dark patinas or rock varnish created by a thin skin of iron or manganese oxides mixed with clay often cover rock surfaces, providing a distinct contrast when this skin is cut through to expose the underlying lighter sandstone. Also, some especially resistant layers within an overall depositional sequence serve as caprock for the material below, resulting in many of the outstanding buttes and mesas of the region along with the overhanging sandstone faces that provide protection from precipitation. These special settings are what allowed painted images to last for millennia.

What we see today likely does not adequately represent just how many rock surfaces were originally marked, at least not for those surfaces that were painted. Images created by chiseling or engraving are more likely to be sufficiently intact for recognition today. Rock spalling, weathering, burial, or other natural processes have doubtless removed some petroglyphs. Humans also might have removed some images, a practice that still occurs on the Navajo Reservation, where *hataɬii* (traditional healers) have systematically eradicated some old petroglyphs ascertained to have caused sickness.[86]

In contrast, painted images may have once existed in many places on the landscape, with only those in protected locations currently left for us to ponder. From trial and error, past artists likely soon learned that direct moisture quickly washes off exposed painted images. Yet loss through time might not have concerned them, at least for some depictions. An image used in a healing ceremony might have a short

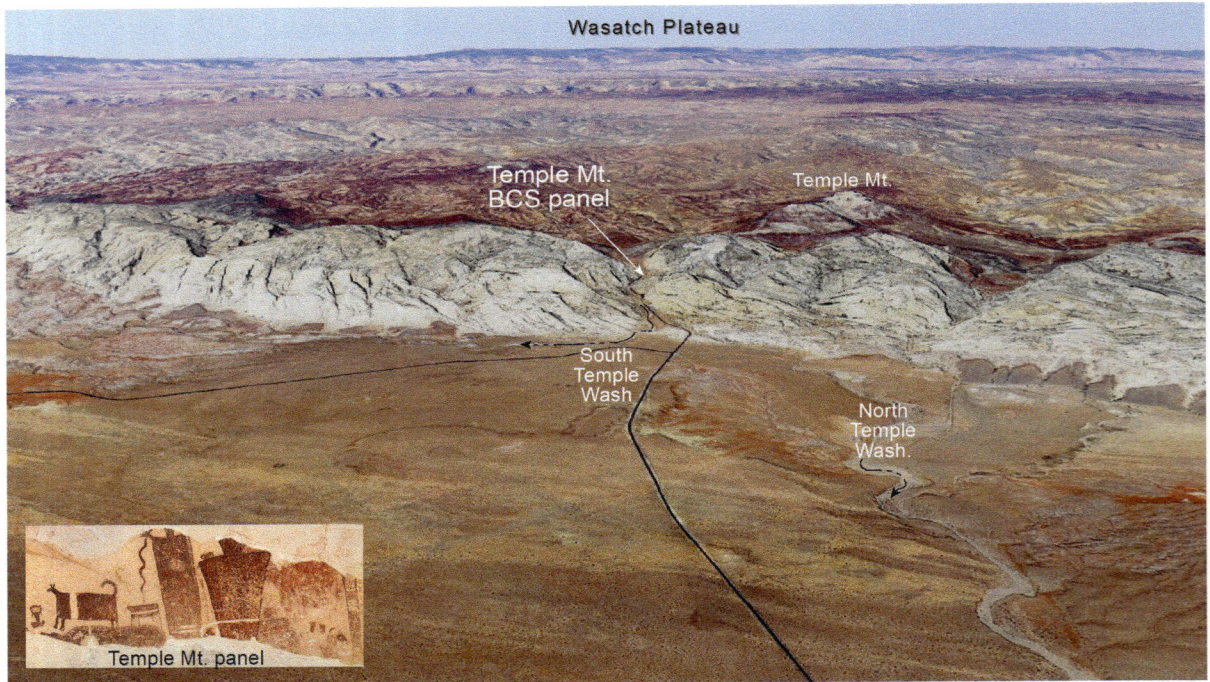

Figure 4.49 Temple Mountain rock art panel general setting along a prominent break in the folded-up sandstone that defines the San Rafael Swell's eastern edge. A modern road passing through this gap likely follows a well-traveled route of past people. Image from Google Earth.

expected existence, analogous to the sand paintings used in Navajo healing ceremonies.[87] Furthermore, the main concern of the maker for some rock art might have been the process, not the product or its longevity.

Once marked, a rock surface might induce subsequent addition of more images. But why were certain rock surfaces selected in the first place? What made a place deserving of human symbols?

Geographic setting provides a potential hint in some cases as to why some rock surfaces were favored over others, though not the specific reason. Travel routes offer one potential link between setting and rock art. All across the Colorado Plateau, the prominent geologic structures that create such scenic beauty also serve to channel traffic, whether by foot or vehicle, and natural breaks in the topography provide inherent travel routes for animals and humans alike.

Consider, for example, the previously shown and discussed Temple Mountain pictograph panel. BCS artists painted images here on a large billboard-like sandstone face at the base of an angled bedrock exposure. Located at the eastern side of an eroded sandstone scarp known as the San Rafael Swell, the setting creates a travel impediment for east-to-west movement. East of the swell there is an extensive grassland that extends to the rim of Horseshoe Canyon and the Great Gallery. Prior to overgrazing, this grassland, with its active dune sands, contained abundant plant foods heavily exploited by Archaic foragers, especially dropseed grass, sunflower, and goosefoot. In the distance to the west side of the swell lie the forested uplands of the Wasatch Plateau, with the contrasting resources of abundant game animals and pinyon nuts, among others. Sites of the plateau such as Sudden Shelter and Aspen Shelter contain rich records of use by Archaic foragers, related primarily to hunting but also to other living tasks.[88]

From what anthropologists have learned about foragers all around the world, mobility is a key aspect of survival. Family groups must move from one area of residence where food has become limited to another setting where food is more readily abundant. There are also seasonal shifts based on the timing of when different foods become available for harvest. For groups living in arid lands with low overall availability of food resources, survival can depend on movement of a hundred miles or more in a year.[89] As such, it is easy to envision that Archaic period hunter-gatherers who used the lower elevation grasslands east of the San Rafael Swell would travel westward on a seasonal basis to the forested Wasatch Plateau and back again, a one-way distance of forty miles.

A natural break through the upturned bedrock created by South Temple Wash is a readymade travel corridor that channels people's movements, today as in the past, as the modern road traces this path of least resistance. Hunter-gatherers traveling east to west would almost invariably pass this way, and the rock face looming above this passage was readily visible to all travelers. Thus, it is possible to envision this location as deriving significance from this quality: a place commonly seen by many. Public viewing perhaps encouraged an appropriately large scale to the images, so all could be appreciated from the ground below. The Black Dragon site, with its massive-scale images, is similarly situated at a canyon chokepoint.

In contrast to the ease of travel through the break created by South Temple Wash is a nearby wash that also provides a breach through the upturned sandstone of the San Rafael Reef. It is also a potential east-west travel corridor, but one far less direct and open. Instead, it is a rather narrow and winding canyon with a southwest jog for about two miles before finally turning back northeast and emerging into the open on the other side of the jagged sandstone fold. A BCS rock art panel known as Ocher Alcove occurs along this route, but it is unlike that of South Temple Wash. The Navajo Sandstone canyon walls are also not like those of South Temple Wash, although there are locations that might have supported larger images. The BCS rock art panel in the canyon is quite small in scale and difficult to spot from the drainage bottom; it is not possible for one to appreciate the images without standing within the small alcove in which they are painted.

Does this divergence in affordances of movement—a major transportation corridor versus a likely transportation chokepoint—account for the differences in the nature of BCS art? The unobstructed passageway was marked with images of a grand scale that can be appreciated from afar, easily seen by any passersby. The sinuous and more difficult passage was not marked with easily seen images, but rather a corpus scaled to a more private viewing, a pattern seen elsewhere in Barrier Canyon Style art. Even at the Great Gallery, there exists a secluded setting above and to the left of the main panel that has small-scale images.

Visibility in travel occurs in the present, for example, when we see billboards in our daily movements, but whether visibility was a motivating factor for BCS artists in choosing their canvases, such as at the Temple Mountain wash location, is impossible to say. Perhaps the travel passage provided by a topographic break had an indirect tie to the significance of this location. The large geographic context is something that modern people can more readily examine than rather small-scale phenomena specific to a location that might have provided the source of power or reason behind rock art creation.

Visibility is something that can be examined by a number of modern methods using GIS and similar technologies. Visibility has a clear relation to travel routes, since the direction and path of travel plays a large role in defining what is highly visible and what is effectively not visible. The South Temple Wash example is an obvious context where there is little choice about what is the most optimal way to travel. It does not take a sophisticated least-cost path analysis to figure out the obvious. Plenty of places in the Southwest are like this: geographic features channel travel in certain directions, thus making cliff scarps or boulders along such a route highly visible.

The Courthouse Wash Panel occurs not only at an obvious geographic choke-point but also at one of the few easily accessible crossings of the Colorado River. Displacement along a major geologic fault named after Moab has created a traffic channel running southeast to northwest between towering cliffs of sandstone and other sedimentary rocks. The Old Spanish Trail came this way, following a Native American path well worn from millennia of prior foot traffic. This crossing allowed access to several distinct environments, including the highlands of the La Sal Mountains. Buckhorn Wash is another example of an apparent relationship between BCS rock art and a likely well-used travel corridor, such that the main panel here might have been regularly seen during a normal annual pattern of band movement.

The Great Gallery might not fit this pattern despite its large scale and impressive imagery. This gallery may have been a site of regular visitation and likely qualified as a destination in its own right, but it is more difficult to make a good case that this location sat along the way of regular seasonal travel. Horseshoe Canyon is not an optimal travel corridor for movement northward toward the Green River or points beyond. You can follow Barrier Creek to where it empties into this river, but the journey is a challenge, one compounded by children and the elderly and when burdened with the baggage of life, as all foragers were when moving from one residence to another. The canyon is also a barrier to east-west travel, hence the creek's name.

A more clear-cut case of rock art not occurring along a travel route is the Perfect Panel. Though there are few images here, they are of impressive size. The canyon setting of this panel does not provide a travel passage to anywhere. The drainage incises ever deeper as it flows eastward past the panel toward Cataract Canyon of the Colorado River. Once added, the art itself may have been the destination, but it is hard to make a case that BCS rock art was added here because family groups commonly passed this way. This is another setting, somewhat like Ocher Alcove, that might have

been visited only by certain individuals, those who were initiated into certain adult roles of their society and perhaps those who were being initiated.

This discussion has focused on travel, yet how does one map travel paths of the past? Today's travel patterns provide just a rough guide to where past people might have commonly traveled. The break at South Temple Wash and the channel of the Moab Fault are modern examples that hold up, and there are others, but in large part this depends on where people live and where they need to travel. The means of travel is also critical. Understanding the movements of Archaic populations seasonally or over longer intervals and mapping the important places of past settlements requires considerably more archaeological survey and excavation data. Even with these data in hand, archaeologists are hard-pressed to deal with issues such as population distribution and density for people that moved often and left scant traces, often residing in temporary brush structures or rock shelters or simply in the open. Also, many Archaic-age sites are hidden, having been buried by eolian sand or other processes or eroded away entirely. How do we even start to estimate where people lived and where they might have wanted to travel?

Figure 4.50 Unnamed drainage incising ever deeper as it flows eastward toward Cataract Canyon of the Colorado River. BCS rock art occurs in canyons like this that are not travel routes to somewhere else. Once added, the art itself may have been the destination. It appears that secluded places were purposefully chosen for some BCS rock art.

Who Was the Audience?

When contemplating why people put images at specific locations, an implicit assumption seems to be that humans were the audience. We have long relied on language to communicate essential information to one another. At some point we also started using imagery for this purpose. A picture is worth a thousand words, or so the modern saying goes. The same was likely true in the past as well. Spoken words are fleeting, but an image can last a long time. Centuries or even millennia after creation, it can still stir the human mind. Eventually, people invented writing, and when combined with images this medium became an important means of mass messaging. The words and images on billboards are designed to induce us to do something: vote for some politician, purchase some special deodorant, accept God into our lives, all communication aimed at humans. But was the same intent true for rock art images? Were they directed just toward humans? Who else might see them? For BCS rock art specifically, who was the intended audience?

Marit Munson, in *The Archaeology of Art in the American Southwest*, asks this rhetorical question: "Without an audience, could there be art?"[90] This query is the opening line of a chapter that examines the interrelationship among artist, art object, and audience. Art occupies space that is on a continuum from public to private, and physical context can limit or broaden audience size. This variable is readily analyzable for rock art because it is fixed in the landscape, with some settings as public as billboards and other settings as secretive as hidey-holes. Accessibility for rock art sites ranges from an easy walk to exceedingly difficult, if not life threatening. Differing degrees of access impact visibility, since how close someone can get to an art object makes a difference in what is perceptible. Indeed, a viewer's perspective is channeled or constrained by their position relative to an image.

Implicit in virtually all discussions about art and audiences is that humans are the viewers. It seems to go without saying that people as witnesses were and are central to art. But is this assumption necessarily true for hunter-gatherer societies or food-producing societies of small social scale? Such societies tend not to make hard and fast distinctions as in Western thought between animate and inanimate, between culture and nature, between human and nonhuman or other-than-human beings.[91] If humans are not the only beings qualifying as "persons" in this world, then the audience for art can be far more than is commonly conceived. Modern Western artists might make art just for themselves or an audience of humans who are culturally similar to them. On the other hand, non-Western artists, say a forager living 5,000 years ago along the Green River, might well have made art for persons represented in the guises of nonhuman animals. Such art might furthermore be directed at various spirits that populate the supernatural world, a substantially broader audience and one with powers unhindered by human limitations of visibility and accessibility.

Munson discusses "several painted rockshelters" in the vicinity of the large Pueblo San Cristobal in north-central New Mexico, a site occupied a few hundred years before Spanish arrival to the area and abandoned shortly after the Pueblo Revolt. Rather small and hidden, these poorly accessible painted rockshelters are characterized as "far more restricted and private" than the plethora of other rock panels that occur on talus boulders more immediately adjacent to the pueblo. She maintains that "making and using rock art within the shelters would have been an intensely personal experience, one in which the artist and the audience is one and the same."[92] Repetitive reuse of stone canvases with limited surface area, tucked away in isolated and poorly accessible settings, seems at odds with the notion of communicating to a human audience, incompatible with having people engage with and learn from the imagery. Why, then, continue with this practice? Munson suspects that rock art at these sites was part of a larger set of behaviors for a nonhuman audience, "the ultimate esoteric audience, the world of spirits."[93]

Munson is likely correct is this interpretation, but why limit the context for such an account? Her conclusion that artists painted imagery for a spirit audience is a supposition that seems worth extending to far more rock art settings than those she considered. Spatial restriction and limited access, along with repeating and retouching the same icons, might provide the sort of "objective" facts that help support her inference, yet spirits likely have little concern for such details. One could make a case that a spirit audience, akin to a human audience, gets drawn in by the highly visible.

Munson also suggests that the act of making rock art, the process itself, might have been far more important than the images.[94] To modern viewers it is the art that has significance, which is why it is tragic when modern people deface rock art. But making and remaking by modifying what is there seems to have been a common practice for BCS artists. Some forms of rock art modification might well have occurred well after the art was originally created, but it still reflects an engagement with images and likely reflects a reenacting of the myths or other central beliefs of the society.

Audience is central to Alfred Gell's argument in *Art and Agency: An Anthropological Theory of Art*, where art is seen as a means of "instrumental action" to influence the thoughts and actions of others; art is about social relations.[95] If you live in a world with many beings, not just humans, then you have a much more complex set of social relationships needing to be created, nurtured, and sustained. The social relations among humans are likely just one part of this and those other relations might be seen as more important, more central to survival and reproduction.

Conclusion

The creators of Barrier Canyon Style rock art left behind haunting, sometimes phantasmagoric images. They secreted away some depictions in places not easily found, at least by us. They placed many on readily visible yet protected rock surfaces that seem to command attention. The fact that these works have lasted for millennia may not have been intentional or in any way anticipated by their makers, but that is what occurred. Symbolic works that survive past the short lifespan of their human creators might ultimately endure long after any that truly understand the original meanings.

Some BCS rock art has already persisted in place for more than twenty times longer than the United States has been a country.

It is unlikely we will ever know the specific meanings for the images created by BCS artists. Yet, this enduring pictorial record upon canyon walls and occasional boulders provides a rare glimpse into the intangible beliefs and worldviews of these past humans, aspects of their cosmology that otherwise would be lost. BCS rock art reveals complex conceptions of the supernatural and natural world, suggesting that the lives of these hunter-gatherers were rich with ceremonies. Few clues to this reality are revealed otherwise in the archaeological record. Hints derive from their clay figurines, prepared paint stick, and inscribed and painted stones, along with a few other traces. But nothing comes close to what is contained in the rich corpus of their rock art. Here we see what were likely important creator forces, spirits, and gods, and the activities of humans trying to propitiate or negotiate with them for assistance. Humans then, like now, fervently hope that some higher power or powers is/are receiving our messages.

Humans in all societies try to understand their world, to create meaning for their life, and to seek advice or assistance from supernatural forces that have special powers greater than those of mere mortals. Depictions on rock surfaces can be a way to instruct or enculturate novices about mythic narratives and supernatural entities. Perhaps more importantly, they can serve as a means to interact with the supernatural. Rock art can provide a powerful symbolic channel, a technology of sorts, for attempting to intervene in the spiritual realm. Tools of flaked stone, bone, and the like work well for manipulating the physical world of lived existence, but accessing and negotiating the spiritual and supernatural realms often require other methods. Rock art might have functioned as one such method: an effective medium for interacting with unseen forces, a likely motivation behind much of BCS rock art in general and some panels specifically.

Threats to individual, kin, and social group survival are ubiquitous but can wax and wane based on the larger ecological and social context. Culture can profoundly influence one's threat perception, yet there can be common patterns when large-scale environmental forces are at work. Causes might be interpreted differently, but a lack of food because of a prolonged drought or other events or processes necessitates action. Hunter-gathers of the early Holocene experienced a long-term drying and warming trend that reduced their ability to maintain viable communities. They made adaptive changes such as shifts in the kinds of resources consumed, with a general broadening of items acceptable as food. They also tried interventions at a higher level, ones directed at rebalancing a world somehow gone out of balance and therefore less sportive of life.

Various rituals and ceremonies were performed directed at supernatural powers that could help. Small clay figurines of spirits were part of this along with many other aspects that left little trace in the archaeological record except for rock art. The art itself was also a critical means of petitioning spirit forces and negotiating with them. The areas at some panels might also have played important roles as grounds for the enactment of group ceremonies.

Barrier Canyon Style rock art proliferated as a symbolic medium for supernatural intervention during the end of the Early Archaic after around 7000 BC. It continued in a similar manner during the Middle Archaic, but foragers also had to take other steps, which included moving to territories far removed from previous stomping grounds. Previously important places like Cowboy Cave were seldom used and the Great Gallery downstream perhaps became a rarely visited location. Overall ecological conditions had improved somewhat by 2000 BC, during the late Archaic, and human populations rebounded. Ancestral places saw renewed use and BCS rock art continued to be painted but with changes. Although the lifeways of these later hunter-gatherers were quite similar in general respects, belief systems and their symbolic representations differed. The later artists had different priorities and different conceptions about the world. A historic connection is detectable, but the style had evolved.

Yet more changes to lifeway and rock art style were coming, as the repercussions of agricultural societies to the south started to infiltrate across the canyon country of Utah. Shortly after the common era some 2,000 years ago, precursors to Fremont rock art are apparent. Some rock art similar to BCS likely continued to be made, perhaps in an attempt to capture or emulate the power that seems to emanate from many of the most impressive ancient BCS images. Modern viewers who venture to the Great Gallery cannot help but be stirred, to ponder not just the lives of those past painters and what they were intending to convey, but also larger issues that humans have contemplated for time immemorial.

Notes

Chapter 1

1. James H. Gunnerson, *The Fremont Culture: A Study in Culture Dynamics on the Northern Anasazi Frontier* (Cambridge: Harvard University Papers of the Peabody Museum of Archaeology and Ethnology vol. 59, no. 2). Jerry Spangler and James Aton provide a highly readable account of the 1931 fieldwork of the Claflin-Emerson Expedition in *The Crimson Cowboys: The Remarkable Odyssey of the 1931 Claflin-Emerson Expedition* (Salt Lake City: University of Utah Press, 2018).

2. For decades, various lines of evidence supported the hypothesis that BCS rock art was ancient, with the style originating 7,000 years ago or more during an interval known as the Early Archaic period. In 2014 Joel Pederson and coauthors challenged this prevailing argument by proposing temporal brackets for the Great Gallery, the BCS type site, based on alluvial stratigraphy dated by optically stimulated luminescence (OSL). They argued that a late Archaic origin between about 2000 BC and the Common Era was the only prior hypothesis not disproven by their evidence. But they went on to conclude that BCS rock art most likely dates to the first thousand years of the Common Era (AD 1–1100), basically leading to and overlapping with the subsequent Fremont culture. Joel L. Pederson et al., "Age of Barrier Canyon-Style Rock Art Constrained by Cross-Cutting Relations and Luminescence Dating Techniques," *PNAS* 111 (2014): 12986–91.

   This publication caused a minor seismic upheaval in the rock art world. "Utah's Famous Canyonlands Rock Art Unexpectedly Recent" read one newspaper headline that broadcast and amplified the conclusion. Others followed. Even *Smithsonian Magazine* got in on the hype: "New Analysis Suggests Utah's Famous Rock Art Is Surprisingly Recent." While the paper looks convincing at first glance, closer examination in conjunction with additional evidence suggests otherwise. For one, not all rock faces painted with BCS rock art in Horseshoe Canyon were buried by alluvium. Even at the Great Gallery, the upstream portion of this panel occurs above the maximum height of the Pleistocene–early Holocene alluvial terrace. The rock art painted in this portion of the Great Gallery is typical for the Barrier Canyon Style. The same is true for the pictographs at the High Gallery down canyon, which were painted on a rock face well above any canyon alluvium.

   Another conundrum and challenge to their conclusion are radiocarbon dates on pigment from the Great Gallery that support the painting of one image around 8000 BC and the painting of another, rather small anthropomorph, after 1700 BC (Alan Watchman, Carol Patterson, and Ann McNichol, "Dating BCS Rock Art at the Great Gallery, Canyonlands, Utah," in *Utah Rock Art* 24 [Salt Lake City: Utah Rock Art Research Association, 2005]). A third problematic aspect is the claim that it took some 4,000 years for erosion to clear the Great Gallery cliff face of alluvium so that it could be painted. This argument does not square with what scientists know about how rapidly alluvial fill was commonly flushed from canyons of the Southwest; the last 120 years of arroyo cutting throughout the region is stark testament to this.

   Finally, there is evidence of probable temporal differences in the four main BCS rock art sites within Horseshoe Canyon. Significant stylistic differences between these panels must be taken into account with the history of canyon alluvial terraces. That history helps make sense of why panels immediately across from each other at the High Panel and Horseshoe Shelter look so different as to suggest temporally distinct artistic traditions. The alluvial evidence indicates that this is the case, but this sort of stylistic change is difficult to reconcile with a painting tradition that was limited to just 1,000 years of the Common Era. It is also difficult to reconcile with a painting tradition limited to the last

2,000 years BC. However, if there are 5,000 to 7,000 years or even more, then it is explicable.

Chapter 2

1. Neil Bennun (*The Broken String: The Last Words of an Extinct People* [London: Viking, 2005], 179–80) provides an account of this for the San people of South Africa, where trance brought on by vigorous dancing often resulted in bleeding from the nose. These trance dances were public events that the whole social group participated in, with trance used for "healing, prediction, rain-making, fighting off malevolent *!gi:ten* (spirits), influencing the movement of game, or other social and spiritual necessities."

2. To see what a portion of the vandalized Buckhorn Wash panel looked like not too long ago, including names and dates of the culprits, websearch "Our Daily Sykes #9," which shows a Kodachrome photo of the panel taken by Horace Sykes in the late 1940s or early 1950s. The difference between then and now is dramatic.

3. Sally Cole ("Origins, Continuities and Meaning of Barrier Canyon Style Rock Art," in *New Dimensions in Rock Art Studies*, edited by Ray T. Matheny [Salt Lake City: University of Utah Press], 36) proposed seven style variants representative for smaller areas of the overall BCS rock art distribution based on formal properties of anthropomorphs such as body shape, interior embellishments, head features, and the like. She saw these as "working hypotheses for identifying internal dynamics and social and cultural relationships." David Sucec ("Toward a Typology of Barrier Canyon Style Spirit Figures," in *Utah Rock Art* 15 [Salt Lake City: Utah Rock Art Research Association, 1997], 61–76) proposed a similar spirit figure typology based on the same sort of variability in BCS rock art but with nine variants recognized. His maps of where these occur reveal considerable overlap in all of them. This result is perhaps expectable for rock art produced by highly mobile and socially fluid hunter-gatherers, especially without temporal control over the images.

4. Jean-Loïc Le Quellec, Paul Bahn, and Marvin Rowe, "The Death of a Pterodactyl," *Antiquity* 89 (2015): 872–84.

5. Alan Watchman, Carol Patterson, and Ann McNichol ("Dating BCS Rock Art at the Great Gallery, Canyonlands, Utah," in *Utah Rock Art* 24 [Salt Lake City: Utah Rock Art Research Association, 2005], 11). Watchman, Patterson, and McNichol report this as over 8520 ± 970 radiocarbon years ago but with no lab number or details. Carol Patterson, who worked closely with Watchman on this project, was able to find correspondence that provided the lab number (OS-35200) and the sample location, which consisted of a tiny sample from the chest area of the right-hand-most of the three large anthropomorphs that are to the left of the black dragon scene.

Chapter 3

1. Michael P. Firnhaber, "Experiencing Rock Art: A Phenomenological Investigation of the Barrier Canyon Tradition," PhD dissertation (University College London, 2007), Appendix D. His motif inventory lists sixty-two BCS sites in total, but he excluded three of these because of poor preservation or vandalism.

2. Unfortunately, the entire hunting scene at the Great Gallery is heavily damaged by "pecking" marks. This sort of damage also occurs on the large spirit figures, but with tiny painted images several marks are enough to almost eradicate them. Sally Cole ("Origins, Continuities and Meaning of Barrier Canyon Style Rock Art," 36) makes an interesting inference about the dents in the sandstone that heavily pepper the hunting scene and most portions of the Great Gallery as well as many other panels. She suggests that this form of obliteration could result from "sharpened stone, bone or hardened wood, possibly in combination with thrust spears, atlatls and darts, or bows and arrows." This makes great sense for the especially heavy damage of this hunting scene where there was an evident focus on the big horn sheep. It might be a form of imitative magic or mimetic prayer where shooting at the animals of a hunt scene on such an important rock art panel brought good fortune in the pursuit of game animals.

3. Polly Schaafsma, "Trance and Transformation in the Canyons: Shamanism and Early Rock Art on the Colorado Plateau," in *Shamanism and Rock Art in North America*, ed. Solveig A. Turpin (San Antonio: Rock Art Foundation Inc., 1994), 52. Schaafsma cites Mircea Eliade's 1964 treatise on Shamanism (*Shamanism: Archaic Techniques of Ecstasy,* 42).

4. David Sucec, "Toward a Typology of Barrier Canyon Style Spirit Figures: Early Findings of the BCS Project (1991-1995)," in *Utah Rock Art* 15 (Salt Lake City: Utah Rock Art Research Association, 1997), 11. Sucec illustrates a few of the horned serpents in BCS art as have others. Nielsen and Helmke ("Reinterpreting the Plaza de los Glifos, la Ventilla, Teotihuacan") review the horned serpent concept in Mesoamerica linking it to the personification of disease.

5. Firnhaber ("Experiencing Rock Art," Figure 4.21) shows a few examples. In his Appendix D on p. 354 no polymorphs are listed for the High Panel in Horseshoe Canyon (his site 616-1). Yet he includes a picture of the flying figure depicted there in his discussion on polymorphs, so evidently this is just a coding error, which means his total count of this motif is 15 instead of 14 and anthropomorphs are reduced by one to 590.

6. Firnhaber, "Experiencing Rock Art," 240.

7. Alan P. Garfinkel et al., "Myth, Ritual and Rock Art: Coso Decorated Animal-Humans and the Animal Master," *Rock Art Research* 26, no. 2 (2009). Garfinkel et al. develop an argument like this for specific images of the Coso Rock Art Complex in eastern California thought to portray animal masters, supernatural entities that could control and replenish game animals.

8. Máire Ní Leathlobhair et al., "The Evolutionary History of Dogs in the Americas," *Science* 361, no. 6397 (2018). Angela Perri et al., "Dog Domestication and the Dual Dispersal of People and Dogs into the Americas," *PNAS* 118, no. 6 (2021): 1–8.

9. Schaafsma, "Trance and Transformation in the Canyons," 54.

10. Polly Schaafsma, *Indian Rock Art of the Southwest*, (Albuquerque: University of New Mexico Press, 1980), 71.

Chapter 4

1. Geologists studying alluvial sequences obtain samples from buried sediment layers to date the episodes of alluvial aggradation and degradation. Wood charcoal or other organic material can be dated by the radiocarbon technique (^{14}C); quartz grains and some other mineral grains in alluvial sand can be dated by the optical-stimulated luminescence technique (OSL). Both methods provide an estimate for the age of the alluvium within some error range: usually on the order of one hundred years or less for ^{14}C dating and often a few hundred years or more for OSL dating.

2. Jon Harvey provides an informative summary of arroyo cutting in the Southwest at https://serc.carleton.edu/vignettes/collection/36633.html. Harden, Macklin, and Baker ("Holocene Flood Histories in South-Western USA") compare alluvial histories in canyon and open valley environments from across the Southwest.

3. Scott B. Aby, "Date of Arroyo Cutting in the American Southwest and the Influence of Human Activities," *Anthropocene* 18 (2017): 76–88. Jerry R. Miller, "Casualty of Historic Arroyo Incision in the Southwestern United States," *Anthropocene* 18 (2017): 69–75.

4. Stephen Hall, "Paleoenvironments of the American Southwest," in *The Archaic Southwest: Foragers in an Arid Land*, ed. Bradley J. Vierra (Salt Lake City: University of Utah Press, 2018).

5. M. Aubert et al., "Pleistocene Cave Art from Sulawesi, Indonesia," *Nature* 514 (2014): 223–27. D. L. Hoffmann et al., "U-Th Dating of Carbonate Crusts Reveals Neandertal Origin of Iberian Cave Art," *Science* 359 (2018): 912–15. A. W. G. Pike et al., "U-Series Dating of Paleolithic Art in 11 Caves in Spain," *Science* 336 (2012): 1409–13.

6. Archaeologists use stone artifacts, especially projectile points, to identify distinct Paleoindian time periods and, by extension, the people who made the tools. When learning to flake stone in early childhood, Paleoindian neophytes internalized cultural standards for how this was done and what was an acceptable shape for a killing point and other tool form. Clovis is one of these Paleoindian cultural groups, so named after a distinctive projectile point style. Clovis culture was once considered the founding population for most people in North and South America, a basal culture. Convincing evidence for people prior to Clovis continues to accumulate, as does evidence suggesting that early migrants came down the Pacific coast some 17,000 to 14,000 years ago, well before Clovis. These pre-Clovis people had different styles of projectile points, even different strategies for how to make those points.

7. Donald E. Brown, *Human Universals* (New York: McGraw-Hill, 1991). Ellen Dissanayake, "Art as a Human Universal: An Adaptationist View," in *Origins of Religion, Cognition, and Culture*, ed. Armin

W. Geertz (Durham, England: Acumen Publishing, 2013).

8. Ashley K. Lemke, D. Clark Wernecke, and Michael B. Collins, "Early Art in North America: Clovis and Later Paleoindian Incised Artifacts from the Gault Site, Texas (41BL323)," *American Antiquity* 80 (2015): 113–33. Lemke, Wernecke, and Collins provide an example of Paleoindian portable art consisting of incised stone and bone from the Gault site in Texas, including Clovis-age artifacts.

9. A recent find of human footprints at White Sands National Park in New Mexico reported by Bennett et al. ("Evidence of Humans in North America during the Last Glacial Maximum") may rewrite this conclusion, though this remains to be seen. At 23,000 to 21,000 thousand years old, this is old enough that humans could have migrated southward on foot prior to glacial ice blockage. If this find is ultimately confirmed, it would be the third time that discoveries in New Mexico have altered our thoughts on the antiquity of Native Americans in the New World—a hat trick of sorts for that state.

10. Gaspar Morcote-Ríos et al., "Colonisation and Early Peopling of the Colombian Amazon during the Late Pleistocene and the Early Holocene: New Evidence from La Serrania Las Lindosa," *Quaternary International* 578, no. 20 (2021): 5–19. The images of the animals suggested to be extinct Pleistocene ones have varying degrees of believability. Some of this is based on the size of animals relative to humans, such as for the possible giant ground sloth. Amy Gilreath and Ken Hedges ("Color Us Skeptical") present a well-reasoned skeptical analysis of this report; their Figures 3 and 4 compare a Columbia pictograph interpreted as Pleistocene megafauna against what the animals actually looked like.

11. Ekkehart Malotki and Henry D. Wallace, "Columbian Mammoth Petroglyphs from the San Juan River near Bluff, Utah, United States, *Rock Art Research* 28, no. 2 (2011): 143–52." Bednarik ("Pleistocene Palaeoart of the Americas") asserts that no mammoths are actually depicted, just a "fortuitous arrangement of unrelated elements" that resemble mammoths, and that a Pleistocene age is not geologically possible with the markings being "less than 4000 years old." He is wrong on the first point. As to the second point, further study is required for geologic dating of when the sandstone cliff face became exposed and if such a surface

could last for more than 12,000 years if marked by Clovis people.

12. A surface Clovis assemblage originally discovered by Margerie Green in the late 1970s during an archaeological survey for proposed mining on Lime Ridge west of Bluff received an intensive surface collection and limited testing several years later, confirming the Clovis age temporal assignment (Davis, "The Lime Ridge Clovis Site"; Davis and Brown, "The Lime Ridge Clovis Site"). A more detailed analysis of the recovered lithic artifacts disclosed further insights to what the Clovis occupants did at this location (Vance, "Stone Without Bones: Reconstructing the Lime Ridge Clovis Site").

13. Solveig A. Turpin, "Archaic North America," in *Handbook of Rock Art Research*, ed. David S. Whitley (Walnut Creek, CA: AltaMira Press, 2011).

14. Ekkehart Malotki, "The Dragonfly: A Shamanistic Motif in the Archaic Rock Art of the Palavayu Region in Northeastern Arizona," *American Indian Rock Art* 23 (1997): 57–72; Ekkehart Malotki, "The Owl: A Shamanistic Motif in the Archaic Rock Art Iconography of the Palavayu Anthropomorphic Style, Northeastern Arizona," *American Indian Rock Art* 22 (1998).

15. Don D. Christensen, Jerry Dickey, and Steven M. Freers, *Rock Art of the Grand Canyon Region* (San Diego: Sunbelt Publications, 2013). Christensen, Dickey, and Freers provide a detailed accounting of rock art in the Glen Canyon region including the Esplanade and related Tusayan styles. Mary Allen started documenting many of the ancient paintings in Grand Canyon in the 1980s and 1990s and called them Grand Canyon Polychrome, a name that she prefers over Esplanade (Allen, "Grand Canyon Polychrome vs. Esplanade Style: Is a Name Change Warranted?").

16. Even archaeologists have sometimes made such a claim as when Alice Kehoe (*Shamans and Religion: An Anthropological Exploration in Critical Thinking*, 71–80) suggested that some rock art might have been the simple doodles of idle children, much to the annoyance of Polly Schaafsma (*Images and Power: Rock Art and Ethics*, 44–45).

17. Richard A. Rogers. *Petroglyphs, Pictographs, and Projections: Native American Rock Art in the Contemporary Cultural Landscape* (Salt Lake City: University of Utah Press, 2018). Rogers provides a thought-provoking exploration of how modern

people impose meaning on Native American rock art. This is not a "western" frame of mind but simply what people everywhere do: try to find meaning and interpret the world around them.

18. Polly Schaafsma, *Images and Power* (New York: Springer, 2013), 1.

19. The edited volume by Chippindale and Eastwood (*Seeing and Knowing: Rock Art With and Without Ethnography*) provides a useful overview of attempts to learn from rock art with and without ethnography. Layton ("Ethnographic Study and Symbolic Analysis"), among others, provides a useful summary of using ethnography for interpreting rock art.

20. Martin Gusinde, *The Lost Tribes of Tierra del Fuego: Selk'nam, Yamana, Kawésqar* (New York: Thames & Hudson, 2015).

21. These Tierra del Fuego groups did not make elaborate textiles though it is easy to envision that rock art depictions of the people in ceremonial attire could easily be misinterpreted as indicating textile wraps were present. This might also be the case for the creators of BCS rock art since some suggest that the intricate decorations on BCS anthropomorphs were woven decorated garments. There is no evidence for this in the archaeological record until after the introduction of cotton in the Common Era.

22. Linda A. Brown and William H. Walker, "Prologue: Archaeology, Animism and Non-Human Agents," *Journal of Archaeological Method and Theory* 15 (2008): 297–99; Patricia A. Helvenston and Derek Hodgson, "The Neuropsychology of 'Animism': Implications for Understanding Rock Art," *Rock Art Research* 27, no. 1 (2010): 61–94; Martin Porr and Hannah Rachel Bell, "'Rock-Art,' 'Animism' and Two-Way Thinking: Towards a Complementary Epistemology in the Understanding of Material Culture and 'Rock-Art' of Hunting and Gathering People," *Journal of Archaeological Method and Theory* 19 (2012): 161–205; Robert Wallis, "Re-enchanting Rock Art Landscapes: Animic Ontologies, Non-Human Agency and Rhizomic Personhood," *Time and Mind: The Journal of Archaeology, Consciousness and Culture* 2, no. 1 (2009): 47–90. Eduardo Viveiros de Castro ("Cosmological Deixis and Amerindian Perspectivism," *Journal of the Royal Anthropological Institute* 4 [1998]: 469–88) provides an interesting account of Amerindian perspectivism.

23. Helvenston and Bahn's edited volume *Waking the Trance Fixed* is just one of several refutations of the shamanic account for rock art, especially Lewis-Williams and Dowson's shamanic Three-Stages of Trance model. Anne Solomon's (2008) examination of southern African rock art attributed to San-speaking people ("Myths, Making, and Consciousness: Differences and Dynamics in San Rock Arts"), a key source for Lewis-Williams's shamanic theory, suggests that there is far more in these than just a universal shamanistic cosmology linked to altered states of consciousness. Sally Cole ("Origins, Continuities and Meaning," 65–66) provides a critique of shamanic interpretation for BCS rock art.

24. Irving A. Hallowell, "Ojibwa Ontology, Behavior, and World View," in *Culture in History: Essays in Honor of Paul Radin*, ed. Stanley Diamond (New York: Columbia University Press, 1960); Graham Harvey, *Animism: Respecting the Living World* (Kent Town: South Australia, Wakefield Press, 2005).

25. Sue O'Connor et al., "Memory and Performance: The Role of Rock Art in the Kimberley, Western Australia," in *Rock Art and Memory in the Transmission of Cultural Knowledge*, ed. Leslie F. Zubieta (Cham, Switzerland: Springer, 2022).

26. Sally J. Cole, *Legacy on Stone: Rock Art of the Colorado Plateau and Four Corners Region* (Boulder: Johnson Books, 2009), 2. Cole disparages the term pictograph and favors instead "rock painting."

27. C. C. Hawley, R. C. Robeck, and H. B. Dyer, *Geology, Altered Rocks and Ore Deposits of The San Rafael Swell, Emery County, Utah* (Washington, DC: US Government Printing Office, 1968). Hawley, Robeck, and Dyer report that the major rock units exposed in the San Rafael Swell include substantial amounts of hematite in one form or another. In the early 1980s I found hematite nodules in large washes draining eastward out of the swell, such as South Temple Wash and Chute Canyon Wash, and also in small washes, such as the narrow, short one leading to Wild Horse Window, a skylight arch in the ceiling of a large sandstone grotto. The largest nodule that I collected was a naturally rectangular chunk measuring three inches long and one inch in width and thickness. I have since used this nodule for a variety of experimental purposes including the painting of small pictographs. According to the Munsell color system, the ocher from the San Rafael Swell is dark red (10R3/6), dusky red (10R3/4), and

red (10R4/8, 4/6, &5/8) when abraded. The ancient, weathered rind on these nodules is always darker, even reddish black (10R2.5/1).

28. Alan Watchman, Carol Patterson, and Ann McNichol, "Dating BCS Rock Art at the Great Gallery, Canyonlands, Utah," in *Utah Rock Art* 24 (Salt Lake City: Utah Rock Art Research Association, 2005), 7; Pete E. Poston and Gary Cox, "Final Report: Raman Spectroscopic Analysis of Rock Art Pigment from the Great Gallery, Maze District, Canyonlands National Park, Utah," (Moab: Canyonlands National Park, n.d.).

29. Evidence that ancient people also collected yellow chunks of uranium ore not knowing the dangers of this material comes from a find at Sand Dune Cave in southeastern Utah, where a chunk of "hot" yellow ore occurred in a Basketmaker II tool cache (Lindsay et al., *Survey and Excavation North and East of Navajo Mountain, Utah 1959–1962*). The ore occurred in a small animal-skin pouch along with flaked stone projectile point preforms inside a larger bag made of dog skin. The ore was so radioactive that it had fused with a few of the bifaces over the nearly 2,000 years that the bag lay cached.

30. Steve Manning ("A Modal Based Classification System for Rock Art Research") critiques the style concept in rock art research, laying the blame for its problematic application in Utah largely at the feet of Polly Schaafsma and ultimately art historian Meyer Schapiro ("Style"). Alan Wallach ("Meyer Schapiro's Essay on Style: Falling into the Void") provides an informed appraisal of Schapiro's concept of style, concluding that it is of little concern for art historians (14).

31. Tim Ingold, *The Perception of the Environment: Essays on Livelihood, Dwelling, and Skill* (London: Routledge, 2000), 89–110; Marianne Elizabeth Lien and Gisli Pálsson, "Ethnography Beyond the Human: The 'Other-than-Human' in Ethnographic Work," *Ethnos* 86 (2019): 1–20.

32. Sally J. Cole, *Legacy on Stone: Rock Art of the Colorado Plateau and Four Corners Region* (Boulder: Johnson Books, 2009); Steven R. Simms and François Gohier, *Traces of Fremont: Society and Rock Art in Ancient Utah* (Salt Lake City: University of Utah Press, 2010); Polly Schaafsma, *The Rock Art of Utah: From the Donald Scott Collection* (Cambridge, MA: Harvard University, 1971); and Polly Schaafsma, *Indian Rock Art of the Southwest* (Albuquerque: University of New Mexico Press, 1980) have all discussed the relationship between Fremont and Barrier Canyon Style rock art.

33. A very crudely mud-painted horned figure is an example of an image that looks like a recent attempt to mimic the ancient rock art. This figure was present when the first archaeologists visited the site in 1930, but cowboys had been there plenty of times previously and many added their names on the back wall of this shelter, a place of welcome shade in summer and protection from wind and precipitation in colder times.

34. Robert G. Bednarik, "The Dating of Rock Art: A Critique," *Journal of Archaeological Science* 29 (2002): 1213–33 Bednarik provides a thorough critique of rock art dating up through the start of the new century including a detailed postmortem of cation-ratio (CR) dating, initially used for relative ordering of petroglyphs and then for providing absolute dates by calibrating the technique with carbon trapped under varnish layers. Bednarik concludes that "CR analysis has not provided any accepted results, its methodology is fundamentally flawed and it does not provide a valid method of estimating the ages of rock art or of geomorphic exposures" (p. 14). Likewise, he argues that radiocarbon dates on petroglyphs are invalid for reasons such as a false assumption of homogeneity in samples even though trapped organic matter was clearly heterogeneous and of different ages (p. 6). A report by Beck et al. ("Ambiguities in Direct Dating of Rock Surfaces Using Radiocarbon Measurements") led to the suspicion that the heterogeneous carbon components in petroglyph varnish samples were not there by accident. Bednarik ("The Dating of Rock Art," 6) correctly cautions that examples of failure do not disqualify the potential of dating carbon trapped within and under rock art accretions such as varnish.

35. Radiocarbon dating and other absolute dating techniques based on radioactive isotopes were stimulated by the World War II effort that split the atom; Willard Libby, who was associated with the Manhattan Project, won the Nobel Prize in 1960 for pioneering the radiocarbon technique.

36. Robert L. Kelly, *The Foraging Spectrum* (Washington, DC: Smithsonian Institution Press, 1995); Dyble et al., "Networks of Food Sharing Reveal the Functional Significance of Multilevel Sociality in

Two Hunter-Gatherer Groups," *Current Biology* 26 (2016): 2017–21.

37. An example of this south of the area with Barrier Canyon rock art is the Cave 7 massacre of Basketmaker II individuals (see Geib and Hurst, "Should Dates Trump Context? Evaluation of the Cave 7 Skeletal Assemblage Radiocarbon Dates"; Geib, "Basketmaker II Warfare and Fending Sticks in the North American Southwest"). The occurrence of scalps in the Moab area dated to the Basketmaker II time interval indicates that social tensions had increased in this area as well with the arrival of farming (Howard and Janetski, "Human Scalps from Eastern Utah"). The practice of taking head skins is also seen in Fremont rock art.

38. Jesse D. Jennings, ed., *Cowboy Cave* (Salt Lake City: University of Utah Press, 1980). The projectile points from the excavation were reported by Richard Holmer ("Chipped Stone Projectile Points") with Joel Janetski ("Wood and Reed Artifacts") describing the wooden artifacts.

39. John C. Whittaker, "Late Survival of Atlatls in the American Southwest?" *Atlatl* 20, no. 1 (2007): 10–12; John C. Whittaker, "Ambiguous Endurance: Late Atlatls in the American Southwest?" *Kiva* 78 (2012): 79–98; Thomas R. Hester, Michael P. Mildner, and Lee Spencer, *Great Basin Atlatl Studies* (Ramona, CA: Ballena Press, 1974).

40. Schaafsma (*Rock Art of Utah,* 49, Figure 49) misattributes this bow hunter pictograph as possibly Fremont in origin, but there is no evidence for recurved bows until post-Fremont times. Also, this attribution ignores the superimpositioning of one of the red painted hunted elk/deer over a series of white dots that extends to the left under an unusual deeply incised horned stick-figure anthropomorph and then across a very faded Fremont anthropomorph pictograph farther to the left, one of two faded Fremont anthropomorphs that occur here.

41. Frank W. Hull and Nancy M White, "Spindle Whorls, Incised and Painted Stone, and Unfired Clay Objects," in *Cowboy Cave*, ed. Jesse D. Jennings (Salt Lake City: University of Utah Press, 1980): 117–25.

42. Nancy J. Coulam and Alan R. Schroedl, "Early Archaic Clay Figurines from Cowboy Cave and Walters Cave in Southeastern Utah," *Kiva* 61 (1996): 401–12.

43. Coulam and Schroedl, "Early Archaic Clay Figurines," 407.

44. Phil R. Geib, "AMS Dating of Plain-Weave Sandals from the Central Colorado Plateau," *Utah Archaeology* 9 (1996): 35–53; Phil R. Geib and Edward A. Jolie, "Rise of Broad Spectrum Foraging on the Colorado Plateau during the Early Holocene," in *The Archaic Southwest: Foragers in an Arid Land*, ed. Bradley J. Vierra (Salt Lake City: University of Utah Press, 2018), 189–214.

45. See Simms and Gohier (*Traces of Fremont*, 98–99) for a photo of the Pilling Figurines; Pitblado and colleagues ("Archaeological Fingerprinting and Fremont Figurines") provide an interesting account of how a stolen specimen was returned and the methods used to demonstrate it being part of the original cache.

46. David Sucec, personal communication 2020.

47. Pederson and colleagues ("Age of Barrier Canyon-Style Rock Art," 12987), reference Schroedl and Coulam's 1994 article titled "Cowboy Cave Revisited" to support their claim of poor stratigraphic integrity. Schroedl and Coulam excavated at the site under Jesse Jennings's direction, with Schroedl overseeing day-to-day activities. These two authors do not characterize cave deposits as mixed and lacking stratigraphic integrity. Rather, they reaffirm that both Cowboy Cave and the adjoining Walters Cave contained well-differentiated layers with natural breaks that excavators followed. This has allowed researchers "to review, reexamine, reanalyze, and reinterpret data [recovered remains] 20 years [and more] after the fact" (Schroedl and Coulam, "Cowboy Cave Revisited," 26). Schroedl and Coulam mention some mixing from prehistoric pit digging, which incorporated early remains into later strata. This is a common issue to stratified archaeological sites in general and is evident at both caves. There are also cases when small materials get intruded up or down by rodents and other processes. With organic remains, direct dating can control for such intrusions and there are examples of this from Cowboy Cave (see Coulam and Schroedl, "Late Archaic Totemism in the Great American Southwest," 61–62n3, and Geib and Jolie, "Rise of Broad Spectrum Foraging on the Colorado Plateau").

48. Pederson and colleagues ("Age of Barrier Canyon-Style Rock Art," 12987) also dismiss the figurines since the "inferred age is much earlier than most

other evidence for the age of BCS." This "other evidence" is not cited, but presumably this is work reported by Betsy Tipps ("Barrier Canyon Rock Art Dating"), which suggested a late Archaic time span based principally on two dates that Marvin Rowe obtained on paint samples from BCS rock art spalls. Figurine inferred age is consistent with the 8655 ± 210 BP average of two contemporaneous radiocarbon dates on a Great Gallery pigment sample reported by Watchman, Patterson, and McNichol ("Dating BCS Rock Art," 11–12, Table 1).

Coulam and Schroedl noted the "more than coincidental similarities between the Early Archaic unfired clay figurines and the anthropomorphs in Barrier Canyon style rock art" ("Early Archaic Clay Figurines," 411). They mentioned three alternative reasons for why these figurines look so similar to BCS rock art even though the dates obtained by Marvin Rowe and reported by Betsy Tipps suggested a late Archaic age: "It is possible that the dating on the rock art is in error, and that it actually dates to the Early Archaic. Another possibility is that Early Archaic objects at Cowboy Cave were moved upward and redeposited in later strata, to be uncovered by later people who depicted a similar motif in pictographs on nearby canyon walls. A third possibility is that the Horseshoe Shouldered motif remained part of the symbolism of the hunter-gatherers in the northern Colorado Plateau from the Early Archaic through the Late Archaic" (Schroedl and Coulam, "Cowboy Cave Revisited," 411).

Restriction of the Horseshoe Shouldered–style figurines to just early Archaic layers in both caves serves to counter the second potential reason. Since the figurines only came from early Archaic layers, none were actually seen by late Archaic occupants. It is actually important to note that the abundant pit digging at the site by late Archaic foragers, and those that followed, rarely penetrated the early Archaic layers at these sites because of rather thick sand layers that accumulated during the middle Holocene. Schroedl and Coulam's first explanation is possible, but the samples processed by Rowe might apply to when late Archaic artists added to previously painted panels. This corresponds with their third reason: BCS rock art represents a long-lasting tradition that started early and that morphed through time.

49. This ledge can still be used and unfortunately has been by vandals who've added their names and junky modern images rather than just appreciating such an up-close experience with ancient art.

50. Polly Schaafsma (*Rock Art of Utah*, 49, Figure 71) interpreted this large superimposed anthropomorph as Fremont in origin based on the blocky body shape. Sally Cole (*Legacy on Stone*, 76, Figure 35h) also believes it to be Fremont in origin. Steven Manning ("42EM65, The Temple Mountain Pictograph Panel," 66–67) argues that it is BCS, though done by a later artist of that tradition. The careful addition of this figure was part of several evident modifications to the right side of the panel. Manning maintains that the superimposed large anthropomorph is closely comparable to anthropomorphs from the Great Gallery and he uses body form outlines to make this point (Manning, "42EM65, The Temple Mountain Pictograph Panel," Figure 27). At this generalized level of comparison he is right, but the anthropomorphs at the Great Gallery that have this outline also have considerable interior body decoration, but not so the Temple Mountain figure. Had such details been added then there would be no doubt as to which figure came from which panel. Manning is perhaps correct about the larger figure being BCS but done considerably later in time than the spirit figure that it superimposes, perhaps done during the late Archaic.

51. Schaafsma (*Rock Art of Utah*, 73) labeled this animal a "large companion dog . . . with a hairy tail" whereas Manning ("42EM65, The Temple Mountain Pictograph Panel," 59) argues that it could be a mountain lion because of its "long curving tail and round paws."

52. Cole (2009:76, Fig. 35h) identifies the animal as a grizzly bear; Manning ("42EM65, The Temple Mountain Pictograph Panel," 58) also thinks it might be a "large bear," although he acknowledges that this does not fit the curved horns.

53. Steven Manning's detailed description of this panel ("42EM65, The Temple Mountain Pictograph Panel") is well worth reading and provides the sort of publicly available record needed for other panels.

54. Cole, *Legacy on Stone*, 65. Also see Betsy L. Tipps, "Barrier Canyon Rock Art Dating," in *Holocene Archaeology near Squaw Butte, Needles District, Canyonlands National Park*, ed. Betsy L. Tipps (Denver: National Park Service, 1995), 153–169.

55. Another key to relative dating in the Alcove Gallery is the vertical position of the rock art panels with regard to alluvial terraces in Horseshoe Canyon. The T1 late Holocene alluvial terrace provides a level floor surface for much of this massive sandstone grotto. The deposit is exposed at the front of the shelter and consists of about fifteen feet of fine layers of washed-in sediment. The accumulation dates from about 3,000 to 800 years ago (Pederson et al., "Age of Barrier Canyon-Style Rock Art"). The talus pile at the back of the alcove used for access to the upper panel rises some thirty feet or more above the top of this young terrace. Plastered against the alcove wall on the upstream side of the talus pile is a small remnant of an ancient alluvial terrace from the Pleistocene known as T2. This slightly calcified sediment is quite distinct from the far younger alluvium. Pleistocene alluvium once filled the shelter like the T1 alluvium does today, but most is now gone, having eroded away in the distant past. The talus pile likely rests upon and preserves a portion of this terrace though some of this rock accumulation may have been in place before T2 deposition.

　　Painting any images on the lower panel could never have occurred until the Pleistocene terrace had eroded away, thereby clearing the rock face where the images occur. But the images painted on the upper panel, which are now largely faded, occur above the level of the Pleistocene alluvium. Using this rock surface as a canvas for painted images was possible for the earliest Native Americans who ventured through the canyon. Whether the talus pile was in place to actually reach this surface is another question, but this was certainly true by the time the Pleistocene terrace reached its full height. An early Holocene age for painting the upper panel is possible.

56. A third piece of a spalled pictograph from this area was determined to be contaminated by kerosene or other recent hydrocarbons after it returned an implausible age of 32,900 ± 900 BP (AA-8747; Chaffee, Hyman, and Rowe, "Vandalism of Rock Art for Enhanced Photography"). There is also a fourth painted block from this area that at some point around AD 1100 either fell from the rock face or was turned over and placed on sediment and some cottonwood leaves. The approximate age of this event is known by a radiocarbon date on the trapped leaves and two corroborating OSL dates for

sediment immediately under the block (Pederson et al., "Age of Barrier Canyon-Style Rock Art").

57. This technique oxidizes any organic carbon to carbon dioxide (CO_2) using a radio wave generated low-temperature and low-pressure oxygen plasma (Chaffee, Hyman, and Rowe, "AMS ^{14}C Dating of Rock Paintings"; Rowe, "Radiocarbon Dating of Ancient Rock Paintings"; Russ, Hyman, and Rowe, "Direct Radiocarbon Dating Of Rock Art").

58. These first attempts to radiocarbon date pictograph fragments from the Great Gallery occurred when Gary Cox, who was then serving as a backcountry NPS ranger for Canyonlands, collected two separate samples of painted sandstone blocks from below the spalled panel to the left of the Holy Ghost group. These two separate samples, 42WN418-1 and -2, were turned over to Nancy Coulam, who was the Canyonlands archaeologist at the time, and she in turn sent them to Marvin Rowe, who was then fine-tuning his plasma extraction technique for recovery of organic carbon from tricky samples such as rock art. This was in the early 1990s.

　　Rowe's lab processed one specimen first (42WN418-1), extracting two separate CO_2 samples (1a and 1b), which they sealed in glass vials and sent to the University of Arizona accelerator mass spectrometry (AMS) facility for radiocarbon dating. The first of these samples returned an unbelievable age of 32,900 ± 900 BP (AA-8747), which prompted a consideration of possible sample contamination from recent hydrocarbons (e.g., kerosene). This they demonstrated in various ways, and it is something that seems to account for the diffusion or bleeding of hematite pigment into the sandstone surrounding the outline of the largest spalled anthropomorphic figure to the left of the Holy Ghost group (Chaffee, Hyman, and Rowe, "Vandalism of Rock Art for Enhanced Photography"). These results have no bearing on the age of BCS rock art but serve as a warning to scientists about some potential difficulties with dating this rock art.

　　For the second sample, 42WN418-2, Rowe submitted two CO_2 samples to the UA lab: one of paint mixed with sandstone from the rock surface and another consisting just of sandstone as a control. Neither sample had evidence of hydrocarbon contamination. In this case, the painted image being dated was the smaller anthropomorph immediately to the left of the larger, spalled anthropomorph with hydrocarbon contamination. The paint sample returned an age estimate of 3400 ± 65 BP (AA-8625) whereas the sandstone sample without paint returned an age of 4010 ± 55 BP (AA-9177). The latter age estimate reveals the presence of organic carbon in the rock, which might well cause the paint assay to overestimate true age. As such, Rowe interpreted the 3400 BP date, which is roughly 1700 BC, as a maximum age for the anthropomorph. Betsy Tipps reported these results in her 1995 report *Holocene Archaeology near Squaw Butte, Canyonlands National Park*. Because of residual organic carbon in the sandstone matrix, the dated image was likely painted at some point after 3400 BP, which means after about 1500 BC.

59. Fremont people also cached an animal skin bag at the Great Gallery that contained tools, food, and a hide pouch that once contained red ocher (Geib and Robins, "Analysis and AMS Dating of the Great Gallery Tool and Food Bag").

60. Watchman found no evidence for hydrocarbon contamination, likely because this block had fallen from the gallery wall well back in antiquity.

61. The two assays are 8630 ± 310 BP from the National Ocean Sciences Accelerator Mass Spectrometry (NOSAMS) lab and 8680 ± 1105 BP from the Rafter Radiocarbon Laboratory (Watchman, Patterson, and McNichol, "Dating BCS Rock Art," 10–11, Table 1).

62. Watchman, Patterson, and McNichol, ("Dating BCS Rock Art," 11) give the Black Dragon date of 8520 ± 970 BP (OS-35200) obtained by the National Ocean Sciences Accelerator Mass Spectrometry (NOSAMS) facility at Woods Hole Oceanographic Institution. A letter from Watchman to the National Pictographic Society dated August 2001 describes the sample as a minute specimen from an exfoliation scar in the chest area of the right-hand, larger-than-life figure that occurs to the left of the "dragon," the figure that somewhat resembles a vacuum tube in outline. This figure has a swath of silt washed across the central part from above. Watchman also obtained a date of 2610 ± 270 years BP (OS-35194) on oxalate covering paint on the foot of the anthropomorph immediately left of the Intestinal Man. This is reported in a letter to Richard Reed.

63. Green and colleagues ("Dating Correlated Micro-layers in Oxalate Accretions from Rock Art Shelters") provide an informative recent paper detailing how oxalate-rich mineral accretions are useful for rock art radiocarbon dating and paleoenvironmental reconstruction using a case study from Australia.

64. Betsy Tipps ("Barrier Canyon Rock Art Dating") reports on White Bird Shelter using its official designation of 42SA20615; different chapters provide details about the overall site including its rock art panels, the results of limited testing, and radiocarbon dating of two mud-painted figures on one panel of the site. Unfortunately, one of the pigment samples was contaminated at the University of Arizona AMS dating facility when a lab technician left a valve open, mixing in modern air with the CO_2 extracted from the pigment.

65. Tipps, "Barrier Canyon Rock Art Dating," 159, Table 28.

66. "The Curious Case of the Invisible Panel," a slide presentation by Dennis DeVore at the 2018 URARA Symposium in Bluff, Utah, is available at http://www.utahrockart2.org/pubs/proceedings/papers/2018-7-DeVoreD-Curious_Case_Invisible_Panel.pdf.

67. Joel L. Pederson et al., "Age of Barrier Canyon-Style Rock Art Constrained by Cross-Cutting Relations and Luminescence Dating Techniques," *PNAS* 111 (2014): 12986–91. Age estimates for alluvial deposition are based on a series of OSL dates on quartz grains from exposures of both the T2 and T1 terraces.

68. Pederson et al., "Age of Barrier Canyon-Style Rock Art, abstract; 12986.

69. Pederson and coauthors argue that once incision of the T2 deposit got started, it took at least 2,000 years or more for the ancient alluvium to be cleared from the sandstone face at the Great Gallery. Figure 2 in their report has the word "incision" and an arrow that runs from just after 8,000 years ago to 4,000 years ago, implying a four-millennium-long process. Given their 8010 OSL date for the top of T2, they reason that gallery painting could not have occurred until after at least 6,000 years ago or roughly 4000 BC and likely much more recently. They maintain that this maximum age constraint makes an early Archaic origin highly improbable.

70. It is also worth noting that the sixteen-foot-high T1 terrace in Horseshoe Canyon, which has a terminal date of roughly 800 years ago, has already eroded

from much of the canyon. Incision and flushing of this sediment likely started in the late 1800s or early 1900s like the rest of the Southwest.

71. The OSL date at the top of T2 is 8,010 ± 1,130 years ago (USU-671; Pederson et al., "Age of Barrier Canyon-Style Rock Art," Table 1). Given the large counting error, there is no necessary conflict with the radiocarbon age on the Great Gallery pigment sample reported by Watchman, Patterson, and McNichol ("Dating BCS Rock Art"). The early half of the two sigma OSL counting error is from 10,270 to 8,010 years ago which overlaps with the radiocarbon date.

72. See Jesse D. Jennings, Alan R. Schroedl, and Richard N. Holmer, *Sudden Shelter* (Salt Lake City: University of Utah Press, 1980), and Jennings, *Cowboy Cave*, 1980. Also see Alan R. Schroedl and Nancy J. Coulam, "Cowboy Cave Revisited," *Utah Archaeology* 7 (1994): 1–34. Cowboy Cave also includes the adjacent alcove known as Walters Cave that was partially excavated at the same time and exhibited a nearly identical depositional sequence (see Geib and Jolie, "Rise of Broad Spectrum Foraging on the Colorado Plateau," for details and dating). Cowboy Cave (with Walters) is especially significant since it is upstream from the Great Gallery within a tributary of Horseshoe Canyon and has well-stratified dry deposits that preserved abundant perishable remains including clay figurines that strongly resemble the large BCS anthropomorphs as argued by Alan Schroedl ("The Power and the Glory," 17) and then again by Nancy Coulam and Schroedl ("Early Archaic Clay Figurines"). The largest of these figurines (FS301) came from Walters Cave and occurs in a deposit (F54) next to a plain-weave sandal (FS576) with a radiocarbon date of 6350 ± 85 bp (Geib, "AMS Dating of Plain-Weave Sandals"). The lowest underlying cultural stratum in Walters Cave (F72), partially truncated by the overlying F54, has several radiocarbon dates on human feces and a sandal between 7400 and 7900 rcybp (Geib and Jolie, "Rise of Broad Spectrum Foraging on the Colorado Plateau") marking the start of human occupation at the site. A radiocarbon date of 7960 ± 50 bp on a small, coiled basket from Cowboy Cave is the oldest reliable date from that site and marks the time of first occupation (Geib and Jolie, "The Role of Basketry in Early Holocene Small Seed Exploitation").

73. Schaafsma, *Indian Rock Art of the Southwest*, 70.

74. Polly Schaafsma, "Rock Art," in *Handbook of North American Indians: Great Basin*, ed. Warren L. D'Azevedo (Washington, DC: Smithsonian Institution, 1986), 225; Alan Robert Schroedl, "The Archaic of the Northern Colorado Plateau" (PhD diss., University of Utah, 1976); Alan R. Schroedl, "The Power and the Glory," *Canyon Legacy* 1, no. 1 (1989): 13–17; Coulam and Schroedl, "Early Archaic Clay Figurines," 411.

75. Jennings, *Cowboy Cave*; Coulam and Schroedl, "Early Archaic Clay Figurines"; Coulam and Schroedl, "Late Archaic Totemism in the Great American Southwest," *American Antiquity* 69 (2004): 41–62; Geib and Jolie, "Rise of Broad Spectrum Foraging on the Colorado Plateau," Alan Robert Schroedl, "The Archaic of the Northern Colorado Plateau" (PhD diss., University of Utah, 1976).

76. Jennings, *Cowboy Cave*. The data tables in this report are informative but in many cases are in need of slight revision based on issues such as the correlation of depositional layers designated as features with the synthetic Strata used for reporting purposes, items not included, and clerical errors with the field specimen numbers (e.g., Coulam and Schroedl, "Early Archaic Clay Figurines from Cowboy Cave and Walters Cave," 403; Geib, "AMS Dating of Plain-Weave Sandals"; Geib and Jolie, "Rise of Broad Spectrum Foraging").

77. Isabel T. Kelly, *Southern Paiute Ethnography* (Salt Lake City: University of Utah Press, 1964), 146.

78. See Marsha C. Wibowo et al., "Reconstruction of Ancient Microbial Genomes from the Human Gut," *Nature* 594 (2021): 234–39.

79. Phil R. Geib, "Sandal Types and Archaic Prehistory on the Colorado Plateau," *American Antiquity* 65 (2000): 509–24. J. Richard Ambler was the first to recognize open-twined sandals as being potentially quite old. Even so, the radiocarbon dates he obtained directly on three sandals came as a surprise since they were more than 7,000 radiocarbon years before present (Lindsay et al., *Survey and Excavation North and East of Navajo Mountain*).

80. Thomas J. Connolly and Pat Barker, "Basketry Chronology of the Early Holocene in the Northern Great Basin," in *Early and Middle Holocene Archaeology of the Northern Great Basin*, ed. Dennis L. Jenkins, Thomas J. Connolly, and C. Melvin

81. An open-twined sandal from Walters Cave radio-carbon dated in the late 1970s produced an age estimate of 8875 ± 125 BP, providing the earliest evidence of human occupation at the site (Jennings, *Cowboy Cave*, Table 3). The dated sandal was part of a pair found together along with some human feces. Recent radiocarbon dating of these items reveals that the 8875 BP date is about a thousand years too old (Geib and Jolie, "Rise of Broad Spectrum Foraging on the Colorado Plateau," 200–201).

82. Cole, *Legacy on Stone*; Schaafsma, *Indian Rock Art of the Southwest*.

83. James M. Adovasio, "Artifacts and Ethnicity: Basketry as an Indicator of Territoriality and Population Movements in the Prehistoric Great Basin," in *Anthropology of the Desert West: Essays in Honor of Jesse D. Jennings*, ed. Carole J. Condie and Don W. Fowler (Salt Lake City: University of Utah Press, 1986), 43–89.

84. Schroedl and Coulam, "Cowboy Cave Revisited." These living structures evidently lack superstructures of any sort, but within a dry cave this is perhaps not surprising. Each of these living basins had hearths or ash pits near their centers. The basins were cleaned out of refuse accumulation several times with the debris heaped toward the center of the cave.

85. Jacob Freeman et al., "Culture Process and the Interpretation of Radiocarbon Data," *Radiocarbon* 60 (2018): 453–67.

86. I have witnessed this with rock art on Paiute Mesa at the large Ancestral Puebloan site of Pottery Pueblo, which is situated on a small sandstone prominence. A large number of petroglyphs once covered a sizable area of cliff face along the east, south, and west sides of this bedrock knob, depictions that likely date to the time when the pueblo was occupied (ca. AD 1240–1285) and much earlier when several nearby Basketmaker II habitations were in use (ca. AD 1–450). When archaeologists with the Museum of Northern Arizona partially excavated this site in the early 1960s, they documented the petroglyphs with an extensive series

of black-and-white photographs. During my first visits to the site in 1977 and 1979, guided by J. Richard Ambler, who had dug there in the 1960s, the petroglyphs were undamaged. It wasn't until a site revisit in the 1990s that I observed that someone had chopped away a vast majority of the images using what was probably a metal axe. I later learned from a Navajo friend local to the Navajo Mountain and Paiute Mesa area that this was done as part of a healing ceremony by a family that lives nearby the site. Similar image eradication for healing purposes has occurred elsewhere in southeast Utah along the San Juan River such as at "Desecration Panel" (Schaafsma, *Images and Power*, 77–78).

Image erasure has also occurred farther south on the Navajo Reservation in northeast Arizona. One location where this occurred is known as Inscription Point where copulation images got singled out for removal as have some probable Hopi clan signs (Weaver, Mark, and Billow, "Inscription Point: Too Little Too Late?," 149). In this case, two different motivations and likely groups of individuals seem to have been involved. Nearby in the western Hopi Buttes volcanic field occurs another interesting case. Here there was a probable Pueblo IV image of a flute player holding his musical instrument upward with twin parrots hanging upside down from the flute. I had shown Ekkehart Malotki an image of the petroglyph but when he went to photograph it the rock face that once displayed this image had been abraded smooth, with an inscribed cross occupying where the flute player once was. A nearby Navajo resident recounted that the image was interpreted as lightning striking a man and the source of sickness for someone living nearby. The image was removed as part of a curing ceremony and subsequently a Christian family member then added the cross, likely as a further apotropaic measure.

87. Nancy J. Parezo (*Navajo Sandpainting: From Religious Act to Commercial Art* (Tuscon: University of Arizon Press, 1983). Parezo provides an informative review of how sand painting among the Navajo shifted over time from a strictly religious act to one used to create art for commercial sale.

88. Jennings, Schroedl, and Holmer (*Sudden Shelter*) report on the Sudden Shelter findings including 453 projectile points, of which 353 could be assigned to a named type and came from depositional strata.

Other significant Archaic-age sites on the Wasatch Plateau include Joes Valley Alcove (Barlow and Metcalf, "1990 Archaeological Excavations at Joe Valley Alcove"; DeBloois, Green, and Wylie, "Joes Valley Alcove: An Archaic-Fremont Site in Central Utah") and Aspen Shelter (Janetski and Wilde, *Excavations at Aspen Shelter: A Deer Hunting Camp on the Old Woman Plateau*), both of which yielded abundant evidence for use as hunting camps.

89. Robert Kelly, "Hunter-Gatherer Mobility Strategies," *Journal of Anthropological Research* 39, no. 3 (1983): 277–306; Robert Kelly, *The Foraging Spectrum* (Washington, DC: Smithsonian Institution Press, 1995), 111–16. Kelly summarizes much of the ethnographic information available that pertains to foraging and mobility by hunter-gatherers.

90. Marit K. Munson, *The Archaeology of Art in the American Southwest* (Lanham, MA: Lexington Books, 2011), 71. As she points out, audiences are a key part to most Western definitions of art. The audience aspect of rock art has been considered by various researchers such as Richard Bradley ("Access, Style and Imagery"; *Image and Audience: Rethinking Prehistoric Art*).

91. Ingold, *The Perception of the Environment* is just one example of this.

92. Munson, *The Archaeology of Art in the American Southwest*, 92.

93. Munson, *The Archaeology of Art in the American Southwest* 93.

94. Munson, *The Archaeology of Art in the American Southwest* 102.

95. When defining what constitutes an anthropological theory of art, Gell (*Art and Agency*, 7) states that "we can roughly define [it] as social relations in the vicinity of objects mediating social agency." Note that he says objects, not artworks.

References

Aby, Scott B.

2017   Date of Arroyo Cutting in the American Southwest and the Influence of Human Activities. *Anthropocene* 18:76–88.

Adovasio, James M.

1986   Artifacts and Ethnicity: Basketry as an Indicator of Territoriality and Population Movements in the Prehistoric Great Basin. In *Anthropology of the Desert West: Essays in Honor of Jesse D. Jennings*, edited by Carole J. Condie and Don W. Fowler, pp. 43–89. University of Utah Anthropological Papers 110. University of Utah Press, Salt Lake City.

Allen, Mary

2003   Grand Canyon Polychrome vs. Esplanade Style: Is a Name Change Warranted? *Vestiges* 23(11):4–5.

Aubert, M., A. Brumm, M. Ramli, T. Sutikna, E. W. Saptomo, B. Hakim, M. J. Morwood, G. D. van den Bergh, L. Kinsley, and A. Dosseto

2014   Pleistocene Cave Art from Sulawesi, Indonesia. *Nature* 514:223–27.

Barlow, K. Renee, and Duncan Metcalfe

1993   1990 Archaeological Excavations at Joe Valley Alcove. Reports of Investigations 93-1. University of Utah Archaeological Center, Salt Lake City.

Barnes, F. A.

1982   *Canyon Country Prehistoric Rock Art*. Wasatch Publishers, Salt Lake City.

Beck, W., D. J. Donahue, A. J. T. Jull, G. Burr, W. S. Broecker, G. Bonani, I. Hajdas, and E. Malotki

1998   Ambiguities in Direct Dating of Rock Surfaces Using Radiocarbon Measurements; with Response by R. I. Dorn. *Science* 280:2132–39.

Bednarik, Robert G.

2002   The Dating of Rock Art: A Critique. *Journal of Archaeological Science* 29:1213–33.

2014   Pleistocene Palaeoart of the Americas. *Arts* 3(2):190–206.

Bennett, Matthew R., David Bustos, Jeffrey S. Pigati, et al.

2021   Evidence of Humans in North America during the Last Glacial Maximum. *Science* 373:1528–31.

Bennun, Neil

2005   *The Broken String: The Last Words of an Extinct People*. Viking, Penguin Books, London.

Bowden, Ross

2004   A Critique of Alfred Gell on Art and Agency. *Oceania* 74:309–24.

Bradley, Richard

2002   Access, Style and Imagery: The Audience for Prehistoric Rock Art in Atlantic Spain and Portugal, 4000–2000 BC. *Oxford Journal of Archaeology* 21:231–47.

2009   *Image and Audience: Rethinking Prehistoric Art*. Oxford University Press, Oxford.

Brown, Donald E.

1991   *Human Universals*. McGraw-Hill, New York.

Brown, Linda A., and William H. Walker

2008   Prologue: Archaeology, Animism and Non-Human Agents. *Journal of Archaeological Method and Theory* 15:297–99.

Chaffee, S. D., M. Hyman, and M. W. Rowe

1993   AMS ^{14}C Dating of Rock Paintings. In *Time and Space: Dating and Spatial Considerations in Rock Art Research*, edited by J. Steinbring, A. Watchman, P. Faulstich, and P. S. C. Tacon, pp. 67–73. Australian Rock Art Research Association, Melbourne, Australia.

1994   Vandalism of Rock Art for Enhanced Photography. *Studies in Conservation* 39(3):161–68.

Chippindale, Christopher, and Edward B. Eastwood

2010   *Seeing and Knowing: Rock Art With and Without Ethnography*. Wits University Press, Johannesburg.

Christensen, Don D., Jerry Dickey, and Steven M. Freers

2013   *Rock Art of the Grand Canyon Region*. Sunbelt Publications, San Diego.

Cole, Sally J.

2004   Origins, Continuities and Meaning of Barrier Canyon Style Rock Art. In *New Dimensions in Rock Art Studies*, edited by Ray T. Matheny, pp. 7–78. Museum of Peoples and Cultures Occasional Papers Series 9, Brigham Young University. University of Utah Press, Salt Lake City.

2009   *Legacy on Stone: Rock Art of the Colorado Plateau and Four Corners Region*. Revised and updated. Johnson Books, Boulder.

Connolly, Thomas J., and Pat Barker

2004   Basketry Chronology of the Early Holocene in the Northern Great Basin. In *Early and Middle Holocene Archaeology of the Northern Great Basin*, edited by Dennis L. Jenkins, Thomas J. Connolly, and C. Melvin Aikens, pp. 241–50. University of Oregon Anthropological Papers 62. Museum of Natural and Cultural History, Eugene.

Connolly, Thomas J., Pat Barker, Catherine S. Fowler, Eugene M. Hattori, Dennis L. Jenkins, and William J. Cannon

2016   Getting Beyond the Point: Textiles of the Terminal Pleistocene/Early Holocene in the Northwestern Great Basin. *American Antiquity* 81:490–514.

Coulam, Nancy J., and Alan R. Schroedl

1996   Early Archaic Clay Figurines from Cowboy Cave and Walters Cave in Southeastern Utah. *Kiva* 61:401–12.

2004   Late Archaic Totemism in the Great American Southwest. *American Antiquity* 69:41–62.

Davis, William E.

1989   The Lime Ridge Clovis Site. *Utah Archaeology* 2:66–76.

Davis, William E., and Gary M. Brown

1986   The Lime Ridge Clovis Site. *Current Research in the Pleistocene* 3:1–3.

DeBloois, Evan I., Dee F. Green, and Jerry Wylie

1979   Joes Valley Alcove: An Archaic-Fremont Site in Central Utah. Ms. on file, Manti–La Sal National Forest, Price, Utah.

Dissanayake, Ellen

2013   Art as a Human Universal: An Adaptationist View. In *Origins of Religion, Cognition and Culture*, edited by Armin W. Geertz, pp. 121–39. Acumen Publishing, Durham, England.

Dyble, Mark, James Thompson, Daniel Smith, Gul Deniz Salali, Nikhil Chaudhary, Abigail E. Page, Lucio Vinicuis, Ruth Mace, and Andrea Bamberg Migliano

2016   Networks of Food Sharing Reveal the Functional Significance of Multilevel Sociality in Two Hunter-Gatherer Groups. *Current Biology* 26:2017–21.

Eliade, Mircea

1964   *Shamanism: Archaic Techniques of Ecstasy*. Bollingen series LXXVI. Princeton University Press.

Firnhaber, Michael P.

2007   Experiencing Rock Art: A Phenomenological Investigation of the Barrier Canyon Tradition. PhD dissertation, Department of Anthropology, University College London.

Freeman, Jacob, David A. Byers, Erick Robinson, and Robert L. Kelly

2018   Culture Process and the Interpretation of Radiocarbon Data. *Radiocarbon* 60:453–67.

Garfinkel, Alan P, Donald R. Austin, David Earle, and Harold Williams

2009   Myth, Ritual and Rock Art: Coso Decorated Animal-Humans and the Animal Master. *Rock Art Research* 26(2):179–97.

Geib, Phil R.

1996   AMS Dating of Plain-Weave Sandals from the Central Colorado Plateau. *Utah Archaeology* 9:35–53.

2000   Sandal Types and Archaic Prehistory on the Colorado Plateau. *American Antiquity* 65:509–24.

2016   Basketmaker II Warfare and Fending Sticks in the North American Southwest. PhD dissertation, University of New Mexico, Albuquerque.

2018   Mesoamerican Flat Curved Sticks: Innovative "Toltec" Short Sword, Fending Stick, or Other Purpose? *Ancient Mesoamerica* 29(1):45–62.

Geib, Phil R., and Dale Davidson

1994   Anasazi Origins: A Perspective from Preliminary Work at Old Man Cave. *Kiva* 60:191–202.

Geib, Phil R., and Winston B. Hurst

2013   Should Dates Trump Context? Evaluation of the Cave 7 Skeletal Assemblage Radiocarbon Dates. *Journal of Archaeological Science* 40:2754–70.

Geib, Phil R., and Edward A. Jolie

2008   The Role of Basketry in Early Holocene Small Seed Exploitation: Implications of a ca. 9,000-Year-Old Basket from Cowboy Cave, Utah. *American Antiquity* 73:83–102.

2018   Rise of Broad Spectrum Foraging on the Colorado Plateau during the Early Holocene. In *The Archaic Southwest: Foragers in an Arid Land*, edited by Bradley J. Vierra, pp. 189–214. University of Utah Press, Salt Lake City.

Geib, Phil R., and Michael R. Robins

2003   Analysis and AMS Dating of the Great Gallery Tool and Food Bag. *Kiva* 73:291–320.

Gell, Alfred

1998   *Art and Agency: An Anthropological Theory.* Oxford: Clarendon.

Gilreath, Amy, and Ken Hedges

2020   Color Us Skeptical. *La Pintura* 46(4):1, 5–9.

Green, Helen, Andrew Gleadow, Vladimir A. Levchenko, Damien Finch, Cecilia Myers, Jenna McGovern, Pauline Heaney, and Robyn Pickering

2021   Dating Correlated Microlayers in Oxalate Accretions from Rock Art Shelters: New Archives of Paleoenvironments and Human Activity. *Science Advances* 7(33):1–15.

Gunnerson, James H.

1969   *The Fremont Culture: A Study in Culture Dynamics on the Northern Anasazi Frontier.* Papers of the Peabody Museum of Archaeology and Ethnology Vol. 59, No. 2. Harvard University, Cambridge, Massachusetts.

Gusinde, Martin

2015   *The Lost Tribes of Tierra del Fuego: Selk'nam, Yamana, Kawésqar.* Thames & Hudson, New York.

Hall, Stephen

2018   Paleoenvironments of the American Southwest. In *The Archaic Southwest: Foragers in an Arid Land*, edited by Bradley J. Vierra, pp. 16–28. University of Utah Press, Salt Lake City.

Hallowell, A. Irving

1960   Ojibwa Ontology, Behavior, and World View. In *Culture in History: Essays in Honor of Paul Radin*, edited by Stanley Diamond, pp. 19–52. Columbia University Press, New York.

Harden, Tessa, Mark G. Macklin, and Victor R. Baker

2010   Holocene Flood Histories in South-Western USA. *Earth Surface Processes and Landforms* 35:707–16.

Harvey, Graham

2005   *Animism: Respecting the Living World.* Wakefield Press, Kent Town, South Australia.

Hawley, C. C., R. C. Robeck, and H. B. Dyer

1968   *Geology, Altered Rocks and Ore Deposits of The San Rafael Swell, Emery County, Utah.* Geological Survey Bulletin 1239. US Government Printing Office, Washington, DC.

Helvenston, Patricia A., and Paul G. Bahn

2005   *Waking the Trance Fixed.* Wasteland Press, Louisville.

Helvenston, Patricia A., and Derek Hodgson

2010   The Neuropsychology of "Animism": Implications for Understanding Rock Art. *Rock Art Research* 27(1):61–94.

Hester, Thomas R., Michael P. Mildner, and Lee Spencer

1974   *Great Basin Atlatl Studies.* Ballena Press, Ramona, CA.

Hoffmann, D. L., C. D. Standish, M. García-Diez, P. B. Pettitt, J. A. Milton, J. Zilhão, J. J. Alcolea-González, et al.

2018   U-Th Dating of Carbonate Crusts Reveals Neandertal Origin of Iberian Cave Art. *Science* 359:912–15.

Holmer, Richard N.

1980   Chipped Stone Projectile Points. In *Cowboy Cave*, edited by Jesse D. Jennings, pp. 31–38. University of Utah Anthropological Papers 104. University of Utah Press, Salt Lake City.

Howard, Julie, and Joel C. Janetski

1996   Human Scalps from Eastern Utah. *Utah Archaeology* 5:125–32.

Hull, Frank W., and Nancy M. White

1980   Spindle Whorls, Incised and Painted Stone, and Unfired Clay Objects. In *Cowboy Cave*, edited by Jesse D. Jennings, pp. 117–25. University of Utah Anthropological Papers 104. University of Utah Press, Salt Lake City.

Ingold, Tim

2000   *The Perception of the Environment: Essays on Livelihood, Dwelling, and Skill.* Routledge, London.

Janetski, Joel C.

1980   Wood and Reed Artifacts. In *Cowboy Cave*, edited by Jesse D. Jennings, pp. 75–95.

University of Utah Anthropological Papers 104. University of Utah Press, Salt Lake City.

Janetski, Joel, and James D. Wilde
2012   *Excavations at Aspen Shelter: A Deer Hunting Camp on the Old Woman Plateau.* Occasional Paper 17, Museum of Peoples and Culture, Brigham Young University, Provo.

Jennings, Jesse D., editor
1980   *Cowboy Cave.* University of Utah Anthropological Papers 104. University of Utah Press, Salt Lake City.

Jennings, Jesse D., Alan R. Schroedl, and Richard N. Holmer
1980   *Sudden Shelter.* University of Utah Anthropological Papers 103. University of Utah Press, Salt Lake City.

Kehoe, Alice B.
2000   *Shamans and Religion: An Anthropological Exploration in Critical Thinking.* Waveland Press, Prospect Heights, IL.

Kelen, Leslie, and David Sucec
1996   *Sacred Images: A Vision of Native American Rock Art.* Gibbs Smith, Layton, UT.

Kelly, Isabel T.
1964   *Southern Paiute Ethnography.* University of Utah Anthropological Papers 69. University of Utah Press, Salt Lake City.

Kelly, Robert L.
1983   Hunter-Gatherer Mobility Strategies. *Journal of Anthropological Research* 39(3):277–306.
1995   *The Foraging Spectrum.* Smithsonian Institution Press, Washington, DC.

Layton, Robert
2001   Ethnographic Study and Symbolic Analysis. In *Handbook of Rock Art Research*, edited by David S. Whitley, pp. 311–31. AltaMira Press, Walnut Creek, CA.

Lemke, Ashley K., D. Clark Wernecke, and Michael B. Collins
2015   Early Art in North America: Clovis and Later Paleoindian Incised Artifacts from the Gault Site, Texas (41BL323). *American Antiquity* 80:113–33.

Le Quellec, Jean-Loïc, Paul Bahn, and Marvin Rowe
2015   The Death of a Pterodactyl. *Antiquity* 89:872–84.

Lien, Marianne Elisabeth, and Gisli Pálsson
2019   Ethnography Beyond the Human: The "Other-than-Human" in Ethnographic Work. *Ethnos* 86:1–20.

Lindsay, A. J., Jr., J. R. Ambler, M. A. Stein, and P. M. Hobler
1968   *Survey and Excavation North and East of Navajo Mountain, Utah 1959–1962.* Museum of Northern Arizona Bulletin 45. Northern Arizona Society of Science and Art, Flagstaff.

Malotki, Ekkehart
1997   The Dragonfly: A Shamanistic Motif in the Archaic Rock Art of the Palavayu Region in Northeastern Arizona. *American Indian Rock Art* 23:57–72.
1998   The Owl: A Shamanistic Motif in the Archaic Rock Art Iconography of the Palavayu Anthropomorphic Style, Northeastern Arizona. *American Indian Rock Art* 22:1–18.

Malotki, Ekkehart, and Henry D. Wallace
2011   Columbian Mammoth Petroglyphs from the San Juan River near Bluff, Utah, United States. *Rock Art Research* 28(2):143–52.

Manning, Steve J.
1993   A Modal Based Classification System for Rock Art Research: Overcoming Stylistic Methodological Problems. In *Utah Rock Art*, Vol. 11, edited by Nina Bowen, pp. 1–32. Utah Rock Art Research Association, Salt Lake City.
2003   42EM65, The Temple Mountain Pictograph Panel. In *Utah Rock Art*, Vol. 21, edited by Steven J. Manning and Nina Bowen, pp. 47–85. Utah Rock Art Research Association, Salt Lake City.

Miller, Jerry R.
2017   Casualty of Historic Arroyo Incision in the Southwestern United States. *Anthropocene* 18:69–75.

Morcote-Ríos, Gaspar, Francisco Javier Aceituno, José Iriarte, Mark Robinson, and Jeison L. Chaparro-Cárdenas
2021   Colonisation and Early Peopling of the Colombian Amazon during the Late Pleistocene and the Early Holocene: New Evidence from La Serranía La Lindosa. *Quaternary International* 578(20):5–19.

Munson, Marit K.
2011   *The Archaeology of Art in the American Southwest.* Lexington Books, Lanham, MD.

Nielsen, Jesper, and Christophe Helmke

2011 Reinterpreting the Plaza de los Glifos, la Ventilla, Teotihuacan. *Ancient Mesoamerica* 22:345–70.

Ní Leathlobhair, Máire, Angela R. Perri, Evan K. Irving-Pease, et al.

2018 The Evolutionary History of Dogs in the Americas. *Science* 361(6397):81–85.

O'Connor, Sue, Jane Balme, Mona Oscar, June Oscar, Selina Middleton, Rory Williams, et al.

2022 Memory and Performance: The Role of Rock Art in the Kimberley, Western Australia. In *Rock Art and Memory in the Transmission of Cultural Knowledge*, edited by Leslie F. Zubieta, pp. 147–70. Springer, Cham, Switzerland.

Parezo, Nancy J.

1983 *Navajo Sandpainting: From Religious Act to Commercial Art*. University of Arizona Press, Tucson.

Pederson, Joel L., Melissa S. Chapot, Steven R. Simms, Reza Sohbati, Tammy M. Rittenour, Andrew S. Murray, and Gary Cox

2014 Age of Barrier Canyon-Style Rock Art Constrained by Cross-Cutting Relations and Luminescence Dating Techniques. *PNAS* 111:12986–91.

Perri, Angela R., Tatiana R. Feuerborn, Laurent A. F. Frantz, Greger Larson, Ripan S. Malhi, David J. Meltzer, and Kelsey E. Witt

2021 Dog Domestication and the Dual Dispersal of People and Dogs into the Americas. *PNAS* 118(6):1–8 [e2010083118].

Pike, A. W. G., D. L. Hoffmann, M. García-Diez, P. B. Pettitt, J. Alcolea, R. De Balbín, C. González-Sainz, et al.

2012 U-Series Dating of Paleolithic Art in 11 Caves in Spain. *Science* 336:1409–13.

Pitblado, Bonnie L., Molly Boeka Cannon, Megan Bloxham, Joel Janetski, J. M. Adovasio, Kathleen R. Anderson, and Stephen T. Nelson

2013 Archaeological Fingerprinting and Fremont Figurines. *Advances in Archaeological Practice* 1(1):3–12.

Porr, Martin, and Hannah Rachel Bell

2012 "Rock-art," "Animism" and Two-Way Thinking: Towards a Complementary Epistemology in the Understanding of Material Culture and "Rock-Art" of Hunting and Gathering People. *Journal of Archaeological Method and Theory* 19:161–205.

Poston, Pete E., and Gary Cox

n.d. Final Report: Raman Spectroscopic Analysis of Rock Art Pigment from the Great Gallery, Maze District, Canyonlands National Park, Utah. Manuscript on file, Canyonlands National Park, Moab.

Rogers, Richard A.

2018 *Petroglyphs, Pictographs, and Projections: Native American Rock Art in the Contemporary Cultural Landscape*. University of Utah Press, Salt Lake City.

Rowe, Marvin W.

2009 Radiocarbon Dating of Ancient Rock Paintings. *Analytical Chemistry* 81:1728–35.

Russ, Jon, Marian Hyman, and Marvin Rowe

1992 Direct Radiocarbon Dating of Rock Art. *Radiocarbon* 34:867–72.

Schaafsma, Polly

1971 *The Rock Art of Utah: From the Donald Scott Collection*. Papers of the Peabody Museum of Archaeology and Ethnology vol. 65. Harvard University, Cambridge, MA.

1980 *Indian Rock Art of the Southwest*. School of American Research, Santa Fe. University of New Mexico Press, Albuquerque.

1986 Rock Art. In *Handbook of North American Indians: Great Basin*, edited by Warren L. D'Azevedo, 215–26. Smithsonian Institution, Washington, DC.

1994 Trance and Transformation in the Canyons: Shamanism and Early Rock Art on the Colorado Plateau. In *Shamanism and Rock Art in North America*, edited by Solveig A. Turpin, pp. 45–71. Special Publication 1, Rock Art Foundation Inc., San Antonio.

2013 *Images and Power: Rock Art and Ethics*. Springer, New York.

Schapiro, Meyer

1953 Style. In *Anthropology Today: An Encyclopedic Inventory*, edited by Alfred L. Kroeber, pp. 287–312. University of Chicago Press, Chicago.

Schroedl, Alan Robert

1976 The Archaic of the Northern Colorado Plateau. PhD dissertation, Department of Anthropology, University of Utah.

Schroedl, Alan R.

1989   The Power and the Glory. *Canyon Legacy* 1(1):13–17.

Schroedl, Alan R., and Nancy J. Coulam

1994   Cowboy Cave Revisited. *Utah Archaeology* 7:1–34.

Simms, Steven R., and François Gohier

2010   *Traces of Fremont: Society and Rock Art in Ancient Utah.* University of Utah Press, Salt Lake City.

Solomon, Anne

2008   Myths, Making, and Consciousness: Differences and Dynamics in San Rock Arts. *Current Anthropology* 49:59–86.

Spangler, Jerry D., and James M. Aton

2018   *The Crimson Cowboys: The Remarkable Odyssey of the 1931 Claflin-Emerson Expedition.* University of Utah Press, Salt Lake City.

Sucec, David

1997   Toward a Typology of Barrier Canyon Style Spirit Figures: Early Findings of the BCS Project (1991–1995). In *Utah Rock Art* vol. 15, pp. 61–76. Utah Rock Art Research Association, Salt Lake City. utahrockart2.org/wa/symp_papers_by_author.html.

Tipps, Betsy L.

1995   Barrier Canyon Rock Art Dating. In *Holocene Archaeology near Squaw Butte, Needles District, Canyonlands National Park,* edited by Betsy L. Tipps, pp. 153–69. Selections from the Division of Cultural Resources 7. Rocky Mountain Region, National Park Service, Denver.

Turpin, Solveig A.

2001   Archaic North America. In *Handbook of Rock Art Research,* edited by David S. Whitley, pp. 361–413. AltaMira Press, Walnut Creek, CA.

Vance, Meghann M.

2011   Stone without Bones: Reconstructing the Lime Ridge Clovis Site. Master's Thesis, Northern Arizona University, Flagstaff.

Viveiros de Castro, Eduardo

1998   Cosmological Deixis and Amerindian Perspectivism. *Journal of the Royal Anthropological Institute* 4:469–88.

Wallach, Alan

1997   Meyer Schapiro's Essay on Style: Falling into the Void. *The Journal of Aesthetics and Art Criticism* 55(1):11–15.

Wallis, Robert

2009   Re-enchanting Rock Art Landscapes: Animic Ontologies, Non-Human Agency and Rhizomic Personhood. *Time and Mind: The Journal of Archaeology, Consciousness and Culture* 2(1):47–70.

Watchman, Alan, Carol Patterson, and Ann McNichol

2005   Dating BCS Rock Art at the Great Gallery, Canyonlands, Utah. In *Utah Rock Art,* vol. 24, edited by Carol B. Patterson, pp. 1–13. Utah Rock Art Research Association, Salt Lake City, Utah.

Weaver, Donald E., Jr., Robert Mark, and Evelyn Billo

2001   Inscription Point: Too Little Too Late? In *American Indian Rock Art,* vol. 27, edited by Steven M. Freers and Alanah Woody, pp. 137–50. American Rock Art Research Association, Tucson.

Whittaker, John C.

2007   Late Survival of Atlatls in the American Southwest? *The Atlatl* 20(1):10–12.

2012   Ambiguous Endurance: Late Atlatls in the American Southwest? *Kiva* 78:79–98.

Wibowo, Marsha C., Zhen Yang, Maxime Borry, et al.

2021   Reconstruction of Ancient Microbial Genomes from the Human Gut. *Nature* 594:234–39.

Index

Italicized page numbers indicate images or content in the front matter.